P9-CEP-659

THE
EXECUTIVE
ODYSSEY

HF
5386
.H26
1989

THE EXECUTIVE ODYSSEY

Secrets for A Career Without Limits

FREDERICK G. HARMON

WILEY

JOHN WILEY & SONS

New York • Chichester • Brisbane • Toronto • Singapore

SOUTHEASTERN COMMUNITY
COLLEGE LIBRARY
WHITEVILLE, NC 28472

Copyright © 1989 by Frederick G. Harmon

Published by John Wiley & Sons, Inc.

All rights reserved. Published simultaneously in Canada.

Reproduction or translation of any part of this work
beyond that permitted by Section 107 or 108 of the
1976 United States Copyright Act without the permission
of the copyright owner is unlawful. Requests for
permission or further information should be addressed to
the Permissions Department, John Wiley & Sons, Inc.

This publication is designed to provide accurate and
authoritative information in regard to the subject
matter covered. It is sold with the understanding that
the publisher is not engaged in rendering legal, accounting,
or other professional service. If legal advice or other
expert assistance is required, the services of a competent
professional person should be sought. *From a Declaration
of Principles jointly adopted by a Committee of the
American Bar Association and a Committee of Publishers.*

Library of Congress Cataloging in Publication Data:
Harmon, Frederick G.
    The executive odyssey : secrets for a career without limits /
Frederick G. Harmon.
        p.   cm.
    Bibliography: p.
    ISBN 0-471-61657-5
    1. Success in business.   2. Career development.   3. Self
-realization.   I. Title.
HF5386.H26   1989
650.1'4—dc19   88-29181
                                                                  CIP

Printed in the United States of America

10 9 8 7 6 5 4 3 2 1

SOUTHEASTERN COMMUNITY
COLLEGE LIBRARY
WHITEVILLE, NC 28472

Gift of Dr Scott 10/96

This book is for
James, John, Kate, and Mike

CONTENTS

PART 2   USING THE SYSTEM FOR MAXIMUM
         PROGRESS

PREFACE: A CAREER WITHOUT LIMITS

Humanity was once led by a strong leader, the king, who ruled by dynasty. Then the world outgrew the monarch, developing democracy, wresting the birthright of freedom from the usurper king.

The flock was once dominated by the priest. People obeyed with a devotion that was submission. Today, individual awareness, not priestly direction, guides the conscience of even those who follow organized religions.

Superstition once enslaved humanity. Then, codified knowledge developed. Science emancipated the individual. Clarity and understanding replaced the tyranny of unthinking belief.

The world of work is now entering a similar period of liberation. The individual executive is struggling to overthrow the weight of the past. In the days of our fathers and grandfathers, rigid bureaucratic discipline dominated the lives and careers of every executive. The price of success was blind obedience.

Today, human aspiration and global competition have jolted us in a sudden awakening. The sleeper is now restlessly half awake.

Self-generated discipline now challenges the power of bureaucratic structure, ushering in an era of individual freedom. There is now hope that the individual can rise above bureaucracy and preside over it.

Executives all over the world are experimenting to find a new paradigm of organization. Before any such new design can emerge it must integrate three dynamic trends: 1) technological revolutions in communications and automation; 2) the demand by employees for more complete and meaningful work; and 3) the rising pressure for efficiency, fueled by fast-paced and increasingly global competition.

Traditional organizations everywhere are suffering acute stress or even psychological breakdown. The underlying cause is the struggle to fit these trends into an organizational design created for a disappearing world. Self-directed change is now the priority for every organization. For the individual manager or professional the priority is exactly the same. For the company or the individual manager to rely on or blame others for his fate signals that he is playing by old rules in a revolutionary new game.

Today's corporate professional is the heir to those who wrested community from the monarch, emancipated religious belief from priestly domination, and rose above superstition into science. Yet, this same richly endowed heir remains under a deep cloud of unconsciousness when it comes to the self-directed career. Like a medieval peasant, the manager is haunted by psychological tyrannies. Success remains a mystery. It can only be explained by such superstitions as luck, being the right person in the right place at the right time, going to the right school, being born into the right family, or becoming a workaholic. And, the greatest superstition of all: At work, my career destiny is in the hands of others.

Every year thousands of individuals abandon these superstitions to achieve astonishing success. Such individuals are not controlled by an environment of rapid change; they consciously or unconsciously follow a systematic approach to success. The time has come for every executive and professional to become fully conscious, to seek personal success and fulfillment the same way humanity became more fully conscious as it overthrew the tyranny of the monarch, the priest, and primitive superstition.

The knowledge of how to rise in life is a process that has now been codified. Its components are the individual, the environment, the work itself, and the method used to carry out that work. The forces employed are personal energy, internal psychological organization, and skill. Any individual can learn to master these components and forces to create success without limits. Once mastered, the process can become a conscious tool to reach any goal at work or indeed in life.

FREDERICK G. HARMON

Wilmington, Delaware
February, 1989

THE
EXECUTIVE
ODYSSEY

PART ONE

THE SYSTEM

Mastering the process of personal growth requires understanding and then applying seven principles:

- Aspiration releases energy; the more deeply felt the aspiration, the higher the energy.
- Channeling energy through a *complete act* is the building block of all success.
- Success expands through psychological effort; the more dedicated that effort, the more significant the success.
- While survival depends on strengths, success is built on overcoming weaknesses.
- Mastery of any environment begins with concentrating on essentials and applying appropriate rules.
- Complete mastery of any environment is achieved by carrying out nonessentials to perfection and knowing which rules to break.
- Values determine the direction of all success.

This section will explain these principles as they apply to your work. Step by step, you will be shown how to use them to achieve your immediate goals. Further, you will be challenged to put them together in a complete system to reach your deepest and most profound aspirations.

1 ASPIRATION: COULD YOU MAKE IT IN SHANGHAI?

For years W. Michael Blumenthal has quietly evaluated some of the world's most powerful men by his own personal standard: Could they make it in Shanghai? By any standard, Blumenthal embodies the American dream of success. He began his career by earning two master's degrees and a doctorate at Princeton. He next combined a brilliant career in both business (vice president of Crown Cork International Corporation and president of Bendix Corporation) and government (chairman of the U.S. Delegation to the Kennedy Round of Trade Negotiations and Secretary of the Treasury). In what he calls his latest incarnation, Blumenthal is chairman and chief executive officer of UNiSYS Corporation. He created this $10 billion manufacturer of commercial information systems, defense systems, and related services by merging Sperry Corporation with Burroughs Corporation.

As with many American successes, Blumenthal's story begins in adversity. "I grew up as a Jew in Nazi Germany. I saw my father barely escape with his life from a concentration camp and then immigrated with my family to wartime Shanghai, China. In that environment I witnessed how people react when they are stripped of all of their possessions and thrust into a totally alien environment. And when I refer to stripping them of all their possessions, I mean not only physical possessions, but of their language because these were German-speaking people, who suddenly no longer found much use for their language, their skills. If you were a lawyer in Germany, it didn't do you much good in wartime Shanghai. If you were a doctor, you couldn't easily practice medicine. If you were a famous journalist whose name was a household word in Germany, it meant nothing in China, nobody knew who you were.

"And I have always thought, after observing how people react in this environment, both those who were rich and famous and those who were poor and uneducated, and observing sometimes that the latter adjusted much better than the former, that what counts in life is not who you are or where you come from but the inner resources that you bring to bear, first. And secondly, that the trick is not how well you deal with success, but how well you deal with adversity.

"Time and time again in dealing with so-called important people in my life here in the United States and in my various professional experiences, I asked myself silently . . .'How would you do in Shanghai, Mr. Ambassador, Mr. Senator, Mr. Chairman of the Board, in the same kind of situation that I saw people? How would you deal with a situation in which the fates conspired against you?' That was very helpful in telling me that *it depends on me and on my inner resources.*"

FULL AND DRAMATIC SUCCESS

The first thesis of this book is that, as with Michael Blumenthal, your success depends on you and on your ability to marshall your inner resources. Blumenthal's accomplishments were fashioned in an effort to bring himself physically, mentally, and psychologically out of Shanghai. He learned how to rely on himself, how to draw on his inner resources, and success followed. Because he learned fully under dramatic circumstances, his success has been full and dramatic. To the degree that you learn and apply these same lessons, your success can be equally full and dramatic.

The second thesis is that not only can you find those inner resources, you can systematically develop and expand them throughout your career. The power of these resources is limitless—the more you use, the stronger and greater the supply available to you. This is true wherever you are today, no matter how little or how much you have achieved.

The third thesis is that development of your inner resources leads to ever-expanding professional success and to personal fulfillment as well. Drawing on your inner resources means, above all, using external circumstances, both opportunities and adversity, to foster your own growth. Once you know how to do this—and this book will show you how—your growth and success can be perpetual.

Aspiration is the gateway to your inner resources. All success, great or small, is conceived in aspiration. Wanting success and being willing to work for it, are the first, indispensable steps. Aspiration comes in many forms—from the basic desire to become rich to the noble ambition to serve others.

An Aspiration To Create

All his life Eugene M. Lang has had one overriding aspiration— to create things. Money has always followed. Lang won a scholarship to Swarthmore College. Shortly after graduating in 1938, he originated a publication that cross-indexed and analyzed groups of stocks by criteria such as 10-year yield and industry. Wall Street brokers could purchase copies in bulk and distribute them to their customers. Then World War II changed all his plans. The day after the Pearl Harbor attack, he tried to enlist in the Army but was turned down for flat feet. He went right back to his office and told his partners they could buy him out any way they wanted because he was joining the war effort one way or another.

Lang took a job as an apprentice machinist at 40 cents an hour. Within a year, he was managing the factory. As the war progressed, the factory's production was slowed by a tremendous shortage of cutting tools and gauges, because traditional manufacturers could not meet the demand. As he was to do again and again, Lang broke the problem into logical pieces and came up with a creative solution.

During the war, hundreds of small garages and automobile repair shops had little to do because of the shortage of spare parts. Lang broke down the manufacture of the cutting tools and gauges into a series of discrete operations that the small shops could handle in sequence. After selling the Navy on his idea, he arranged for boxes of blanks to move from shop to shop for successive operations until the final cutting tool emerged.

After the war, he opened a factory to produce one of his inventions—a screw thread fastener that could make durable threaded connections between soft metals and plastics. The product took off as the age of light metals and plastics dawned. As his plant boomed, Lang recalls, "We got these people from overseas coming in. They wanted our product, but it was no good overseas because we made screw threads only to inch standards."

Lang searched for an agency "that would take our technology, our patents, our know-how and arrange to make [them] operate in other markets." Finding that no such agency existed, Lang decided to create one. In 1952 he sold his share in the fastener company, retaining the foreign rights ("which no one placed any value on"), and created the Resources and Facilities Corporation. He rented an office, hired a secretary, put $3000 in a bank account, obtained the foreign rights for several other patents, and took off on a three-month, round-the-world trip. By the time he came back, Refac Technology Development Corporation, as his company is now known, was in business.

Helping one small company after another license its products and patents overseas has made Lang a wealthy man. "My $3000 investment grew to the point where it has been possible for me to give away more than $25 million and I'm going to give that over again in my lifetime."

Like his businesses, Lang's charities are creative. Invited to make a commencement speech at East Harlem's Public School 121, from which he graduated in 1928, Lang threw away his prepared speech. No doubt recalling his Swarthmore scholarship, he offered each of the 61 graduating sixth graders a four-year college scholarship if they completed high school. The next year he established the "I Have a Dream" Foundation to provide a way for others to adopt graduating elementary school classes in inner cities.

From the beginning, Lang knew "you can't just hand out money and walk away." He hired a social worker to counsel both his adopted class and their family members. Most important of all, he spent his time showering personal attention on the youngsters, offering advice and support. Both the counselor and the personal attention are now integral parts of the foundation's programs. More than 50 of the original "Lang's Gang" are scheduled to graduate from high school by June 1989. By the fall of 1988, 34 had been accepted to college. And the program has spread to 24 cities and involves 8000 students.

Lang believes his life centers on the idea, first instilled in him by his father, that the highest aspiration is to create—"creating enterprises, creating new industries, creating jobs, creating new products for the market." These days, Eugene Lang spends most of his time creating opportunities for disadvantaged youngsters. His life demonstrates that a deep aspiration never runs out of opportunities to express itself through both inner and outer resources.

Lifting the Bar Every Day

Deep aspiration is so powerful that it can even substitute for a natural endowment. "The first thing I can ever remember wanting to do was to be a great football player," recalls Alexander Kroll, chairman and chief executive officer of Young & Rubicam, Inc. "I used to imagine that when I was six or seven years old." But in his first high school season, "I was pummeled and slammed and rocked and also I had the wonderful advantage of not being able to see very well." Over his mother's objections, Kroll invested all his savings in a set of barbells. To work out three times a day, he had to get up at 2:30 AM. "I was obsessed. I had a vision, a picture of myself as a great athlete. I really was willing to do almost anything in the way of hard work in order to make that happen."

Several years later, Kroll was All-American and captain of his undefeated team at Rutgers. "The final game of the season was on my parents' 25th wedding anniversary. It was the 25th day of the month and we came from behind to score 25 points in the last quarter to win. It was such a terrific day and I was on such a roll that I immediately proposed to Phyllis, my wife." Kroll's exuberance in retelling this story years later suggests the power and joy of a great aspiration fulfilled.

Having learned how to succeed in a self-directed challenge, Kroll brought the same technique to his work at Young & Rubicam. What is the key to his success in rising to the top of the largest independently held advertising agency in the world? "Persistently try to lift the bar or put a little more weight on the bar every day. Set a big goal, something very inspiring, and then go after it." To be a worthy aspiration, that goal "should scare you some and be something that takes your breath away."

Kroll's example shows how learning to draw on inner resources at one time, in one field, creates a capacity that can be transferred infinitely, in almost the same way that a franchise is spread to multiple locations.

When Frederick A. DeLuca was 17 years old, he opened his first Subway sandwich and salad shop to pay his way through college. By 1987 Subway was the fastest growing franchise in America, having opened 578 units that year. DeLuca has set a goal of doubling his units to 5000 stores by 1994. Why 5000? Because his aspiration is to be the first founding entrepreneur to take a fast-food company to that size.

Reversing Adversity

Aspiration can be triggered by desperation, so much so that we often create our most meaningful successes in adversity. It took 27 years for John C. Koss's stereo headphone company to become the industry leader. By 1981, with sales of more than $25 million, Koss

Corporation dominated half of the domestic and a quarter of the international market. Then, between 1981 and 1984, the company was buffeted by market shifts and internal control problems. It plummeted from $11 million in net worth and no short-term debt to a negative net worth and a $15 million debt.

"This was my life's work," Koss remembers. "It wasn't just some business I was running." Koss, then in his mid-50s, filed for Chapter 11 bankruptcy, rallied his family around him, bought time from the banks, introduced a successful series of new products, and worked his way back to a profitable, stable company. "You have this terrible desire to go into your house and shut the world out. You have to fight that feeling or you aren't going to win. There are a lot of people out there who want to help you, but they aren't going to come busting through your door to help you. You have to go out and stay out and give those people a chance to help you."

The Highest Aspiration

Every executive understands the power of aspiration. It takes a considerable measure of aspiration to get and hold an executive job. It took inner resources to create the energy, concentration, and dedication that resulted in a college degree, a good recruiting interview, and satisfactory performance in those initial assignments. Aspiration created those early promotions.

Then, for many, something starts to go wrong. *Newsweek* noted in a recent issue: "For all its action and glamour, today's business world has generated corrosive ways to wear down bodies and spirits. The buzz around the modern water cooler is full of anxiety and paranoia."[1] In other words, many previously successful executives find themselves stranded seemingly overnight in their own personal versions of Shanghai.

Ironically, this demoralized retreat occurs in the midst of one of the great epochs of human liberation. "Freedom," wrote the

---

[1]*Newsweek*, "Stress on the Job: It's Hurting Morale and the Bottom Line," April 25, 1988, p. 40.

Indian sage Sri Aurobindo, "is the final law and the last consum-
mation." Throughout the world, in virtually every aspect of life,
one feels a pressure toward that final law—here with the force of
a flood, there with a trickle. The 45 years since the end of World
War II have seen nations, indeed whole continents, strike the hour
of freedom from colonialism.

On the issue of self-determination, small nations defy super-
powers and win. In the United States, we have witnessed mass
movements such as End the Vietnam War, Civil Rights, Women's
Rights, and Gay Rights challenge the Establishment's right to dictate the rules and norms of life. In the 1988 primary elections, the
Reverend Jesse Jackson brought thousands of new voters to the
polls by appealing to the demand for greater freedom for U.S.
minorities. In religion, the Catholic Church stood for centuries on
the principles of faith and obedience. Yet today clergy and laity
alike feel free to argue with a popular Pope on Church dogma. In
management, Tom Peters has become the world's most popular
business writer and speaker as he challenges organizations to overhaul their bureaucracies to meet human needs.

Technology creates and fuels the aspiration for human freedom. Recall the battle cry of the 1960s: "Power to the people!"
Today, more than ever, knowledge (that is, information) is power.
A small portable computer today can link you inexpensively to
databases far greater than any enjoyed by the industrial giants of
the 1950s.

Freedom ebbs and flows in the daily headlines, hurls forward,
is forced back, and moves forward again. This should neither blind
us to the aspiration of the age nor discourage us from seeking that
aspiration within ourselves. We can clearly see part of the problem:
the external establishment that seems to limit our freedom in new
ways every day. Following the imperative of survival, corporate
America has sweated and strained through a long nightmare of
restructuring and cost cutting, while lower level managers complain bitterly about unfeeling bosses and a system that seems designed to program them for failure.

THE ESTABLISHMENT WITHIN

The road out of Shanghai is not an external route but an internal highway; and on that highway we confront another establishment that is far more powerful and far more intimidating than anything or anyone found at the corporate office. John Koss felt the power of this "Establishment Within" when he wanted to retreat to his house and stay there. Alexander Kroll feels it when he sets a goal "that takes your breath away." Michael Blumenthal battled it during his "very frustrating" period as Secretary of the Treasury when he found it necessary "to keep coming back to Shanghai very often" to remind himself that the important thing was not the "unjustifiable nonsense the newspapers were writing," but rather the ability to deal with adversity and "deal with it as best I can."

The Establishment Within is our own personally constructed set of limitations, barriers that seek to define us and entangle us far more securely than rules and regulations found in the most oppressive U.S. organization. Every success cited in this book rests at its core on a struggle by someone, frequently quite an ordinary person, to rebel once, twice, or perhaps many times against the Establishment Within.

John E. Jacob is an executive who understands overcoming barriers, within and without. A black man, raised in the era "when my parents preached that in order to make it in America, you've got to be at least twice as good as white people," Jacob overcame an internal barrier in his own organization to become the first president of the National Urban League, Inc., ever selected from within the ranks of the organization. In his final interview for the job, Jacob was asked why he thought he should be president. "My response to that was because for every second, every minute, every hour, of every day, of every week, of every month, of every year for the last 17 years, I have been preparing for this moment."

Jacob's effort was a deeply conscious one. For many the effort is unconscious. However, regardless of whether the effort is conscious or unconscious, you should experience an exhilaration when you develop your inner resources to release more and more aspiration. You can measure how well you are doing by one simple barometer: how much energy you bring to the job, all day, every day. If you are drawing solely on external resources, each new assignment or promotion will decrease your energy. Inner resources lift your energy, strength, and spirits.

The Workaphiles

The term "workaholic" has become a great American putdown. Even people who should know better apply it to themselves. The suffix *-aholic* joined to the noun *work* implies an unhealthy addiction—people's inability to stop doing what they know they should not be doing or what they do not even want to do. Yet in the past 20 years I have met hundreds of executives in the United States and elsewhere who work long days year after year and who seem able to draw more energy and indeed more joy from their work every year. Hard workers, yes; workaholics, no. Workaphiles—lovers of work—would be a far more accurate term.

To be sure, I have met a fair share of workaholics—joyless, sometimes bitter people driven by some private obsession. On the surface, the difference is hard to detect. Both workaphiles and workaholics come in early, work late, start their business trips on Sundays, interrupt weekends for important meetings, and relax by reading work-related periodicals. To understand the difference, ask yourself which one shows the most genuine enthusiasm for the work? The test here is who has the most energy at the end of the day. People who love their work are working from an inner center and it shows. They are growing through their work, expanding their inner resources, and releasing aspiration and energy. Their work is not an obligation but a joy.

A common example will illustrate the difference between inner and outer work. In the past 10 years, many executives have learned to use the personal computer—a small but significant growth. It is significant because, in the words of one executive, "the computer empowers you in so many new ways." While you are learning to use a computer, even the simplest clerical chore such as a routine business letter can suddenly change from drudgery to a suspenseful adventure. As you work, you feel a sense of inner achievement and growth with the mastery of new skills. You can become so absorbed that you completely forget the time or even where you are. You experience these reactions because you are growing— expanding your inner resources and your confidence in learning a new skill—even though, all along, you have been doing a routine and somewhat boring piece of work. The external results, while important, are secondary.

Hard-working executives are workaphiles to the extent that their work focuses primarily on extending their capacities, and they are workaholics to the extent that their work focuses solely on the external results.

Managing Your Luck

With few exceptions, everyone is born with a reasonable inheritance of good health. As the years go by, some dissipate, some develop, and some slowly spend this inheritance. Similarly, almost everyone in today's executive ranks was born with enough aspiration and inner resources to rise to the rank of CEO. Your initial selection as an executive, particularly if combined with subsequent success, establishes your capacity for the work you have chosen. Then, according to the conventional wisdom, random chance begins to shape your career.

It wasn't very long ago that we thought good health was largely a matter of chance. In some European countries in the last century, people called the physician the "messenger of death." Now the physician, together with an informed patient, is the delayer of death. Today people recognize that their health is in their own hands. "The wellness movement is not a fad," says Owen J. Lipstein, the young entrepreneur, president, and publisher of *American Health* magazine. "It isn't for vegetarians, it isn't for vitamin freaks, it isn't for athletes, it is for you and me. . . . the limits that we thought were true physically aren't there. You can essentially function like a young man until you are about ready to drop is what biology is telling us. . . . It is in your control." Lipstein believes further that the rise of the personal health revolution and the rise of the entrepreneurial movement are one and the same. "They are both about taking control of your life yourself."

If we can control our health, why not our careers? To do that, we must first face down the myth that luck—the bad boss, the wrong industry, the takeover threat, or, in positive terms, the good fortune of being in the right place at the right time—controls our destiny. If luck wasn't the factor we thought it was in health, maybe it's not the factor we think it is in career success. When we thought it was mostly luck in health, the people who lived longer in better health unconsciously behaved differently. If we take the trouble to look, we will see many highly successful executives acting differently and then attributing their success to luck.

One of the executives interviewed for this book begins every workday at 5:30 AM, has showed enormous inner strength in backing his people and his products in a period of corporate upheaval, and loves his job so much that his idea of a good evening is a couple of hours of work after supper. "But, of course," this executive explained, standing up to end the interview at precisely the agreed-upon minute, "it's mostly a matter of being at the right place at the right time."

If such a disciplined, self-developed executive believes that luck is the major factor in his career success, it is not surprising that many far less successful people explain their fate by luck. How important is luck? The answer is best defined by a common definition: Luck is where opportunity meets preparation.

This brings us back to Shanghai. In the end, your career success depends on you—on how well you develop your inner resources, on how willing you are "to lift the bar a little bit every day," and on how much and how fast you want to grow. Success is not a secret prize awarded to a lucky few: it is a birthright available to every executive. All that is required is aspiration, a knowledge of the process, and the will to go forward.

2 THE COMPLETE ACT: THE BUILDING BLOCK OF SUCCESS

"She was a wild boss," Kendall Lockhart recalls, "just incredibly weird but very smart and a hard worker who understood the common sense approach to doing tasks." Incredibly weird or not, Lockhart was stuck with her. He was 19, had disagreed with his parents over the direction of his education, and needed $20,000 to continue at Princeton.

Searching for a job with high pay where it didn't matter that he looked like a high school runaway, he ended up as a cold caller for an executive recruiting agency. "You would call up a company's personnel executive and you would ask 'Do you have a vice president's job in banking?' " At first, Lockhart made the mistake of taking no for an answer and hanging up. Completely unsatisfactory, according to the wild boss. A no answer was the beginning, not the end, of the negotiation.

"She would really embarrass you. 'Call them back,' she would say, 'and ask them if they have an assistant vice president; see if they have a cashier.' The next time you remembered, because she would make you call back 20 times until you had asked for every job."

Today, at 31, Kendall Lockhart, the self-financed Princeton graduate, is a vice president at Bank of America. He achieved that goal only five years after joining BOA with no previous banking or even financial experience. "The system of inquiry and persistence that I learned at 19 is something that stayed with me to this day."

Lockhart has risen rapidly at the bank by exploiting a knack for putting together complicated, multi-million-dollar financing deals and a tenacity that won't quit. "I have my own 90 to 100 rule. I'll bet you 90 times out of 100 there's a way to do it. People at the bank know that I am going to keep harping on them until we find a way to do it."

BUILDING BLOCK OF SUCCESS

The complete act, which Lockhart learned at 19, is the fundamental building block of all successful careers. Whether fired at point-blank range by a terrorizing boss or taught more gently by a kindly mentor, the lesson is always there. Every successful executive remembers both the curriculum and the price of tuition.

"I will take it with me until the end of my days as a lawyer," says Peter W. Bruce. Another fast rising executive, Bruce at 34 became general counsel of Northwestern Mutual Life Insurance Co. "It was right here in this office. While I don't remember any more what the issue was, I distinctly remember [then general counsel] Dick Mooney asking me what the contract provided. And I had been busily working in the law library and I had all this casework, what the courts had held in similar cases and I had written those up and was reciting them. But I hadn't read the contract. Dick said 'You haven't read the contract' in a certain tone of voice. He was a very proper fellow and looked much more the part of a general counsel than I do. And he looked as if he would bite through his pipe. I felt a quarter of an inch tall . . . and went and read the contract."

The complete act was preparing the opinion for his boss. Bruce had left out one obvious step, making the act incomplete. Mooney actually did very little except to reinforce the lesson that was immediately apparent to Bruce himself. This one incident left Bruce, who is both bright and conscientious, with a vivid reminder that will shape his approach "until the end of my days as a lawyer." One such traumatic experience for a dedicated executive will fully open consciousness to the reinforcing experiences that are part of every day's work.

Bruce later worked with Mooney on a massive updating of Northwestern's articles of incorporation and bylaws. The effort involved hundreds of drafts of provisions. "There was never any word of it that was too small to change, to do again and do better. . . . I guess the lesson in all that to me throughout my career has been to try to get it right and think about it and to do it again and to try to overcome the temptation that we all have that it's good enough. It may be good enough, but it can be better. Until you're satisfied that it's of the highest quality, you're not finished with it and maybe you had better go back and do it again."

Both Kendall Lockhart and Peter Bruce have risen fast in corporate life partly because they learned early how to carry out a complete act. As the micro-unit of the body is the simple cell, the micro-unit of success is the complete act. Both micro-units have the capacity to replicate themselves, with more and more complexity, at higher and higher levels. Both are building blocks for future growth. The complete act is always complete in appropriateness, not only in effort. Ironically, unnecessary work can spoil it.

Douglas J. MacMaster, Jr., senior vice president of Merck & Co., Inc., started his working life as an attorney with a top New York law firm. A partner once asked MacMaster to research a particular point in contract law. About a week later, MacMaster sent him documents that included a survey of every state and the federal statutes as well. "It wasn't as big as a phone book but it was very thick. He called me in a state of shock and told me that the matter involved only about $3000 and what he had really wanted was just a quick brush by the subject. He pointed out that we couldn't bill my time because even though it was rather inexpensive time, it was worth far more than the actual value of this claim for the client."

Asking the right question is the first step toward a complete act. "When I ask questions of people here today where I really need detailed answers, I tell them exactly what I want," MacMaster says, summarizing the lesson of that early experience. "Sometimes . . . I just want an opinion on the spot, particularly if it is a question that has only two answers and you can flip a coin and be right half the time. . . . In other cases, you obviously want in-depth research."

MacMaster has built a reputation at Merck for superb decision-making skills. He sees the key to the complete act in decision making as "learning to put it together." He recalls going to see one of the partners in the law firm "after I had done a piece of research, telling him I really didn't know the answer. I had done all the work but I just didn't know. He started asking questions. After five or ten minutes of his asking questions, I knew the answer and so did he. I had all the information, but I didn't know how to put it together." Thoroughness can involve not only getting the data together, perhaps really more data "than you can possibly assimilate," but also learning how "to get to the heart of things, learning how to get the job done."

In executive work, getting "to the heart of things" is often the ability to perceive a complete act with all its ramifications. This is why high-level decision making is most effective when carried out by executives who have learned to see the completeness of an act at a lower level.

COMPLETE PREPARATION

In learning the complete act, a young executive with an able boss sees routine actions in a new light. Take meetings. Randel S. Carlock, today president and chief executive officer of his own company, Image Retailing Group, Inc., started his career at a Dayton

Hudson department store in Minneapolis, Minnesota. He calls a former boss at Dayton Hudson "the best executive I ever worked for" because she taught him how to prepare for every situation.

"She would never go into a meeting for which she had not been totally briefed and that was my job so I got to see it. You don't see it normally. You sit at a meeting with senior management and you think, boy, are they smart. They are no smarter than the rest of us but, boy, are they prepared. . . . Before any topic was covered at a management meeting that she attended, I would have to do a complete background, not just on our department, but on what was going on in other companies in the same department. She would have that background information, all the facts, all the information, before the meeting ever started."

Learning such preparedness instills discipline, but even more important, it instills a knowledge of the grammar of a successful piece of work. You can have a large vocabulary of individual words, but without an understanding of the structure that holds the words together, you will have no command of the language. If you cannot see a piece of work whole, your individual actions are like individual words without grammar.

Conscious study pays big rewards. If you learn unconsciously to carry out a complete act, you will always perform well. If you learn the structure of the complete act, you can evaluate and improve the performance of others.

Completing the Act Begins at Home

Executives arrive at work the first day with varying degrees of commitment to the complete act. Parental discipline is clearly the most powerful influence before work begins. In the childhood home of the National Urban League's John Jacob, "there was no electricity until I was in the eighth or ninth grade, but my father said, 'You can see by kerosene lamp.' You could not tell my Daddy that you couldn't do anything that anybody else could do."

Also, act and result were rigorously linked. "My father—the

older I get the more I quote my father now—my father ran his house by four fundamental rules. 'I'm a rules man,' my father said. 'If you live in this house, you've got to go to school. If you're not in school, you've got to have a job. If you get a girl pregnant, you're going to marry her. If you go to jail, you're going to stay there. Very simple. These are the rules if you live in this house, these are the rules.' "

For Sara Westendorf, growing up in a comfortable middle-class home, the words and cadences were far different, but the message was fundamentally the same. Be responsible for yourself and for the completion of anything you undertake. Westendorf is Research and Development Manager for Advanced Manufacturing Systems Operations at Hewlett-Packard in Sunnyvale, California. She supervises the work of project teams working in plant and factory automation on contract to such companies as Ford, Rockwell, Fiat, and GM. Responsible for the work of 80 to 100 people, she is, at age 37, one of the highest ranked women at Hewlett-Packard.

She attributes her aspiration to "admiring my mother and what she had accomplished." After having been an engineer during World War II and then getting her Ph.D. in math, Westendorf's mother became dean of Smith College. From her mother, Westendorf first learned "not to be afraid of success, because all the talent in the world isn't going to get you there if you don't believe that you can succeed."

As for the complete act, "we bought an old house, for instance, and the plaster and wallpaper were stained and falling off the wall. If I wanted to have my room remodeled, then I had to do it myself, from the planning to the finished job." Many youngsters would have taken a stab at such a job, only to have the paint peel and the panels fall off the walls six months later due to faulty preparation. "If you are going to remodel a room," Sara Westendorf learned, "you realize that you've got to handle things like trim and lots of other things to get the job done. When you think you are 80 percent finished, you are only 20 percent. You learn the lesson early that if you really want your room to look nice, you must attend to all of the details . . . you've got to follow through on every last loose end."

Thinking Backwards

Think! Whenever Denise Lloyd, a 32-year-old publisher for Babcox Publications, faces a big problem today, "I hear my father say 'Think!'" Lloyd's father worked in sales in a variety of areas. "Even though I was a little girl, he would discuss his business with me." She vividly remembers her father's advice: "Read the directions. If you don't know how to do it, then find out. If you don't know, there is somebody out there who does know and all you have to do is find them."

For Lloyd today, the complete act is a whole magazine. She is the publisher of *Bodyshop Business*, a national, monthly magazine for the collision repair industry. "In publishing you have a magazine and it comes out with all your 100 pages or whatever, but when you start, it is a blank page. It is just a piece of paper in a typewriter. You have to see that magazine completely in your head before you start the project. Many people just don't do that no matter what their function. They can't see the finished job and you have to see the finished job and work backwards."

The same see-the-end-product thinking dictates Lloyd's annoyance with sloppy problem-solving methods. "A lot of people in business have a tendency to take the easy way out, to do a Band-Aid approach so they can solve problems right now. They don't ask, 'Does it solve the problem six months from now?' They are not solving the problem, they are covering it up. They aren't thinking."

Completing the Act at School

Next to the home, school—elementary, secondary, and college —is the most influential source of early discipline in the complete act.

Asked about major influences in his business life, Northwestern Mutual Life Insurance Company president and CEO Donald J. Schuenke answers without a second's hesitation: "Basic education in the parochial schools from the nuns. . . . This idea about excellence and doing it right, that was taught right from the beginning in school. . . . I clearly remember from a very early age there were really strict rules for performance, strict rules for accomplishment, and it started with the nuns."

In the seventh or eighth grade, Schuenke recalls, "we had compositions that we had to write. Each week you had to write one page and you were on your own. You wrote them and you put them in this certain file on the desk of the teacher. I was writing mine, but I was putting them in the wrong file, so when grades came out I got [a] zero in these compositions. . . . At the time I thought it was very silly to take that attitude, but the message was there. The lesson was, by God, you've got to put them in the right place. Just writing them is not enough. I've never forgotten that; it was an important lesson."

By high school, the lessons of the complete act can be bruising experiences that scare off the timid and scar the strong. Cathy Pokorny has excelled all her life. At 37, she is president of PRO-CONSUL, a rapidly growing public relations agency based in Cleveland. Her parents set exceptionally high standards. "You had to excel at whatever you did. If you weren't going to do it right in the first place, then don't bother getting involved. I got almost all A's all the way through school, but that was never good enough. The question was what could I do above and beyond that?" Above and beyond meant honor courses and graduating from college in three years instead of four while holding two jobs.

Pokorny grew up taking this kind of pressure for granted. Even so she recalls every painful detail of her first three days at a journalism course at the University of Michigan during the summer of her junior year in high school. Assigned to interview the university's track coach, she turned the story in on schedule. "The first thing they did was rip it to shreds. Then they sent me out again and told me to do it all over. When I came back the next day, they ripped it to shreds again. Finally, when I came back the third time, they said 'you are improving.' " Although she had second thoughts because "I don't like to be bad at anything," she decided to stick with writing because "nobody was going to tell me at that point that I wasn't going to make it."

Root Causes

By college the complete act already appears in a more complex, conceptual form. John A. Betti, executive vice president of Ford Motor Company's $13 billion Diversified Products Operations, says that, for him, engineering school was a turning point. Betti remembers "coming to the conclusion that the only way that I was really going to understand what was going on was to make sure that I understood the fundamentals instead of trying to memorize them. . . . once you can do that and then derive the equation, it becomes a lot easier to apply."

While such disciplines as engineering and law seem to promote more systematic thought, rigorous liberal arts can produce the same result. When Bank of America enrolled Kendall Lockhart in a high-powered finance course, he was one of only two class members without an MBA, yet he ranked second at the end of the course. He had to work harder in "the basic accounting sort of things." However, his rigorous education as an English major at Princeton enabled him to grasp more complicated concepts quickly. During a long and detailed lecture on present value, "I said, 'Excuse me, but aren't you really saying that a dollar is worth more today than tomorrow?' He said, 'Yes.' I said, 'Thank you.' That was all I needed because then the rest was only math."

In studying English in college, Lockhart learned "to find what the concept is. What is the point of the paragraph?" The fundamental building block of his success, Lockhart adds, "has always been meticulous implementation once you know 'what the concept is.' "

ENERGY CHANNEL

Aspiration unlocks inner resources, producing energy appropriate to the aspiration—the energy for Alex Kroll to lift the barbell, for John Jacob to study without electricity, for Sara Westendorf to remodel a room, and for John Koss to pull his company back from disaster. The most effective channel for that energy is a *complete act* because a complete act both avoids any need to waste energy redoing an incomplete job and promotes personal growth and capacity. To achieve that, a complete act must involve far more than simply seeing the work through to the end. That is just the beginning, not the end, of completeness.

To be complete, any act, no matter how simple, must first achieve the desired result—the room must be remodeled, the decision must be correctly reached on the contract, the order must be obtained for the employment company. *Beyond this, the truly complete act achieves the desired result fully at three levels: physical, mental, and psychological.* If you accomplish this, routine acts can become career accelerators.

The Physical Component

Early training, in home or school, usually focuses on achieving results with physical perfection. Sara Westendorf learned when you remodel a room, the job is only 20 percent complete when you think you are 80 percent finished because there are so many physical details that escape your attention at first. The nuns taught Don Schuenke that he had not completed the mental work of the composition until he physically placed the paper in the right folder.

All work in an organization has a physical component. The higher the organizational level, the less visible this component is, but it is always there. At the lowest level, the physical component dominates. The jobs of the assembly line worker, the forklift operator, the fast-food attendant, the company mailman, and the construction worker are all dictated and dominated by a series of repetitive physical actions.

The senior executive job, no matter how high, can never fully eliminate the physical component. The CEO has her in-box to deal with. She must physically sign requisition and personnel change notices. She must personally review the papers requesting board action on a billion-dollar merger. The luncheon for the board must be ordered with an eye to the finance committee chairman's cholesterol problem and the vice chairman's kosher diet. While traveling, the CEO must keep track of her expenses and receipts just as the lowest junior executive does. The microphone and podium from which she will announce approval of the billion-dollar merger must be checked and double-checked before the press conference. Whether she delegates these actions or carries them out herself, all are physical components vital to the success of her job.

Our public ceremonies employ the smallest physical act to symbolize the levels of work that have created a complete act. The President of the United States, surrounded by legislative and administrative leaders, TV cameras, and newspaper reporters, physically signs a landmark legislative act into law. The governor, with a similar ceremony, physically cuts a ribbon opening a new bridge or highway. These staged events celebrate the completion of an important act and subtly remind us that work is never complete without physical effort.

All successful executives have learned that, in the words of one popular proverb, "the devil is in the details," and these are frequently the physical details. Consciously or unconsciously, people who arrive at the top have learned that physical details count, while many far more brilliant people level off because they perceive small physical details as either unimportant or beneath them. Merck's Doug MacMaster puts it like this: "When you touch a job, you want to ensure that it's completed. . . . somebody has asked you to get tickets to a play. If you get the tickets and then throw them into your out-basket that doesn't mean that the person in Oshkosh has the tickets. You have to follow through on these things."

Attention to the Smallest Detail.

Poor handling of physical details can wreck the best conceived plans, as every military officer is taught again and again. An army that runs out of gasoline and bullets cannot execute the general's brilliant strategy. However, in courses for public and private sector managers, much time is devoted to the mental and psychological aspects of executive work, as if the physical component were something that even the most inexperienced manager had learned to handle smoothly. In their eagerness to get managers to delegate more, course instructors sometimes imply that the physical details are a dull and somewhat unimportant part of management work.

The reality back in the office is vastly different. Management crisis time most frequently involves cleaning up messes created when a sloppy or wrong physical component delays or spoils a complete act—the promotional mailing that went out late or, worse, went to the wrong place; the new product launch held up by one 85-cent part; the typographical error in the press release; the important report not circulated to the right executives in time for the approval deadline.

American Health magazine almost failed at the outset because the printer who was contracted to mail out the all-important first issue used inferior mailing labels that fell off the magazines. The work of Owen Lipstein and his partners in creating a bold new concept, the design work of their artists, the creativity of their writers, and the skill of their production people all meant nothing as the magazines sat, undeliverable to the potential subscribers. *American Health* had no money for a rerun and the printer at first refused to correct the error. After a heated confrontation with Owen Lipstein, the printer replaced the labels at a cost to himself of $300,000, and the successful launch continued. Every executive can recount similar, if not so dramatic, examples of significant efforts delayed or destroyed by careless attention to physical details.

Not just every job but every act has a physical component,

and it is here that the effort to be complete begins. Think of any task, no matter how seemingly abstract, and find the physical components. Consider, for example, strategic planning. There must be premeeting documentation; announcement of the meeting schedule; pencils, notepads, and blackboards available; coffee and food ready at the right time; and notes transcribed and distributed. Delaying or mishandling one of these components can cause either a minor annoyance (the coffee is late) or a serious waste of time (without proper documentation we may waste 40 minutes in an argumentative discussion that could have been settled in 5 minutes with the right set of figures). Either way, the completeness of the act of strategic planning is spoiled.

An Invisible Cord

When Garry Jacobs and I visited and analyzed companies for our book *The Vital Difference*,[2] we found that attention to the smallest physical details was one clear distinction between companies that grew and developed steadily and companies whose growth was flat or uneven. The same holds true for individuals. It is as if brilliant concept and mundane execution are linked by an invisible cord. If that cord breaks, no matter how brilliant the concept, no significant performance will occur.

Rear Admiral David M. Cooney, who retired after a 30-year career in the U.S. Navy to become president and chief executive officer of Goodwill Industries of America, Inc., learned this lesson aboard ship. He recalls a shipmate who had a Ph.D. in engineering physics from MIT as "one of the brightest people I've ever known. But he was absolutely incapable of expressing the concepts that he had in his mind in a way which was meaningful to the people he worked with." This officer had the capacity to analyze the sche-

---

[2]Frederick G. Harmon and Garry Jacobs, *The Vital Difference: Unleashing the Powers of Sustained Corporate Success.* Published by AMACOM, a division of the American Management Association, 1985.

matics of a new missile system and explain to the manufacturer's engineers why it didn't work. However, when confronted with a small, but deadly, physical problem, he could not translate his conceptual knowledge to a simple physical solution.

The specific incident involved a paint-scraping device that was improperly plugged into 220 volts of current. The man holding the device had stepped into a puddle of water and had become frozen to the device as a result of the electric current. Several sailors, not thinking, grabbed the man, inadvertently saving his life by absorbing some of the current in their bodies. The officer with the Ph. D. in engineering physics arrived on the scene where now several sailors were locked in the grim electrical embrace and he, too, made exactly the same mistake. A few moments later, another sailor, probably with a grade school education, ended the incident by unplugging the device.

No matter what your level of theoretical achievement is, it means nothing if you cannot reach down and physically pull the plug when the occasion demands.

The Mental Component

Beyond the physical level, each act of executive work has a mental component. The effort here is to organize physical labor in new and more productive ways. At the highest level, this is Henry Ford thinking through the work of building automobiles in a new way and changing manufacturing forever. It is Alfred Sloan creating a new organizational system that left General Motors unchallenged as the symbol of a well-managed company for two generations. It is General Robert Wood integrating purchasing and distribution to make Sears Roebuck & Co. the world's largest retailer. It is Michael Blumenthal responding to the new global marketplace in computers by integrating, not just merging, Sperry and Burroughs.

The company president, entrepreneur, or middle-level manager all must organize their mental work at their current level before further progress is possible. A sudden job change can expose a huge gap in mental readiness with gut-wrenching speed.

At age 27, Randy Carlock left Dayton Hudson, sold his BMW, and bought a small stereo retail store, Audio King. He immediately made plans to open another. After a short time, the new owner/president "sat in the office on the second floor and looked at the ceiling. I had made a terrible strategic error. I didn't know where to find the accounting department, the legal department, the personnel department, the advertising department. I had come from a big corporation and everybody did everything for you. All you had to do was run the merchandising and advertising and the people. If you needed new people, you called personnel. If you needed an ad, you called advertising. If a new contract came in, the legal staff looked at it for you. The accounting was all done for you."

Carlock had been promoted quickly at Dayton Hudson by performing complete acts at a lower level. Inevitably, his work became part of a wider complete act for the corporation. Now he had to manage the complete act for an entire company. Even though the company was small, the difference shook him.

Carlock's example is dramatic because the lesson hit him all at once, but the principle can be found in any expanding career. The mental component of the complete act suddenly expands, leaving a gap and tension in its wake. In an orderly, planned succession, there has been training to ensure that this gap is minimized. However, when people are rapidly or unexpectedly promoted or embark on new careers, the gap can seem like a chasm.

If aspiration is strong, the inner resources will release abundant energy for the extra effort now required, energy that can flow in several directions. Commonly, it converts into simple physical energy, providing stamina for a stretch of 16- to 18-hour days until the crisis is manageable. This is the time-honored approach to crisis management that is followed by entrepreneurs and corporate executives alike. While it will work most of the time, it merely draws on the inner resources without expanding them. The executive

weathers the crisis but with little or no growth except for a somewhat fanciful belief in an expanded capacity for crisis management.
Growth comes only when the executive manages the crisis *while
learning the complete act at the new level*.

Carlock had little time to waste. As he surveyed his new
empire, he found "we had a couple of divisions that were losing a
lot of money. There was no organization, no coordination between
the two stores, and we had no business plan. And the worst part,
the worst realization that I had was that I wasn't prepared to do
any of those things. . . . I'd come out of this big corporation and
I was a hot shot and I knew everything. And I came into a small
corporation that was just a fraction of the size and I didn't know
what to do. I didn't know what to do first because everything
needed to be done. There was no computer, there was no control
system, there were no regular inventory systems, no anything."

So what did Carlock do first? "I went back and started work
on an MBA at the University of Minnesota." He invested the
energy summoned by the crisis both in immediate problem solving
and in increasing his capacity to complete the expanded mental
component of his job. "I realized that if we were going to build
this into a real company, we had to have an understanding, a global
view of business and a view of how strategically all the pieces fit
together."

In the crisis, Carlock had by experience and instinct grasped
what many entrepreneurs and even some corporate presidents never
understand—that the complete act for the company president and
CEO is the whole company's business, not just a favored part that
this individual does well. He recognized that education would provide him with the mental expansion to see his new responsibilities
whole.

Money or Smarts

Carlock recently sold a public offering of his company's stock for
$3.2 million in a deal that made him a millionaire. He is starting

his doctorate in leadership and plans eventually to become a full-time professor. For Carlock, there are only two tools for success: financial and human capital. "As I tell my students, you've got to have either money or smarts."

Smarts for the successful manager means mastering the mental component of every part of each job. Success is measured by a mental mastery of jobs of steadily increasing complexity. Richard J. Markham, 38, vice president of marketing for Merck Sharp & Dohme, joined Merck in 1973 as a professional representative, calling on doctors. His first boss, John Traw, finding a willing student, began coaching Markham not just in sales, but also in sales management. Traw took the unusual step of keeping his protégé in the field for nearly four and one-half years, rather than the customary two. Although Markham admits to some frustration over this, the additional training paid off. "I ended up skipping one of the jobs people normally went through to become district manager . . . so I ended up no further behind and maybe a little bit ahead of some of my peers." Thanks to a generous mentor, Markham learned the complete act at the next level. Almost.

Appointed district manager in New York City in 1978, Markham found himself supervising 12 sales representatives. Again he reported to a boss with a clear mental concept of the work to be done. "I came up to meet him and he offered me the job. We were talking afterwards and he asked me, 'Why do you think we have district managers?' Having just been appointed district manager, I thought it was an unusual question. . . . I came up with a lot of answers that one might come up with, such as plan the activities of the district. . . . Finally, I could see I wasn't coming up with the answer he wanted so I said, 'I give up. Why, in your opinion, do we have district managers?' He said, 'The only reason we have district managers is to help the representatives be better representatives. Otherwise, I could have all the representatives report directly to me.' It turned out he was right and it set me off on a course in the right direction as a manager."

His career accelerating, Markham became a product manager

at age 29. Now the task was to get things done without anyone actually reporting to him. The mental component was technical knowledge and communication skill. Markham quickly analyzed his deficiencies. "I thought I had learned about writing as a district manager but I had to learn a lot more in that job." He also found he was "terribly deficient" in the critically important product manager's skill of speaking before large groups. Coaching from his boss improved his writing, and an outside course improved his speaking to a satisfactory level for the job.

The product manager's job also taught him to aim for perfection in physical as well as mental acts. "So many of the things that we did that were seemingly small points at the time ended up coming back as big things two or three years later. . . . It's what I call avoiding the that's-good-enough syndrome. . . . Even if it's something as simple as writing a one-paragraph memo, you have a tendency to look at it and say, 'If I redid it, I could do it better but for this purpose it's good enough.' You let it go, and sure enough three months later, it turns out you should have fixed it. . . . What I picked up primarily as a product manager was that you shouldn't say, 'That's good enough.' You shouldn't quit until you can say, 'That's the best I can do.' "

"Is It Good Enough?"

Markham has a good test to evaluate the completeness of an act, which he uses to teach younger managers at Merck. Take anything you do and pretend the chairman of the board is going to evaluate your whole career on that one thing. "Now," says Markham, "is it good enough?" Underlying this technique is a deep truth. "You never know which thing you do is really going to make a difference."

Reflecting on his rapid rise, Markham gives abundant credit to the strength of the Merck career development system and to his string of able bosses. Even so, to reach vice president of marketing in the sales and operations division of one of the world's premier pharmaceutical companies well before the age of 40 indicates performance that is far more than just the product of a good system.

The most important key to Markham's success is one trait he always looks for in those he now hires: "people . . . who are able to concentrate on the task at hand for a long time. They are not easily distracted. . . . To me the people who are most successful really have an ability to concentrate. . . . There have been lots of smart people who have been my peers in the jobs I have had. There have certainly been people who could do any of the jobs that I have done as well or better than I could do, if you just looked at the qualifications. There are people who have the ability to concentrate whatever level of intellect they have on the task at hand and not be distracted. . . . This ability to concentrate their grey matter on the topic is something that separates some of the very top performers from the others."

What Markham calls the "ability to concentrate the grey matter on the topic" is the mental component of doing the complete act—organizing the task at hand in a way to maximize results, while carrying out the physical details to perfection. This, indeed, is a major factor separating the very top performers from the others. As Markham's career illustrates, the good news is that the ability to complete the act on the mental level is not an innate knack or talent, but rather a technique that can be learned by anyone aspiring to become one of those top performers.

The Psychological Component

Top performance on a complete, act requires still one more level —psychological. The physical details can be perfectly arranged and the mental work may be conceived, organized, and implemented with imagination, but still there remains the way in which the act is communicated and coordinated with others, and how the feelings of others are considered at each step. Every act carried out by a human being has this psychological dimension.

Take a fundamental human act such as preparing and eating

a meal. At the most basic, physical level, the *desired result* is that the meal be successfully ingested so that life may continue. However, everyone who has ever learned how to cook or has taught "company manners" to children knows there are many more levels than this. The *physical* skills of handling knife, fork, spoon, and glass must be mastered. There is also a *mental* level of deciding what foods to prepare and in what order to present them. Every novice cook has struggled with the problem of the meat dish being ready too early or late. The social or *psychological* component raises a basic act of survival to a subtle and joyful experience. (It is here that we wage the intergenerational wars with teenagers over such issues of self-restraint as elbows on the table, slurping the soup, and talking with one's mouth full.)

The psychological component of a complete act always involves self-restraint, checking the desire of the rampaging ego to get on with the job without regard to the feelings of others. "Will you eat like that when you go to dinner at the White House?" asks the exasperated parent. "Then, I'll remember what to do" is the teenager's invariable answer. There is truth on both sides of this dialogue. The teenager is right: We can all exercise psychological restraint when we must. After all, a nasty temper is seldom directed at the boss. The parent also has a strong argument. Situational rather than habitual self-restraint is always a strain. The enjoyment of the conversation and cuisine at that White House dinner is sure to be spoiled if the teenager has to concentrate on which fork to use.

Self-Mastery

At work, a missing or faulty psychological component always causes a strain. Failure to master the psychological component subtly shifts control of the situation from an inner feeling of self-confidence to externally dominated anxiety. Self-mastery lets us relax and focus on results even in tense situations. The world-famous tennis star does not lose her concentration because she is behind in the deciding set. Long practice in controlling her emotions permits her to continue playing at her peak. The practice of self-restraint in making common everyday acts more perfect builds up a similar inner calm on which one can rely in any crisis.

Everyone in management knows people who can be relied on 100 percent to carry out the physical and mental components of a complete act, but who seem totally incapable of considering the feelings of others in delivering their work. If they are brilliant enough and their individual efforts are critical to corporate success, their behavior will be largely overlooked; in fact, wise managers may even assign individuals of lesser talent to "run interference" for them. We find such exemptions from the normal rules in the star salesperson with the knack of writing million-dollar orders in the middle of recessions, the researcher with the unbroken string of profitable new products, and the advertising genius whose inspired copy always moves the customers to buy more right now. These are the legendary "big gorillas" of business, who, in the words of one executive, "sit where they damn well want to sit."

After exempting those few, we find many more whose progress is clearly frustrated by an inability to carry out a complete act without annoying or actually infuriating others. There is the market researcher whose arrogance blocks reception of her valuable insights; the foul-tempered manager whose skills keep his results high despite the highest staff turnover and lowest morale in the organization; the politician/glory-seeker who will take not only his well-deserved share of credit for the project, but also the share of everyone else on the team as well.

In such talented individuals, aspiration has touched inner resources, producing energy in abundance. However, they have learned to use only the physical and mental components in expressing their energy. Their work on the surface may be perfect, but its value is limited by a failure to consider the impact of their words and behavior on others. In the washrooms, dining rooms, and boardrooms, the private word on such Charlies and Charlottes is that they have come as far as they will go. They are hard workers, to be sure, and valuable individual performers within marketing, finance, sales, or research and development, but they are absolutely "incapable of working easily with others." The current "Age of the Entrepreneur" has provided a creative escape valve for the energy and talent of many such individuals. Left to depend solely on their own ability, they will succeed brilliantly until the size of their own company requires the self-restraint of achieving results with others.

In large organizations with a commitment to the development of people, individuals without enough concern for others are likely to be told so with unmistakable clarity. Others, without such coaching, discover the importance of inner restraint and develop the personal techniques that make it possible. The many successes of such learning, with or without coaching, show that the psychological component, like the physical and the mental, can be learned by anyone who understands its importance.

The Complete Psychological Act

As with the physical and mental components, the psychological component can be carried out partially or even fully in one situation and poorly in another. Teenagers may display their company table manners for Aunt Mary, whom they rather like and respect, while reserving their worst behavior for Cousin Eddie, whom they consider a bore. Similarly, a manager may communicate with one colleague with a full appreciation of how she likes to receive information, while ignoring the same preference entirely with one of her own team members.

Making the effort to put yourself in the other person's position is the first and indispensable step in mastering the psychological component of the complete act. This essentially is the art of friendly persuasion. Frank Popoff, president and chief executive officer of the $17 billion Dow Chemical Co., remembers that during the first of two assignments in Europe, one of his team members was a top Swiss salesman, "a very good man who had longish hair, who dressed a little differently, who wasn't the quintessential archetypal representative of a U.S. company."

This is the kind of problem that causes sleepless nights for many inexperienced managers. Popoff's situation was complicated by its being an international assignment where "you're just another American who's come over, especially going over for the first time. . . . They were testing you. They wanted to see how far they could push."

The situation offered Popoff a wide variety of options from ignoring the challenge entirely to an autocratic show of authority. He chose to raise the psychological level of his response by looking at the situation from the other man's viewpoint. "So I said, 'You know, Gene, you've got a situation here where you're damn good. We know that, I know that, you know that. The results speak for themselves. But you're doing a lot less than you could.' He said, 'I work like hell, what are you talking about?' I said, 'Well, if you were calling on me and your business card said The Dow Company and I looked at you in your kind of burnt orange suit and your long head of hair and all the idiosyncracies that you have in manner and dress, it would take me at least one or two calls before I became comfortable with you. You've lost a lot of time on the way to getting the order.' This was a very commercial guy and that got his attention. He said, 'You're right, by God,' and he really cleaned himself up. He didn't get his hair cut though."

When Popoff was reassigned to the United States, his team assembled to wish him goodbye at a Paris airport hotel. Each man gave him a small memento. Gene was late for the gathering, "and this other guy, one of his friends, says 'Gene will be with us in a minute but he wanted you to have this.' " Popoff opened the corsage box and found a mass of hair with a big red rose on top. When Gene arrived, he said, "You know I couldn't think of a more significant goodbye gift to give you than this goddamned haircut of mine." Popoff adds, "He kept his hair short and I was touched."

Popoff had gracefully succeeded by making this small but potentially disruptive incident a complete act. The *results* had been achieved at the *physical* level (more sales, better image for the company) by a *mental* process of thinking through all the options and choosing the highest possible *psychological* response, which was putting himself in the other man's position. Popoff could have achieved the same results in many ways, but no other way would have been so perfect an act, a fact subtly acknowledged by Gene in his own complete act in response.

THE HEART OF ALL GROWTH

Skills are essential to progress at work. From the lowest (filling out an expense account) to the highest (creating a strategic plan), skills can either advance or hinder executive progress. However, skills are not the heart of growth; they are the limbs that do the work well or poorly as growth progresses or stalls.

The heart of all successful growth is the perfectly complete act. At the lowest level, the complete act is reflected in how well a manager achieves a desired result in a tricky personnel situation by coordinating the basic physical, mental, and psychological components. At the highest level, it is reflected in how well a CEO coordinates the physical assets of the company such as cash, factories, and patents through the mental process of thinking through the company's mission, direction, and opportunities in a manner that expresses the highest psychological concern for customers, workers, managers, suppliers, and the communities in which the company operates.

In every complete act, the physical/mental/psychological synergy is complete, if not perfect. Remove one component at the lowest level and you have the perfectly planned and physically beautiful mailing piece that does not go out on time because of discontent and low morale among the workers assigned to the project. Remove one at the highest level and you will find that the brilliant merger combining the physical assets of two giant firms in a new, imaginative way never lives up to expectations because of psychological anxieties among managers and workers.

In the anatomy of success, the complete act is the basic cell, containing within it the seed of all future growth. Like the simple cell on which all life rests, the complete act is a building block that can be replicated again and again or combined in higher and higher forms. In business terms, the complete act is the franchisable entity with the billion-dollar future; once successfully created in one place, it can be rapidly expanded everywhere.

We Are Born Into a Complete Act

A successful family is a complete act. The family was created to nurture and raise children and to support and protect its adult members. That result must be achieved at the physical level—the family works to provide food, shelter, and security. At the mental level, it plans for the future and decides how to employ its assets to create that future. At the psychological level, it offers reassurance, comfort, and support to its members.

From this one complete act, replicated millions of times with endless variations, comes a power on which American society rests, a power so great that we take it for granted. Our industries and our educational and government institutions draw every day on the inexhaustible power of the family. If you read profiles of political, business, or sports leaders; listen to financiers or developers; or talk to bosses, colleagues, board members, or assembly line foremen, you will often learn identical responses to such questions as "Where did you learn this skill or that attitude? Where did you acquire that ability or this knowledge?" The answers are so common and so true that they have become clichés: "From my father, my mother, my grandfather, my aunt, my family; from living with my brothers and sisters."

We are born into a complete act, which shapes us and is our inheritance. When John Jacob quotes his father's rules or when Sara Westendorf remembers redecorating her room, they are evoking far more than a fond memory of incidents long past; they are touching the center of a complete act that has been the wellspring of their success.

Getting a college degree is a complete act. For some, the

physical component can dominate, the need somehow to assemble the money to pay for books, a place to live, and food to eat. The mental component is not just the studies themselves but the organization of the studies so that the work can be accomplished before midterms. On their own for the first time, many students find the need for self-restraint difficult to handle. The "freshman 15" is the code phrase for the sudden weight gain that often signals the first extended period away from home cooking. Enrollment often drops by a quarter or more in the first year of college as the combined pressures of finances, self-directed studies, and relationships not supported by the family take their toll. Many students return after a year or two, having learned elsewhere how to complete an act.

Despite these difficulties, millions of Americans earn college degrees because they understand the power of this complete act. Educators, of course, see this power as coming primarily from the effort to strengthen young minds, but the reminiscing at any college reunion tells another story. Classmates relive together not just their studies, but the total college experience, which involved sharing physical adversity and learning how to work with others.

Employers are correct to emphasize college degrees in hiring. The degree may or may not show intellectual eminence, but it certifies that the graduate has a capacity to carry out a complete act. Also, as the top companies emphasize in their recruiting, the tougher the school, the more rigorous the curriculum, the higher the grades, the wider the scope of extracurricular activities and, the more perfect the complete act of earning a college degree.

The power of this complete act, like the power of a successful family, is self-evident. In the early years of a career, an executive depends heavily not only on the information obtained at college, but also on the social skills, work habits, and commitment to deadlines that he or she developed during those college years. *American Health*'s Owen Lipstein once asked a college English professor: "When I understand the idea, do I really have to write it down?' But then I learned writing it down can teach you something, too."

Some executives will tell you they learned nothing in college except how to mix a good martini. Whatever the student's motives and however minimal the performance, the degree represents an aspiration fulfilled. The higher the aspiration (for example, to be first in the class or captain of the team), the greater the energy released; the more complete the act in channeling that energy, the greater the achievement; the greater the achievement, the greater the power to propel the individual forward in life.

You hold an executive position today because you have achieved one complete act or many. If you aspire to move up, you need only to use the energy generated by your aspiration to make every act at your present level more and more perfect.

Start With One Act

Start with one act, preferably something you believe you do well. Take the example of running a departmental meeting. First, write down in exhaustive detail every physical component (for example, agenda, meeting room, advance documentation, and minutes), every mental component (for example, objectives to be achieved, sequence of topics to be discussed, and how follow-up is to be organized), every psychological component (for example, each participant's overt and hidden anxieties regarding each item on the agenda). Then, in planning the meeting, try to improve every single item within every component by one small step.

Next try to run a meeting that successfully integrates all these components at the highest level. Aim for perfection. Study the response of the participants. Study your own response. You will feel an undeniable surge of energy and enthusiasm. Beyond that you will feel a calm confidence, which should indicate to you just how much anxiety actually surrounded this task that you do well.

Suddenly you will see that your individual and management work is a mass of incomplete acts. On one particular task, a poor filing system hinders good mental work. On another assignment, inadequate planning created unworkable deadlines. On yet another job, neglect of a colleague's obvious sensitivity is causing friction and delay. If we can gain such an infusion of calm, steady energy by perfectly completing the act on something we do well, what would be the potential of applying the complete act to every single aspect of our job, to the parts we do well and the parts we do poorly? The potential, of course, would be a career without plateaus.

3 PSYCHOLOGICAL EFFORT: THE WILL TO WORK

We all know the drudgery of a tough day at the office and we have all felt the exhiliration of a good day's work. What essentially is the difference? One difference concerns external achievement: in a good day, we have accomplished something worthwhile; in a tough day, we have not. A second difference concerns inner achievement, that is, a sense that we are, in some perhaps not fully explainable way, more than we were. At a deeper level, growth occurs during a good day, not during a bad one. The path to that sense of inner achievement and growth is psychological effort.

Physical effort is important, but because it is so visible, it gets disproportionate credit as a primary source of success. "You should have seen the boss," recounts the admiring middle manager. "We got off that plane after 12 hours. I was absolutely exhausted and he says can we schedule a meeting tonight?"

What the younger manager does not fully comprehend is that this formidable energy does not spring from some secret reservoir that is not available to ordinary humans. Rather, it is the physical manifestation of energy created by aspiration; the more intense the aspiration, the greater the energy. The press marvels at the inexhaustible energy displayed day after day by the candidates for the presidency, the highest political aspiration in our country.

Throughout primary and election campaigns, these politicians are in perpetual motion, never showing fatigue. Then, at the final press conference, when they announce they are withdrawing from the race, they seem barely able to stand upright. Without the force of high aspiration, superhuman energy quickly fades.

Mental effort also counts, but it is not the major determining factor in business success. One successful president told me that "there is not a single thing involved in any executive job that any of us can't learn. The only difference is our willingness to learn and the speed of our learning curve. Some will take six days, others six months, but there's nothing involved that's so complicated that any of us can't learn it if we want to."

The executive's hours at work are visibly dominated by physical and mental work. However, the single greatest work involved in career advancement is psychological effort, the below-the-surface, behind-the-scenes battle that individuals wage in restraining their ego, in working to improve the impact they have on others, and in shaping themselves to the requirements of the work.

CIVILIZING YOURSELF

Psychological effort is the hard, private work of molding and, at the deepest level, civilizing yourself. Because it is hard, there is always the temptation to let up or abandon the effort after a few years on the job. Any encouragement is important for motivation. Training courses are a powerful motivator not only because of the information they provide, but also because at heart they all sell one fundamental concept: You don't have to settle; you can become more!

Because it is private, psychological effort often remains invisible until its results emerge full-blown in a crisis or opportunity. In some careers, the results of this steady inner effort appear slowly in the form of more perfect mastery of external situations of increasing complexity, but the real mastery is always within. This is the real growth behind those careers that seem to progress in a preordained manner from success to success or, conversely, in those careers that for years are beset with external barriers only to brilliantly flower at the point when most careers are ending. In the latter case, the individual has held onto aspiration and continued to work on tasks dictated by psychological effort, but has somehow missed until very late some single step that brings it all together. Everything is waiting for that single ingredient.

Such late success is not as rare as we think. In 1953 Colonel Harland Sanders owned one restaurant valued at $165,000. Three years later he sold the restaurant for $75,000 (barely enough to clear his debts) after a new interstate highway was scheduled to bypass his cafe. At age 66, Sanders set out in his 1946 Ford to establish his franchise business. He would drive up to a restaurant and offer to cook his chicken for the manager and employees. If they liked it, he would cook the recipe for their customers for a few days, hoping to sell his specially prepared blend of spices to the manager on an informal contract basis. In the first two years he had signed up only five franchises. So, to promote business, Sanders adopted his famous attire—all-white suit and shirt, white mustache and goatee, with a black string tie and a cane. By 1960 there were more than 200 outlets; by 1963 some 600 franchisees were paying Sanders $300,000 a year. In 1964 he sold out for $2 million plus a lifetime annual salary of initially $40,000 (later $200,000) for advertising and publicity work.

In another well-known example, Raymond A. Kroc was 52 and still selling milkshake mixers for someone else when he saw the possibilities in a small hamburger chain called McDonald's.

Psychological Restraint

Psychological effort is essentially the work of civilizing yourself because it mirrors the way civilizations were created. Civilization developed on a foundation of physical effort, as tribes of hunters and, later, farmers learned to combine individual physical strength to produce a higher yield for all. Later, such mental creations as tools, money, and writing enabled the original discovery of combining group physical effort to be replicated and expanded at a higher level in towns.

As society organized at higher mental levels, humans developed greater psychological restraint, establishing laws to govern behavior. Society has progressed through all three kinds of effort —physical, mental, and psychological—through the course of history, with the shift from physical to mental effort becoming more pronounced in the last 100 years. The need for greater psychological self-restraint is also unmistakably growing in an age of nuclear proliferation. However, humanity is far less willing to make this psychological change than it is to shift from physical to mental effort.

Business Evolution

We find the same evolutionary process in American business. Our economy was established by the back-breaking physical toil of the slave, the farmer, and the pioneer. Simple survival dominated. The only customs imported from the Old World were those that worked in the harsh realities of the New World. American business, unencumbered by outdated customs, free to apply the results of a period of heretofore unparalleled technological change, and able to use the tremendous human energy of a society eager to encourage individual aspiration, became the wonder of the world. As business grew, it dominated and dwarfed other aspects of American life, often with unhealthy effects. "The business of America is business," proclaimed President Calvin Coolidge. Intellectuals ridiculed the President's statement without denying its essential truth.

The shift from physical to mental effort was speeded by what some called American ingenuity, as if it were an innate American asset. Whitney's cotton gin and Fulton's steamboat, to name two examples, were mental innovations that upgraded the results of human physical effort. Henry Ford's mental effort organized physical work at a still higher level. In our own era, the computer wizards of the Silicon Valley have eliminated the physical work of thousands of workers and managers. As with any major technological revolution, these changes simultaneously have created social upheaval, new opportunities, and an urgent need to upgrade basic skills within society.

For most of our history, the free spirit of American business has entertained few self-directed efforts at psychological restraint. However, external forces have imposed considerable discipline. Labor unions forced greater restraint in dealing with workers. Government regulations attempted to keep business's values aligned with society's evolving norms. Competition created enormous pressures to improve quality and lower costs. In recent decades, better managed companies have begun to apply more self-directed psychological restraint, reflecting a growing awareness that society's franchise to business involves more than just creating profit.

The individual manager grows by psychological effort in three ways: overcoming personal traits that get in the way of success at work, reshaping well-established work habits and biases as the requirements of the job change, and putting oneself at psychological risk in order to get the job done.

OVERCOMING PERSONAL TRAITS

Early in his career, Michael Blumenthal became aware that he had a problem. "I had the reputation when I was young, and it is something that dogged me for a good many years, of being considered rough, tough. The word that was used when I was in my early 30s was 'abrasive.'" Blumenthal's initial reaction was a common one. "For awhile, I thought it was probably a bum rap, but maybe that was just self-protection." Eventually Blumenthal acknowledged his shortcomings. "I was not terribly skillful in thinking about how other people would react to what I wanted to do. I did not tolerate fools gladly or lesser lights gladly or other options gladly. That hurt me, and I made a conscious decision to learn from that."

For years Blumenthal worked to overcome, or at least minimize, the negative impact of this trait. "[I would] consciously check myself when I had a tendency to rush in or to brush somebody off or to be brusque, to say, hey, wait a minute, that's going to sound bad or when I felt I sounded bad, to go back to the person and to try to make amends in some hopefully subtle way."

Blumenthal served in government under Presidents John Kennedy and Lyndon Johnson, eventually rising to chairman of the U.S. Delegation to the Kennedy Round of Trade Negotiations. His first tour of government service was "an exercise of six years of give and take, of diplomacy, tact, and skill." Being able to work cooperatively with others is especially important in government, Blumenthal learned. No matter how important your position, "You are always . . . negotiating with people. You have only a piece of the action."

Blumenthal learned his self-imposed lesson well. As he led the Burroughs-Sperry merger, Blumenthal was able to maintain an exceptionally low level of abrasiveness. He skillfully avoided any winners-and-losers mentality in the merged companies. How did he dramatize this?

"Everything I did and said was designed to dramatize it. I did it by not picking a name, but having a contest where everybody participated in picking a new name with a very visible program of rewards. I did it by making sure that the process of deciding how to organize the new company was done in a way which ensured the full participation of both groups of prior executives in the prior companies. I did it by preaching that it doesn't matter where you come from. It matters what you can contribute. The same point that I made with regard to Shanghai. I applied that, not by talking about Shanghai but merely by saying 'I don't care where you come from. I don't care what job you've had. What I care about is what you can contribute now.' "

Blumenthal always tried to speak candidly in order to lessen anxiety. "Up front, we let people know, yes, we're going to have to reduce employment. And let me tell you by how much and let me tell you how we're going to determine where it is. We're going from 102,000 to 92,000, but it's going to be done by attrition; it's going to be done with early retirement. After that we think there will be a residual of 3000 or 4000 jobs [to reduce] and here are the areas where we'll work. We'll do it quickly, but we'll give you a golden handshake. Now relax. And let's go to work."

Blumenthal's success is built on energy, intelligence, an ability to draw on his inner resources through high aspiration, and, finally, on the effort he made to overcome an abrasiveness that could have severely limited the impact of his other strengths.

A Caring Boss

Unlike Blumenthal, many executives either miss or see and then ignore the need for the psychological effort that is part of every executive success. Some pay a terrible price in lost career potential. Others have a boss to thank for driving home the sometimes unwelcome facts of life.

Harvey Golub, president and chief executive officer of IDS Financial Services, Inc., came to IDS after American Express acquired the Minneapolis-based company in 1984. With American Express's backing, the company's performance has improved dramatically, with assets owned or managed valued at a record high of $36 billion in the first quarter of 1988.

Golub's earlier career was with the management consulting firm McKinsey & Co., Inc., where he eventually rose to senior partner. That might never have come to pass except for the advice of J. McLain Stewart, an early mentor at the firm. "When I was a principal and was up for election to director, Mac called me into his office and said, 'You aren't going to get elected as director unless you change.' That got my attention. I said, 'Why, what is going on here?'" Stewart told him that despite his well-recognized analytical skills, he intimidated people. "'You intimidate them by a number of your behaviors and you've got to change those behaviors or you won't be elected.' "

The problem, Golub says, was that people were getting the impression "they were talking to a computer." When people discussed an important issue with Golub, they would get absolutely no physical reaction. "I would sit back with a blank face, taking everything in. What you would get back then was something like, 'I hear what you are saying and there are three reasons you are wrong. The first reason is, and here are two supporting pieces of evidence' and so on with reasons two and three."

Even before his counseling interview, Stewart had made an appointment for Golub with a New York communications specialist. Stewart told Golub, "I already know the things that he is going to tell you to do and work with you on. They are going to be very hard for you to do, but I also know that if you decide that you can do them, you will execute them even if they are uncomfortable for you." Working with the specialist was "painful because I was viewing myself on videotape, and I saw how the consultant and others saw me," but that course "got me elected director of the firm."

Golub learned that "at the start of a conversation, I couldn't say 'There are five points that I want to make' and then go through the five. I would practice saying 'There are several points that I want to make.' It was a loss in precision, but a gain in empathy. People still call me stone-faced, but a lot less than they used to." Golub found that people "didn't mind that I was intellectual, but what they did mind was that I was so explicit." Was it hard work? "Very hard," Golub replies, with no smile, "and it still is."

From this experience, Golub learned the importance of independently learning how others see him. Each year he hires his former mentor, Stewart, to interview all the people who report to him. "Mac talks to all the people about what's going on, what they're feeling, what they like and dislike, what things they would like to see me do differently." Stewart also talks informally to Golub's bosses at American Express. Then, without identifying the source of any individual comment, "Mac gives me my report card."

What kind of things come up? "He might say, 'People are concerned about the pace of change. You need to do a better job of bringing them along. There are some who are not comfortable in their jobs, and they could use some more encouragement from you. You aren't getting out and patting people on the back enough.' "

Golub is a seasoned executive with every reason to trust his ability to understand people. Yet, with the guidance of a shrewd and caring boss, he has made a continual acknowledgment that he needs to improve in this area. The steady effort he has made to improve his skills in working with others has enabled him to use his unquestioned and early recognized intellectual brilliance to full effect.

"A Growing Pain"

The search within for the traits that block effectiveness on the job can lead in surprising directions, sometimes right to the most positive attributes of the personality. Robert F. Smith, president of the management consulting company Strategies & Teams, Inc., in San Diego, has a magnetic personality; meet him for an hour and you will feel you are talking to one of your oldest friends. Between 1964 and 1981, Smith served with great success as president and later as chairman of Phillips-Ramsey, Inc., a rapidly expanding San Diego marketing, advertising, and public relations firm. The firm had an open, friendly style that Smith found very congenial. Still, in any fast-growth organization, even the most open and friendly, sooner or later the CEO must deal with tough performance problems, "none of which were easy or pleasant, nor did anyone else want to do it."

Smith used his empathy toward others first to be sure "Am I perceiving this situation correctly and to double-check myself on that and to feel satisfied that I was." Before crucial meetings with the individuals involved, Smith made detailed notes and then explicitly reminded himself to "be careful when under stress that you don't meet your own needs to have harmony, shall we say, and affability; but rather you meet the needs of what you perceive to be required here. And that really was a conscious thing. It remains so to this day." Smith aptly describes this kind of psychological effort as "a growing pain. And the passage of years has, for me personally, meant growth in my ability to confront those situations, understand that they have to be faced and dealt with, and then do my damnedest to deal with them straightaway."

The irony of psychological effort is that what is easy and natural for one executive is "a growing pain" for another. Any trait, no matter how productive in one situation, will become a deep hindrance when carried to an extreme. Smith struggled with an empathy so deep that it threatened his need for performance, whereas hundreds of other executives are so rigorously committed to performance that they are blind to the human needs of their team members.

Frequently, a single trait is simultaneously an executive's greatest strength and greatest weakness. Many have followed with fascination the career of Steven Jobs, the legendary founder of Apple Computer who was eventually fired by Apple Chairman John Sculley. Christopher Espinosa was Apple's eighth employee. When asked to describe Steve Jobs's greatest strength, he replied: "In a word laden with irony, intolerance. Intolerance of inadequate quality, intolerance of compromise, intolerance of bureaucracy, intolerance for doing something because 'That's the way we always do it.' A constant, maddening, frustrating drive to do it better than you've already done it or better than you want to do it. On the one hand, that is a tremendous creative force. And on the other, it is despotic."

As this example shows, it is impossible to exempt any trait, positive or negative, from self-scrutiny. It is often in our areas of greatest strength that we find the widest field for psychological effort. The first and most important step for any executive is to accept that everyone has weaknesses that need work, areas that right now are hindering performance. The safest move, as Michael Blumenthal found, is, when a number of people complain, to accept the complaint as true whether you agree wholly or not. In life and at work, perceptions do count and they can form a reality of their own.

MATCHING BEHAVIOR TO THE JOB

Psychological effort involves more than just working on personal weaknesses. It also focuses on changing behavior to match changed conditions or a changed role on the job. Alex Kroll has consistently reshaped himself to match the requirements of his job ever since he had to learn how "to work in a small rectangle indoors. It was a major effort for me in 1961. When I came here, I was largely a physical person. The idea of being a sedentary person was actually a discipline for me that had to be learned." Kroll acknowledges that, 25 years later, "I still don't like to sit at my desk very much. I like motion and I used to believe that you were immortal as long as you were moving; when you stopped moving, you were dead."

Learning to sit at a desk and complete your work is a psychological effort that some executives never really master. Walk into a senior manager's office that is filled with stacks of papers in disarray and notice how quickly he jumps up from his desk, almost as if he has been suddenly liberated from a prison cell. Concentrating on the work at hand rather than jumping from thing to thing is basic psychological work. Putting things away in the right place is basic psychological work.

Pure physical effort simply produces results. The executive who can't sit at his desk will put in long hours later tonight to get his work done, making the physical effort to handle papers he has read or glanced at two or three times already.

Mental effort enables us to produce more results better and quicker, whether it is Henry Ford thinking through mass production or the effort our restless executive makes once a year to "get organized." Psychological effort produces more results, better and quicker, and strengthens the executive for future growth. Even such a small thing as staying at your desk means you are placing the requirements of the work ahead of personal preferences.

The Most Difficult Skill of All

It takes psychological effort to learn how to use a skill or talent with greater and greater effect and then, hardest of all, to learn when not to use it.

In 1961 Doug MacMaster left his law firm and went to work for Merck. Asked what he thinks Merck saw in him, he replies: "They were looking for a well-trained lawyer. A technical job, but also somebody who could deal with people." During his early years with the company, MacMaster found that much older executives often wanted to discuss problems with him. They undoubtedly consulted him because of his growing reputation as an able decision maker who was willing to take the heat on the tough calls.

Theoretically, corporate lawyers advise and leave the decisions to the line executives. However, every corporate lawyer knows that the advice can frequently determine the decisions, especially if the lawyer is a good decision maker. "On every job you do," says MacMaster, "there are tough things that have to be done." MacMaster and his colleagues discovered early that Doug was prepared to decide and to take responsibility, to be what he calls the "paid bastard" when the occasion demanded.

After a decade as a corporate lawyer in the United States and the United Kingdom, MacMaster got his first opportunity for line management in 1971. In the years since, the scope of his responsibilities and the impact of his decision making have steadily expanded. Today, as senior vice president of Merck & Co., his effort is focused more on getting decisions made correctly at lower levels than on making them himself.

Echoing the phrasing of the former athlete, Alex Kroll, MacMaster says decision making "is like lifting weights. You start with the little ones and you can lift the bigger ones. If you don't make any, you suffer the consequences, you never develop any muscle . . . and if you don't learn to make decisions that can have some adverse fallout, then you are never going to make tough decisions."

Letting others do it is not easy for any born decision maker with a superb track record. For one thing, you are denied the satisfaction that comes from accomplishing something you are good at, one of life's great joys. You also must take the blame for some things you know would have been handled better had you done them yourself. When decisions go wrong, MacMaster notes, "It's mine and I've got to take the heat. I can't let [the subordinate] take any heat at all, because next time around he won't be willing to stick his neck out."

As Doug MacMaster's success illustrates, each promotion means making the psychological effort to give up something you are good at, something you like to do. Each promotion also requires the psychological effort to acquire a different behavior.

Learning To Listen

Effective communication skills is one trait that is always included on lists of attributes that lead to executive success. Normally this means the ability to convey information in some form. As they rise, executives get better at this, so much better that many cannot summon enough psychological effort to shift from sender to receiver of information. The complaint about senior executives not listening is so widespread that it should be considered universal.

C. Hale Champion's career has been spent working closely with some of the nation's top political leaders and has included nearly a decade as executive dean of Harvard's John F. Kennedy School of Government. The straight-talking Champion says he knows no older good listeners, and, at 66, he includes himself in that harsh assessment. "You gradually get yourself so filled up that it gets harder and harder to keep your mouth shut."

Why can't senior executives see this weakness? Perhaps it is because they do periodically have to listen. Anyone starting a new assignment would be foolhardy not to listen. Perhaps such short bursts convince many executives that they are better listeners than they are. Champion describes one prominent executive, now on his current job for more than a decade, as "a pretty good listener, not a sensitive listener but a pretty good listener when he took the job, but now he can't hear anything anymore because everybody's already told him everything and it just slides in the grooves and slides out."

J.W. Marriott, Jr., is one senior executive who works hard to improve his listening skills. Marriott, chairman, chief executive officer, and president of the Marriott Corporation hotel and res-taurant chain, says he is "less and less impressed with the ability of CEOs of major companies to listen." He calls some of his fellow CEOs "talkaholics," recalling: "I was with one a few months ago. I went in his office and I sat down. He started talking and he never shut up until I left. I didn't even get to say hello or good-bye. It was incredible. He said to me, 'You know, I talk too much.' He came right out and said it. I said, 'Yes, probably.'" The CEO's admission is revealing. In truth, we all know which of our traits require more psychological restraint. If we believe the trait is ob-vious to everybody, we may well admit to it openly, as if admitting it obviates the necessity to do anything about it.

In the 24 years since Marriott became president, his com-pany has grown at an annual compounded rate of approximately 20 percent in both sales and net income, rising from sales of $84 million to $6.5 billion in 1987. Employment rose from 9600 to 200,000 in the same period. How has Marriott personally expanded his capacities during this period? "I learned by getting out and doing it. I learned by seeking out people for advice, talking with other people, associating with other people, trying to listen to my people."

Marriott arrived at his dedicated commitment to the power of listening 14 years ago, when he was elected a bishop in the Mormon Church, responsible for 750 people. "Not all of them came to see me," he recalls, "but a lot of them did. It seemed as if 750 did, with all kinds of problems. What did I know as a 42-year-old business executive about dealing with marital problems, about dealing with father/son, mother/daughter relationships, all these kinds of family problems, emotional problems, psychiatric problems . . .? The only way I could counsel these people was just to let them talk. Every now and then, I'd interject something, but in an hour's conversation, I may have talked for five minutes. I found out that probably the great majority simply just wanted to talk out their problems. They really weren't coming to me for a solution. They were coming to somebody who would listen to their particular problem and maybe give a few words of advice, ask a few penetrating questions to help them think through what they had to do. And, I think at that point in time, I became more attuned to listening."

Marriott had learned a powerful lesson—the quiet listener can play a far more important role in effective decision making than the forceful talker with the best advice. Fred DeLuca's career provides an unusual example.

The original idea for the first Subway sandwich shop came when DeLuca met Ph.D. Peter Buck, a nuclear physicist, at a family picnic. DeLuca wanted to go to college, but he realized that his below-minimum-wage hardware store job didn't bring in enough to pay his bills. After the picnic, DeLuca approached Buck for advice, "secretly hoping he'd just give me a big stack of money. He looked me right in the eye and said, 'What you should do is open a submarine sandwich shop and you'll become a millionaire.' "

Buck's idea was that even though there were many sub shops around, none of them had the quality of the sandwiches he remembered from his childhood. Before the afternoon was over, Buck and DeLuca had become partners and had established a goal of opening 32 sub shops over the next 10 years. "I was too young to be afraid," DeLuca remembers. With $1000 start-up capital provided by Buck, they launched the venture in 1965.

Buck is still a partner, but he has never actively participated in the business. Rather, he has contributed primarily by being an effective listener for the highly creative, but at one time highly inexperienced, DeLuca. "He was always positive about things," DeLuca recalls. "Basically, his input was always broadbrush and then he'd say things like 'Well, don't worry so much about everything.' . . . I'd often talk about employees in the office and should we have this or that rule? He'd say things like 'Don't worry so much about it. They are only going to work X number of hours and get Y amount of work done and you're not going to have a great influence on that by structuring specific rules. That isn't going to affect them so much as their internal motivation.' "

The basic message, reinforced again and again, was that DeLuca was doing a fine job and shouldn't "worry so much." Where are there managers who would not welcome and profit by that kind of mentoring throughout their careers?

Bending the Frame

Good listening is far more than a simple skill. It is an intense psychological effort that shapes the whole way in which the individual reacts to the external environment. The problem for even the good listener, says Hale Champion, is "there is an incredible amount of noise out there and if you are not selective, if you are not careful, you'll get overwhelmed by it. So you need your own resonating mechanism. What resonates? What ties into what you know? What do you pick out of all that noise that ties into you? You don't try to listen to everything, read everything, and so on. If you [did] that, you'd go crazy, and it doesn't tie into anything."

The risk is that if you insist that the information must "tie in," then all the information you receive will reinforce your existing prejudices. However, Champion says effective listeners, once something resonates, "really give you their attention. They are really working it through, trying to fit their frame of reference to your frame of reference."

This is the real secret of truly effective listeners. The poor listener hears the other person's words only as a signal that it would be impolite to break in just yet. The good listener pays attention as she puts everything into an existing framework, gathering useful information but throwing out anything that doesn't fit. The effective listener waits, in Champion's apt word, for something to "resonate." From then on, he "isn't trying to put everything in his frame of reference but is instead trying to get his frame of reference adjusted to the person he is listening to."

Here is the explanation of why there are so few (Champion says there are not any) older first-rate listeners. It is not that the skill diminishes. Rather, the rigidity of the frame of reference, constructed so carefully over decades, is no longer flexible enough to bend to match the new framework presented by the speaker.

Effective listeners are well aware of this risk and consciously fight it. Apple Computer, Inc., Chairman and CEO John Sculley says, "My real title is 'Chief Listener.' " When Sculley first arrived at Apple, "someone handed me a business card and I looked at it with sort of a double take, because it said 'Hardware Wizard.' And I said I'd better check some of these other cards and I found 'Software Evangelist' and 'Product Champion.' So when it came to my own title, I said, 'What do I do most?' And what I do most is listen, so I'm the 'Chief Listener.' "[3]

Michael Blumenthal cherishes "the capacity to continue to learn" despite his concern that "at age 62 it may be getting a bit rusty." This capacity depends on "the consciousness of the fact that we all tend to become prisoners of our experience and that is a danger. . . . What worked in a business environment in the fifties and sixties or, for that matter, in the computer information industry in the seventies is unlikely to work in the eighties. . . . I am very conscious of that and I've always tried to discipline myself to listen and think about ideas that other people come up with, people much younger than I who say we ought to do it differently now."

Any executive looking for a place to test the power of psy-

---

[3]Interview with John Sculley, *Pinnacle*, Cable News Network, New York, December 12, 1987.

chological effort should consider creative listening. Dozens of people were interviewed for this book, on occasion at a rate of three or four a day. Yet no interviewing day ended with psychological exhaustion. Rather, the mind was so richly stimulated that it was difficult to obey the body's demand for sleep. Each interview demanded moment-by-moment concentration. Time was limited, and the listener had to determine for each comment whether the incident was useful, did it fit the framework, or was it something that required the listener to bend his frame?

There was absolutely no time for personal comments or observations, so the listener had to demonstrate interest and concentration largely by nonverbal signals, a terrible strain for the listener, who, no longer being young, has the usual difficulty in keeping his mouth shut. Yet the struggle to keep the mind simultaneously alert and open was absolutely exhilarating, and even many of those being interviewed felt themselves full of energy and enthusiasm, sorry to see the interview end.

Conceptually the technique is easy to describe. Creative listening begins with a clear understanding of what you hope to achieve in the conversation. Without that, you are merely engaged in random, social conversation. You should begin by sharing your purpose with the other person. Determine that there is common understanding, which is not at all as easy as it sounds. After one of these explanations at the start of an interview for this book, the interviewee said bluntly, "If I had understood your purpose fully, I never would have agreed to the interview. I never like to talk about myself." Fortunately this individual agreed to go on and provided useful insights, something that might not have happened if the cross-purposes had not been uncovered at the start of the conversation.

Once having established the purpose, ask one leading question and shut up. Normally the other individual will answer the question and stop. Say nothing. The other person will begin again if you wait long enough. An interesting thing will now occur. The mind of the other person, having had more time to reflect on your original question, will now provide a richer, fuller, deeper answer than the first answer you received. The person will stop again. Wait again, but be sure to show by almost exaggerated body language your acute interest in the conversation.

Try to keep your mind open, avoiding any prejudices or biases about what you are hearing. Avoid the temptation to think of a story of your own that wonderfully illustrates the point the other person is making. When you are absolutely sure that the person has completed answering your first question, ask another. Ask for examples. When you get one, ask for another. Avoid the tendency to summarize; if a summary is appropriate, ask the other person to summarize.

Try this technique with colleagues, team members, or even spouses and children, and you will feel its power. Remember what J.W. Marriott, Jr., learned as a bishop. Remember the power of Fred DeLuca's partner's advice: "Don't worry so much." You will feel the support you can bring to others by using the power of your silence. One consciously planned experience will demonstrate the force of psychological effort, a strength you can extend to many other parts of your work and life.

PUTTING YOURSELF AT RISK

In its third and most dramatic form, psychological effort involves putting yourself publicly at risk when the job or the occasion demands. Public speaking, one of the highest ranked phobias on the American scene, is a common example. John Sculley had to overcome a severe stammer as a boy. When he became PepsiCo.'s marketing vice president he was determined "to build a strength out of what was originally a weakness. I'd practice for hours. I became obsessed with the idea that I was going to become better than anyone else as a business communicator."

Three months prior to his first speech before the all-important Pepsi bottlers, he began working on a 40-minute presentation so

"I could do it without notes, center stage in front of several thousand people. I memorized every one of over 200 slides which appeared in a complex animated format on five screens behind me. . . ." In theory, this degree of preparation should have greatly relieved his mind. "But I recall my anxiety as I was standing in the wings. I remember thinking that maybe I would go out there and my mind would go blank. There was nothing to fall back on, no notes, nothing. I had to keep my composure and just go out and do it. It was only after a few seconds on the stage that I got the strength to continue, and the speech was a great success."[4]

Sculley had completed the act—the physical components of how to stand and the way the slides should look, the mental component of thinking through and then memorizing the ideas in the speech, and the psychological components of understanding the viewpoint of his audience and shaping his material to fit its needs. Beyond this, the carrying out of this particular act had involved a deep psychological effort, particularly for someone burdened with painful memories of a childhood stammer.

Not using notes means that a speaker has taken the care to master the material in the speech not 95 percent but 100 percent, freeing the mind to concentrate entirely on communicating with the audience. The focus shifts subtly from "Let *me* check my notes to see what *I* am going to say next" to "Are *you* understanding this? Am I speaking too fast for *you* to follow me? Do *you* want me to say that again?" Audiences always respect this concern for their needs and pay more attention to a speaker without notes, increasing both the speaker's confidence and the flow of energy between speaker and audience. It was from this interaction that Sculley received what he calls "the strength to continue" once he had started his speech. Modern lecterns can hide the use of notes,

---

[4]Sculley, John with John A. Byrne, *Odyssey, Pepsi to Apple: A Journey of Adventure, Ideas and the Future.* New York: Harper & Row, pp. 111–112.

but such an artifice cannot compare with the strength that flows when great psychological effort becomes visible.

If you ask any executive to recount the most dramatically difficult moment in a career, you are likely to hear a story of psychological effort. Robert Widham's story begins in France: "The day I arrived at the plant, there was a great big sign: *Widam, American Capitalist Pig Go Home.* There were people lying all over the steps, they were all in their blue union uniforms. I had to step over all these bodies to get inside, but since they had misspelled my name, I figured it couldn't be me they were complaining about. It had to be somebody else."

Today, Robert G. Widham, spelled with an *h*, is group vice president at Stanley Works and is responsible for seven major divisions of the $1.8 billion, New Britain, Connecticut, tool and systems manufacturer. On that day in 1976, he had just arrived at Besançon, France, to take over as managing director of Stanley's troubled French subsidiary. Bob Widham already had more than 20 years of experience handling difficult jobs at Stanley. He met this crisis as he had learned always to meet a crisis, with straight talk, hard work, and an empathy for the opposing view.

Widham found that the unions had physically taken over the plant. "I got in there and they brought in the union representatives and I said, 'Look, I don't understand your language or your culture, would you give me a month?' They said they would, and they all went back to work. I knew what it would take to learn another language after learning Spanish [on his previous assignment in Mexico]. People think you pick it up by osmosis, but you don't. It takes a great deal of effort. I spent about four hours every night learning French, and after two weeks I wouldn't let anybody speak to me in English at all. And within four weeks I was able to have a working knowledge of French."

If you don't speak the language on a foreign assignment, you are the prisoner of the information you get from those who speak your language. You can receive virtually no direct input from the lowest level worker. You are blocked from true communication or empathy with any employee or colleague who does not speak your language. Even so, anyone who has ever learned a foreign language under pressure can appreciate what Widham was up against. Beyond the pure physical strain of adding four hours of hard work at the end of a day crowded with new and urgent priorities and the mental effort of struggling to master French irregular verbs, a very special psychological effort was required here, an effort that many executives would have refused to make.

The foreigner learning a new language always knows he sounds a bit foolish. Even in a noncrisis situation, surrounded by people of goodwill, the foreigner feels uncomfortable, especially at the beginning. Judging by his welcome, Widham had absolutely no reason to believe he was surrounded by people of goodwill. On the contrary, he was facing tough Communist union leaders who had not the slightest wish for his success. Further, these were Frenchmen, and the French are a people possessed of a fierce pride in their language and an often not-so-subtle contempt for people who speak it poorly.

Knowing all of this, Widham could have hired a simultaneous interpreter for his union negotiations or asked a bilingual Stanley executive to interpret for him. He could have rationalized that the issues were too serious to risk miscommunication through his weak French. He could have argued that his time was too valuable, that he would learn French later when things settled down. Instead he put himself on the line and rose to a challenge that was really set by no one except himself.

One of Those Peak Experiences

Widham's challenge was far from over when he learned French. He had to confront the organizers, while winning over the workers. He had learned how to make a great psychological effort earlier in his career when he had managed a Stanley plant in Newark, New Jersey, an environment so tough that his life had been threatened four times.

Widham's style consists of never backing down an inch while simultaneously showing his deep regard and concern for the lowest worker. He had the Newark plant cleaned up from top to bottom, and to raise his own level of empathy with the workers, he had spent a day working as a drop forger. "Quite an experience in itself. You have a 2400 degree furnace; you've got a bar that weighs about 110 pounds; you have this drop that scares the daylights out of you. You just slam it about five times and it would go on this great press that goes crunch and you have to do that 90 times an hour. . . . So I got a feel and I did the grinding, I did the polishing, and I went through the whole plant doing all the operations."

His mandate was to double production, and he had to deal with five unions in a plant rigidly divided by racial and ethnic boundaries. He started out by holding communication meetings with the workers—common today, but unusual in the 1960s. "The first one I held I could just feel the hostility coming from this group. They couldn't express themselves very well because they weren't very well educated . . .[they were] rough, tough guys, about as tough as you'll find anywhere and they had some really good gripes." From the sessions, Widham discovered that the men had only one locker for both their filthy forging clothes and their street clothes. "So we got them two lockers. . . . We spruced up the shower room so it wasn't a dirty, filthy mess. . . . We got Coke machines out there . . .," created a small cafeteria, "and just showed respect for them."

Then came the battle of the hard hats. "We were having all these injuries, it was like a battle zone. . . . So we got them the right gloves, we got shoes for them, and then we got hard hats." However, nobody would wear a hard hat. So Widham mandated the wearing of the hats for two weeks. Midway through the second week, "a drop rod fell and hit this guy right in the head—he had his hard hat on—and it came down and broke his collar bone. After that everybody wore the hard hats. It really got to be a feeling of pride with them. They would really have them spotless, and they would actually wear them home at night." By the time Widham left the Newark plant, "I felt it was humming. It was doing well, and it had a future ahead of it at that time. So that was, again, one of those peak experiences."

Making Work an Adventure

At the beginning, France looked like anything but a peak experience. Widham confronted the unions in an unheard of way—he sued them for defamation of character. This was after the Communist unions in their demonstrations put up pictures of Widham and his managers, calling them robbers. The news of the suit traveled fast. "The next thing you know, they were out there with a truck and they had pictures of the union leaders in striped prison uniforms with signs saying we are persecuting them."

Next the union announced that a massive demonstration was to be held in front of Widham's office. "They were going to have 40,000 to 50,000 workers. Then I guess cooler heads prevailed in the union movement itself. They came in and they offered an apology. They said they would stop attacking my managers, but they would always have to attack me because I was the representative of the profit system which they were against. So, it worked out."

It more than worked out. By the time Widham was promoted back to the home office four years later, the plant was a top performer within the Stanley system. All through his tenure, despite periodic storming of his office by 60 or 70 militants, Widham continued to strengthen his rapport with the workers, holding communication meetings and sponsoring sporting days and American-style open houses for the families of the workers.

Widham's whole career illustrates the power of psychological effort. At every stage, he has made, beyond what the physical and mental effort demanded, the psychological effort to mold himself to the requirements of unusually difficult jobs. It takes enormous effort not to give way on a principle when you are all alone and under heavy attack. The strain of making that lonely effort can easily turn into a rigid, blind adherence to principle above all, a position that can easily deny the basic humanity of anyone opposing either you or the principle. Long before quality control circles and worker participation were the rage in management, Widham was using psychological effort to understand and empathize with the lowest worker, while absolutely insisting on the principles required for greater productivity and growth.

Today, Widham exudes the enthusiasm, optimism, and confidence that comes when high aspiration is consistently paired with great psychological effort. This contagious feeling, the legendary good attitude so highly and correctly prized in management, is available to anyone who wants it. It is this combination that makes work satisfying, an adventure rather than a drudgery.

Whether it is overcoming a weakness as Blumenthal did with his abrasiveness, reversing ingrained habits and fears as MacMaster did with decision making and Sculley did with speaking, or, at the highest level, putting yourself publicly and dramatically at risk as Widham has done again and again, this is the process of using work not just as a way to produce results, but as a medium for your own growth and development.

At the end of every day, you should ask three questions: What did I accomplish? What did I learn? How did I expand and grow through my answers to the first two questions? The happy, expansive life is not a life free of adversity nor a life spent in contented leisure. Rather, it is the life of accomplishment, learning, and growth, which are three individually shining goals that can be truly and deeply integrated only through psychological effort.

TURNING WEAKNESSES INTO STRENGTHS: THE HIDDEN 4 POWER WITHIN YOU

In the freedom of nature or the confines of the board room, survival depends on strengths, but success depends on handling weaknesses.

As this is being written, the dominant sound outside is the chattering of more than 40 crows. In nature, for example, the crow survives even though it lives close to several relentless enemies, most notably human farmers. This survival depends exclusively on formidable strengths, including a wide range of sound signals and a surprising ability to learn.

For any species, survival is the first law. Success for a species is measured by the number of the next generation it is able to bring to adulthood. Here, the crow like most birds can be vulnerable. In the nest the young are fragile and defenseless, especially at the perilous moment when they must first try their wings. At the deepest level of existence, the crow acknowledges this weakness and handles it instinctively by cooperation.

The noise outside, rising in volume and stridency over the past few days, signals that the nearby nest is ready to yield its treasure. Although crows mate for life, the dangerous task of launching the young is not left to the parents alone. For several days a tense community has been gathering to stand guard near the nest as the young begin to stretch their wings. In overcoming this desperate

68

moment of weakness, no effort, no matter how extraordinary, is too great.

Yesterday, a human female, a representative of the dangerous and feared species, wandered too close to the nest and was physically attacked until she retreated. Today, a circling bird of prey crossed some invisible line defined by the noisy sentinels and was driven into ignominious retreat by a squadron of crows less than a third its size. By tomorrow, the crisis will pass, the nest will be empty, and the normal patterns will reappear. Then, at the first sight of human or bird of prey, the crows will sound a warning and make a dignified retreat, until another nest stirs with life and success will once again be determined by overcoming a dangerous weakness through extraordinary effort.

AWARENESS IS THE FIRST STRENGTH

In the wilds of corporate life, the same pattern can be clearly observed: executives survive through their strengths and succeed by their ability to deal with weaknesses.

In their early years, most careers are really all about finding strengths and learning how to employ them with greatest effect. In his twenties, Doug MacMaster discovered that his ability to make decisions was both unusual and valuable. Alex Kroll found that his talent was not only to do creative work, but also to organize it. Harvey Golub became aware of the power of his analytical mind and Robert Smith of his pleasing personality. Robert Widham learned he could handle both people and situations of unusual variety and difficulty.

Such self-discovery is so important that every young executive should be willing to change jobs in rapid succession if that is what it takes to test one's potential strengths. This learning phase is not the automatic process it so often appears in hindsight. Early in our careers, we are severely limited by a lack of experience, both our own and that of those around us.

My wife was once a visitor in a home deeply divided by the

issue of the younger son's career. The young man had a mechanical aptitude that seemed absolutely brilliant in a home where, in the words of another family member, "changing a plug on a lamp was a talent bordering on genius." Based on this aptitude, the young man had enrolled in an engineering course, which he hated. At the moment my wife arrived, he had announced that he would not be returning to school for the next term.

My wife suggested the now quite common step of aptitude testing, which in this case produced surprising results. Although the young man's mechanical aptitude was higher than average, it was in no way his real strength. That turned out to be a talent for figures, suggesting a career as an accountant. The family was stunned since they knew no accountants and had only the vaguest notion of what accountants actually did. On faith, the young man changed his major, suddenly enjoyed his studies, and went on to become a CPA with a successful career in finance. Without the test he would have sooner or later discovered his strength, but the process would have been far longer and likely quite painful.

No one has made it to the executive ranks without clear strengths. To ultimately reach that level, however, requires that the young career person first understand what these strengths are and second build them up as quickly and powerfully as possible. There are many fundamental strengths of business success, some of which have already been mentioned: decision making, a natural sense of organization, tenacity, a pleasing way with people, a capacity for hard work, an analytical mind, a creative mind, steady judgment, self-discipline, and an ability to recruit and inspire an effective team. No executive starts out with all these strengths; however, none starts without at least an inherent capacity for one or more of them. The task of one's early career is to understand one's natural endowment and then to develop it.

FINDING LOST STRENGTHS

Every inherent strength will last for life and, if developed widely enough, can by itself be the single source of career survival. Everyone knows examples: the executive with the iron trap analytical mind who becomes indispensable; the colleague who survives near the top year after year with no discernible strength except an exceptional capacity to like and be liked by others; the clean desk executive whose organizing ability has become legendary.

Before these strengths had the survival power we can now observe, they had first to be honed by skills. The woman with the analytical mind had to master finance and the skill to put her information across to others; the man with the pleasing personality had to take a memory course before he could so effortlessly recall the names of colleagues' spouses and children; the organized administrator had to learn the principles and practices of good recordkeeping. For each individual such learning is always a pleasure since it uses, reinforces, and builds up an inherent strength. The more skills are added, the more embellished the strength becomes.

The power of this basic strength is never so clear as when an executive loses the chance to use it. In recent years, as executive redundancies at the senior level have become more common, a new type of consulting firm has grown in popularity. Called outplacement firms, these consultants help fired or redundant executives find new jobs. Their record defies belief, with the majority of their clients, many in their 40s, 50s, or even 60s, finding new jobs at the same or higher pay within six months. How is such magic accomplished with people who for one reason or another are unwanted in their present organizations? Despite individual terminology and techniques, the success of all outplacement firms is built on three basic assumptions:

1. All senior executives possess well above average strengths or they would never have reached the senior ranks.
2. An executive who is let go for any reason has probably been working in a position where some or all of those strengths are not of full value or on full view.
3. Any executive career can be relaunched if precisely defined strengths can be matched with a job where those strengths represent the key components of success.

The first task is to define strengths. Then, there must be a clear understanding of how those strengths have contributed to past success. The next task is to find people who currently have a need for that strength or strengths, largely ignoring whether those people are in the same industry, field, or specialty where the executive has been working.

Outplacement firms are successful because they reverse the traditional way in which redundant senior executives look for a job. The usual philosophy is, "I was marketing vice president for a consumer foods company, so I must find another consumer foods company with a need for a marketing vice president." What is ignored in this approach is that the strength that got this executive promoted, for example, a talent for creative problem solving, was in all likelihood not in full play at the job that was just lost.

Displaced executives going through outplacement pass through several well-defined stages. At first, they become frustrated with the outplacement process that at first prohibits them from actually looking for a new job, but eventually forces them to think through their real strengths, perhaps for the first time. At a later stage, the process of getting back in touch with their real strengths by reliving successful experiences produces a surge of optimism, a feeling that "Those fools were just plain crazy to fire someone with my capacities."

At this moment, with the individual reunited with the true source of earlier success, the outplacement consultant will declare that it is time to start calling on prospects for a new job. Appropriately enough, the résumé carried by the job seeker will be organized entirely around strengths, not chronological experience.

In the world of work, we are our strengths. I once met a man who operated an executive search consulting firm in Britain in the days when the U.K. was drastically cutting back one of the world's largest professional armies. This executive was not in outplacement, so there was very little he could do for the dozens of mustered-out career officers who showed up at his doorstep at the suggestion of mutual friends. "Spending a great deal of time with them would have been a wasted effort for me and would have led to false hopes for them," he told me. "I couldn't do anything much, except ask one question. I would ask, 'Who are you?' They would reply that they were Major so and so, late of Her Majesty's such and such, and I would repeat 'Who are you?' over and over to anything they told me about where they had been or what they had previously done. This would go on for several minutes before they stalked out of the office. Out of a dozen or so, one would come back later and say, 'I can answer your question now,' to which I would reply, 'You, I can help.' "

It was a short, brutal form of the outplacement technique, but the underlying principle was exactly the same: rebuilding or maintaining a career depends first on knowing your strengths and then on finding the right opportunity to use them.

HOW TO PICK WINNERS

In management, the golden strengths of all strengths is being able to assess accurately the strengths of others. You have to like people to be able to see their strengths, but if you like them too much, you can easily exaggerate a strength or minimize a lethal weakness. You have to be able to evaluate past performance, but often the most brilliant strengths are not immediately evident in the earlier track record.

How does one accurately assess strengths? It can be done by following one of the three techniques favored by those who have mastered the art of finding strengths in others. Successful executives develop the skill of picking winners by system, by instinct, and by learning to listen with an inner ear.

By System

General George C. Marshall was the master of the systematic choice. When Marshall became Chief of Staff in 1939, he understood that his job was to prepare the U.S. Army to fight a major war for which the resources were not yet available. A student of the Civil War, Marshall knew that Lincoln and the North had been severely handicapped in the first two years of war by obsolete commanders from the Mexican War, while the South, creating a new army, had been able to promote younger men with higher energy and newer ideas. Determined that the United States would not undergo the fate of the North, Marshall retired many older commanders, most of whom were senior veterans of World War I. Always prepared, Marshall had for years kept a notebook with entries about every young officer who impressed him. When the need arose to replace the older commanders, Marshall chose such names as Eisenhower, Patton, Bradley, and Clark from that book.

Many senior executives today use a similar system. If you were to ask an alert vice president where tomorrow's top performers are within the organization, she could list them and tell you why. Not all this promise will be realized, but because the mental search process is continuous, systematic, and based on performance over time, enough names will be there when the need arises.

By Intuition

Other executives toss out this systematic approach and replace it with an almost uncanny intuition about how people will perform in certain jobs. This approach can result in the unorthodox or unpopular choice who later turns out to have been perfect for the job. Herbert Baum, president of Campbell, USA, the largest operating unit of the Campbell Soup Company, has learned to trust his intuition in launching products and picking people. At one point he had to assemble a team in a hurry for a Campbell assignment, and he likens that team to the 1927 New York Yankees, simply the best that unit ever had. He had to fight for many choices, several of which were unpopular with his superiors, but "they all worked out, every one."

While Baum openly relies on his intuition, he is an endless gatherer of facts. At a dinner party, he will not talk about sports or politics, preferring to ask instead what people like to eat and why. Before assembling his star team, he knew a great deal about each person; the surprises came in which individuals he chose for which jobs.

Relying on your intuition in picking people's strengths is creative rather than systematic, but despite the seemingly nonrational aspect, to be successful, you must depend heavily on information. David Ogilvy, the founder of the Ogilvy & Mather advertising agency, once said that although the creative process is seated in the unconscious, "nothing is more dangerous than an ignorant unconscious." Thousands of facts are needed and then the conscious mind must develop "telephone connections," said Ogilvy, with the unconscious (on long country walks, for instance).[5]

The executive who picks people by gut feeling alone, without taking the trouble to gather facts, is unlikely to assemble the 1927 Yankees but rather the 1988 Yankees, a fifth place team with a few brilliant stars and little teamwork or cohesion.

By Listening With the Inner Ear

The third way of spotting strengths is by learning to listen with an inner ear to what people are really saying. "I'm an Original" is the button worn by entrepreneur Nancy Vetrone, president of Original Copy Centers, Inc. Vetrone started her Cleveland copying business with a single leased Xerox copier, and within a decade her firm appeared on the *Inc.* magazine list of the 500 fastest growing private companies in the United States. A good measure of this success story is based on Vetrone's ability to bring out people's strengths, what she calls "sparkle."

A Vetrone job interview is highly unorthodox. Calling herself "a good reader of people," she will still talk to a serious candidate

---

[5]*Fortune*, March 26, 1979, selection David Ogilvy, Business Hall of Fame.

for three or four hours looking for sparkle, a special glimmer of excitement. "If they have that, you know you can take them to unlimited heights."

Not long ago, a young man from out of town kept badgering Vetrone's secretary for a job interview. Impressed by his persistence, Vetrone agreed to see him even though she was not hiring at the time. "He filled out an application and said he could be a production person, he wanted to run the machines. I took him on a tour and then sat and talked with him. As he was talking, I wondered, 'Why would you think you are a production person? You don't have anything about you that is a production person.'

"Then I started talking with him about how he felt about life and what really excited him and stuff like that. I thought, 'Holy Cow! This kid is a miniature Bob [her husband Robert Bieniek, who runs Original's marketing].'' I looked at him and said, 'Do you really want to work here?' He said, 'Yea, yea!' I said, 'Good, because we are going to put you to work right now.' " Vetrone pulled Bieniek out of a conference and introduced him to his new assistant. Trusting Vetrone's judgment, he put the young man right to work.

As Vetrone continues the story: "He had just arrived in Cleveland that morning. He worked until 11:30 that night. We had meeting after meeting. We taught him right from the beginning: this is how it is; open your mind; see everything." Within a month, Vetrone overheard the young man talking on the phone with a friend: "This isn't like going to work," he said. "It is like going to life!" That is the exuberant cry of someone who quite unexpectedly has found his strength and been given the gift to use it.

IDENTIFYING YOUR OWN STRENGTHS

In finding your own strengths, you can follow system or intuition, or you can listen with an inner ear (like Vetrone).

For the systematic approach, simply follow your own version of the well-perfected system of the outplacement specialists:

1. Write down the 10 most successful experiences of your life. Ignore whether the experience was large or small, whether it was at work or elsewhere, or when it occurred. Being a captain of a sports team or leader of a scout troop in high school definitely should make the list if it was a peak experience.

2. Challenge yourself on each item before leaving it on the list. Was it your own genuine achievement? Did you really make a significant contribution? Were you simply carried forward by a favorable market circumstance?

3. Analyze the 10 solidly successful experiences to find the two or three strengths that form a pattern underlying all the achievements. (Outplacement consultants say that for many people that is the most difficult part.) Executives insist that the successes are random, and there is no pattern. The consultants know better and send their clients back again and again until the telltale strengths are suddenly visible. In any record of success (and executives are almost by definition more successful than the average person), these telltale strengths are always there.

The intuitive method requires a careful gathering of facts. Begin by identifying the strengths of others. On what specific strengths has the president of your company risen? The chairman of the board? Your immediate boss? Your colleagues? We are all experts at identifying the weaknesses of others, but our skill of seeing strengths is nowhere near as well developed.

The work and style of any organization favors certain strengths and devalues others. This is one reason why there is so much turmoil when a new CEO arrives with a mandate to change things. Almost overnight, strengths that used to be highly valued (perhaps creativity and teamwork) fade from view and other strengths (such as adherence to discipline, orderliness, and punctuality) move rapidly to the forefront. Without the opportunity to use the strengths that made them famous in the old organization, the weaknesses of many senior executives are painfully exposed. When the CEO poses with his top team for the annual photo four years later, the faces and the strengths are new.

If you learn to analyze the strengths of others, never stopping until you understand how each person rose, then, as Ogilvy puts it, on one of those long walks in the country it will be clear to you which strengths are moving *your* career forward.

Finally, you can simply listen to yourself with an inner ear. Ignore the compliments you get for a task; they may come to you for external reasons that have little to do with your strengths. Pay attention to how you feel about different tasks. Which ones really bring a true sense of joy, not just in the completion but in the actual doing? At such moments of joy we are very close to an inherent strength. Much of pleasure in executive life is built on external reaction—the opinion of bosses, colleagues, and even customers. Real joy is something deeper and more fundamental—something that means you have come not to work, but to life.

EXPANDING STRENGTHS

Having identified your strengths, your urgent priority is to ask yourself what you have done to develop these strengths in the past six months. Although inherent strengths never disappear, they grow in usefulness only through effort, particularly the effort to add skills and scope to express them more fully. If your strength is decision making, have you investigated the latest computer models for analyzing decisions? If it is discipline, can you find one area in your work that would be enriched by greater discipline? If it is pleasing people, what skills would improve your capacity as a host or hostess? If it is team building, what course on interpersonal skills would expand its scope?

For expanding and building up a strength, absolutely nothing beats teaching it to others. Look around at your colleagues and team members to find someone who would welcome advice on your strength. If that is not practical, consider volunteering as a teacher at a community college or in one of your company's courses. When one of my early mentors was a fast-rising executive in a major company, he volunteered to teach the fundamental skills of every new assignment he received because there was no faster or more effective way to learn.

An inherent strength is a gold coin presented to you without condition in early life. Properly invested in your career, it can, on its own, ensure your survival and, in some cases, even your success.

DISCOVERING WEAKNESSES

An inherent strength is so powerful that many executives believe that success is strictly a matter of working on strengths while ignoring weaknesses. However, the one thing that no executive can do is to ignore weaknesses. You can isolate weaknesses, compensate for them, or overcome them, but ignoring them is the most dangerous of all career strategies.

You discover your weaknesses by reversing the process by which you found your strengths. You can go through the systematic approach, analyzing each case where your performance fell short of your expectations and finding the common thread. You can use the intuitive approach, measuring yourself against the strengths of others in your company or unit. You can again listen with your inner ear for answers to questions like: Why am I really avoiding this task? What really caused me to perform in a less-than-expected manner in that assignment? Am I consciously or subconsciously pushing off my work on others, and if so, what is the common weakness revealed here?

As we are skilled in seeing weaknesses in others, we have learned to be blind to them in ourselves. If they are so blatant as to be unavoidable, we find subtle ways to brag about them, as was the case with the talkaholic CEO who told J.W. Marriott, Jr., that he talked too much. This is the "that's just the way I am but at least I'm honest about it" school of handling weaknesses.

Honest about it or not, every executive must handle weaknesses in one way or another. The choices are to isolate, to compensate for, or to overcome the weaknesses.

Isolating Weaknesses

In any organization there are many individual performer jobs that can be subtly shaped to isolate the impact of a weakness. The advertising copywriter does not have to be orderly as long as the copy comes out brilliantly and on time. The researcher does not have to report to work punctually or be pleasant to colleagues as long as the new products come out on schedule. For the individual who wants to exploit strengths fully while isolating weaknesses, the individual specialties are the surest haven and the greatest opportunity for personal development.

The problem is that most organizations put a premium in pay and status on those jobs requiring frequent interaction with others. As a result, many strive to get these jobs without understanding that the new business card with the word "Manager" on it signals that many weaknesses must now be confronted. This is the quiet desperation of the high school principal who is poor at administration and who secretly longs to return to the classroom, at her present pay, of course. If you are not good at working with people and you don't plan to get better, avoid any management job. Certainly don't be disappointed if you're not promoted to sales manager—be grateful.

Organizations that depend on a certain specialty, the way pharmaceutical companies depend on research, for example, often create dual career ladders that permit specialists to grow in their discipline and still rise in pay and status. This is delightful and rewarding for the individuals involved, who are able to successfully isolate certain weaknesses for a whole career and to concentrate on their strengths. The organization, in turn, is rewarded by the work of highly motivated individuals without being disrupted by their weaknesses.

Proving Yourself

For most, however, no such option is available. Before taking on a new and higher assignment, you should ask yourself which of your weaknesses must now be confronted. In each new assignment, says Dow Chemical's Frank Popoff, "you have to prove yourself all over again to a new group of people. You have to continue to demonstrate that as you are asking people not to live off their laurels, you are certainly not interested in living off yours." How do you demonstrate this? Popoff replies: "You have to get up early and work late and roll up your sleeves and get involved and not delegate all the nasty stuff, delegate some of the fun things and hang on to some of the nasty stuff."

The easiest way to compensate for a weakness is simply to work longer and harder, a common technique used by executives on a new job. Popoff remembers when he became business manager of Dow's Agricultural Department, a field where he had no technical knowledge or even the correct vocabulary: "I burned the midnight oil. I studied enough to get to the point where I could ask questions." Popoff had to study longer and harder on his own because he had another deeper barrier to deal with: He doesn't like to ask questions.

"That's very hard for me. I really have a hard time admitting that I know less than I ought to. Some people are very good at saying, 'Boy, help me out, I don't know a damn thing about that.' That comes hard for me." Like most deep-seated barriers, this one comes from Popoff's childhood. When he came to the United States as a child from Bulgaria, "I couldn't speak English. They just dropped me off at school and I started in school sitting there, having no idea of what was going on. I knew when the bell rang, you got to go home, that was about the size of it. Maybe that instills in you some pride or some, I don't know what, where you find it hard to say I can't or I don't or I won't or I don't understand . . . So that says you have to try to find out what you need to know by swallowing hard and asking questions or doing homework on your own. Obviously, that's the first prerequisite."

A Talent for Disorganization

When one begins to really analyze one's weaknesses, the first discovery is that all around there are people who handle this particular weakness with such verve and ease that it is a major strength. Frequently such people are quite close. As long as I can remember, I have carried the weight of a lack of organization, a talent for disorganization would describe it more accurately. When I became a manager, the weakness could no longer be isolated. I compensated for it by working longer hours, extra time that I could have reduced at any point by better organization.

As I became conscious of this weakness, I simultaneously became aware of my wife Nancy's enormous capacity for organization. I am sure this is not a coincidence. At some level we seek marriage partners who compensate for and, we hope, round out our personalities. Despite this, I didn't understand the real force of her capacity until I actually contrasted her approach with mine.

The most obvious difference is that she uses far less energy in organizing a project than I do in coping with my disorganization. It is as if there is an invisible line between a weakness and a strength. Until you cross that line, you are wasting physical and mental energy; once you cross out of the weakness zone into the area of strength, the effort is reduced by becoming more concentrated. A Doug MacMaster will spend far less energy making a $5 million decision than a poor decision maker will on a $50,000 decision.

I also learned that when one deals from strength, one immediately goes to the heart of the issue. In planning our daughter's wedding, Nancy knew in one day that every detail of the wedding would grow out of the decision on the bride's dress. The formality of the dress would influence everything, from the color of the bridesmaids' shoes to the size of the wedding cake. No irrevocable decisions were made until the dress was purchased, and therefore no time was wasted in false starts and stops.

Having discovered the heart of the issue, the rest, as Kendall

Lockhart might say, "is just math." Whether planning a seminar for her consulting firm or a day of errands for the home, Nancy will make a list, extract the critical items in seconds, and organize the balance of items around the critical few. It sounds so simple, and when it is your strength, it is. It genuinely baffles my wife that anyone could have trouble with organization, just as it baffles me that she could have difficulty handling something that is a strength for me and a weakness for her. Since discretion is one of my strengths, I will go no further on this track.

Compensating for Weaknesses

Once you have discovered your weaknesses and have determined that you can't or won't isolate them, your next choice is to compensate for them. This is commonly handled in management by rounding out your team with someone with the strengths you lack. Success at doing this hinges on your ability both to know yourself with unusual thoroughness and to delegate and control a whole task.

As Frank Popoff warns, it is not just a matter of delegating "the nasty stuff." This is wise advice because many managers view compensating for weaknesses as mostly a matter of dumping what they can't or don't want to do onto someone else. That is far less likely to happen to a manager who has taken the time to think through strengths and weaknesses rather than just responding to superficial likes and dislikes.

J. McDonald (Don) Williams is managing partner of the Trammell Crow Co., one of the largest real estate firms in the United States. Williams has made a persistent psychological effort to develop himself in four dimensions: physical, mental, social, and spiritual. He jogs daily and has what he calls an intellectual recreational program, which includes reading four or five books at a time. He divides the subject matter of the books among classic literature (Shakespeare this year, Dante last year), contemporary novels, business books, and spiritual readings. In the social area, he works consciously to strengthen relationships in his family and in his company. "One of the crucial things for all of us," Williams says, "is to get some insight on yourself," a process that never ends.

One of those insights led Williams to the realization "I'm not good at strategic planning," a critically important task for a firm with $14 billion in assets. Williams handed that assignment to co-managing partner Joel Peterson. "You've got to work with people who are good at what you are not good at. It's sort of the ying yang theory and trying to have a complete team approach rather than some one-man, Lone Ranger deal, which is an illusion. So for me, it was important to know what I was not good at, and that's a long list, and then you try to have close associations with people who are really good at those things so the firm doesn't suffer from my weaknesses."

Effective teams are a time-honored way to compensate for weaknesses. The power of organizations, the force that makes them one of humanity's most productive discoveries, is this ability to bring together strengths and compensate for weaknesses.

Overcoming Weaknesses

The third way of handling weaknesses is to overcome them, sometimes even actually converting them into strengths. This requires the greatest effort, sometimes a seemingly futile effort. "I've wasted a fair amount of time trying to be good at things I'm not good at," says one highly successful president, echoing the views of many. But for a significant minority, this effort has not only been worth the strain, it has marked major turning points in career success.

For Alex Kroll, dealing with weaknesses is another form of lifting the bar another inch higher. When he became Y&R's first worldwide creative director in 1970, there "was nothing written on how to do this." Did he feel tension, a gap between the scope of the job and his capacities? "Tension? Desperation was more like it!" His first priority was to create a "uniform system or process for making advertising strategies that we could institute worldwide." Up until then Y&R had "106 strategy systems in the New York office depending on which client we were dealing with."

Here Kroll was using one of his major strengths. "While the Italians [in the Y&R Italian subsidiary] were better at speaking Italian and the Germans better at speaking German, I was better at creative work plans than anybody. . . . I can see strategy as geometric shapes of different kinds . . . I was also good at directing people toward executions and then letting them do it. I think that has a lot to do with having played team sports for as long as I can remember. It was very easy for me to help people think through the issues and develop a concept." Once Kroll developed the general worldwide concept, he encouraged the national account executives to provide their own individualistic execution. "The concept strategy can be general and it should be . . . but the way it is expressed should be very particular."

In building this system, which endured for 17 years without major overhaul, Kroll was relying on clear strengths. However, the job also had facets where he had clear weaknesses. "I had to learn about salaries, bonuses, expenses—things which I had never paid any attention to." Many executives, presented on their 33rd birthday with a sudden and glorious opportunity to demonstrate their strengths around the world, would have quickly found someone to handle these seemingly more mundane aspects of the job and would have applied their whole energies where, as many would say, "the action is." Kroll chose otherwise.

Asked directly whether he liked or disliked the administrative part of the job, Kroll offers an indirect but revealing answer: "I found it interesting because it was an opportunity to construct an environment. Really it seemed to me that these were tools for having either a more or a less creative environment. The administrative parts of it were very important." Once he had mastered the details, Kroll brought in a manager to handle them.

At first in "creating an environment," no detail was too small for Kroll to handle. "I really got involved in the initiative of how we bought desks or moved furniture to the point of being a real

pain to everyone. How did we spend everything? . . . I knew that
compensation was very important, so I had to understand that."
What was the smallest thing he had to understand? "Draperies,
stationery, paper, typewriters."

In 1975 Kroll was placed in charge of all Y&R advertising
offices in the United States. "I don't think that I had the job 30
minutes before we ran into an economic recession." Kroll decided
"against all advice" to run both the U.S. company and the New
York office himself. Since he had never run a U.S. office, he felt
he needed to master many details and gain new skills, particularly
financial skills. "I was just beginning to grasp issues like cash flow
and receivables." Every month we sat down with the financial
people and worked through every detail of the budget—the var-
iances, how the figures explained what was happening, and so on.

Why did he choose to deal with his weaknesses like this? "I
couldn't do it any other way." Once he had command of the details,
he again brought in a manager to handle them. In this difficult
process, Kroll was rewarded by discovering that "I really had a
latent gift for mathematics that I never knew. It is an ability to
identify a strange number among many other numbers." What had
been a weakness emerged as a considerable strength. "It is totally
bizarre. I don't add or subtract or do any of the basic mathematical
functions the way that you are supposed to. It is impossible to
explain how I arrive at the number."

Nonetheless, colleagues confirm that if the number is wrong
or represents a problem, Kroll will spot it immediately, a talent
that might never have emerged if it were not for Kroll's decision
to confront his weakness head on. How many managers have similarly valuable skills they will never find because they ignore or
are deprived of opportunities to uncover them?

Kroll's case is exceptional because large organizations are designed to compartmentalize work to maximize individual strengths
and isolate weaknesses. This is their great strength. There is an
individual or whole department always available with just the skill
you need. Want to purchase a desk? Call purchasing. Hire a sec-

retary? Call personnel. Need an analysis of the monthly results? Call accounting. Want to understand what's behind that sales drop in Detroit? Call market research.

For the senior manager to insist on doing tiny specialist tasks simply to learn how to do them makes that manager, in Kroll's understated words, "a pain to everybody." The young manager gets even greater pressure to stay with her strengths and within her job description and is reminded again and again not to be "so eager to reinvent the wheel." One young marketing manager in a Fortune 500 company wanted to widen his understanding and use of the computer. When he requested equipment to help him do this, he was asked pointedly: "Do you want to be a marketing specialist or a computer specialist?" The question defines both the strength and the weakness of the large organization.

In confronting this magnificent specialization, the individual quickly learns that success means maximizing your strengths while neutralizing your weaknesses through personal or professional networking with the specialists. What is a power for the organization ends up depriving the individual of a wider field for personal development.

Like Kroll, many other individuals have successfully broken out of the corporate mold, sometimes on their own, sometimes with the help of shrewd mentors. Stanley's Robert Widham added an important strength when he was temporarily steered out of marketing into finance early in his career.

Painful Lessons

Campbell Soup's Herbert Baum remembers vividly one overnight lesson that added an understanding of pricing to his formidable marketing skills. Baum was 40 when he came to Campbell, as "just a little advertising agency person who had never thought that much about this total business thing." His first boss was A. M. (Bill) Williams, then president of the Campbell's Canned Food division.

"He really taught me almost every element of running a business," Baum recalls. "Sometimes it was painful. He put me through exercises that he knew were for my benefit." A later boss, Harold Shaub, reinforced the lessons.

On one occasion, Baum spent the night on a pricing study after taking Shaub a staff-prepared pricing recommendation. "I went into his office, this was at five or six in the afternoon, and he said, 'This is totally wrong. You need to check every element of this pricing study and I want it by tomorrow morning.' " Baum went home and stayed up all night. "I thought I was in college. I went over that thing with a calculator and a pencil. I had to call people about the price of tomato paste and glass and how does this cost relate to that." Baum finished the job and went in blurry-eyed the next morning to see Shaub and "he wasn't even in that day. He just wanted me to go through it."

At first Baum was annoyed, "but when I thought about it afterwards, I knew exactly what he had done. To this day, I am an expert on pricing studies. Someone can walk in here with a pricing study with labor rates, benefits, ingredients, etc., and when I look at that number I can tell you instinctively if that number is high, low, or right on."

Baum's rise at Campbell has been meteoric. After joining the conservative New Jersey company in 1978, it took him only seven years to reach the presidency of its largest unit. Baum arrived as Campbell was shifting from a production-oriented to a marketing-oriented company. Baum was one of the first outside marketing experts recruited in line with the new direction. His first and hugely successful product launch, Prego Spaghetti Sauce, represented Campbell's first really *new* product, not one that was just an extension of Campbell's soup line.

Brought in from the outside with a clear strength that was on the ascendancy at Campbell, Baum made a great effort not just to base his career on being "that advertising guy," but to become also "a student of manufacturing." Over time, what started as a weakness in a heavily manufacturing-based company has become a real strength. He misses no opportunity to expand his working knowledge. "To this day, I would rather go into a manufacturing plant than look at an ad or work on a new product concept. I am fascinated by how products are made." On his desk today, there is always a manufacturing book and only an occasional marketing book.

How far has he come to date? "If there was something lower than a weakness, that was it, since I didn't know the front door from the back door on a manufacturing facility. I won't say I am an expert now, but I certainly understand manufacturing."

In their own highly individualistic ways, Kroll and Baum have broken through the trap of always letting the experts do it for them, choosing instead to become enough of an expert to convert clear weaknesses into equally clear strengths. Can there be any doubt that they and the organizations they head are far stronger because of this unusual effort?

A Nightmare of Success

One of the appeals of leaving a large organization and going out on your own is the opportunity to test and extend your strengths in all directions. But as Randy Carlock found when he left Dayton Hudson, the sudden gap of not having the experts around can be traumatizing. Having worked in a large company, Carlock knew what was missing. Many other entrepreneurs start a business without ever having worked somewhere else. When they rise on favorable market trends, their natural strengths come rapidly, almost poetically, to the fore, and the business grows as if by magic. The business press extols the owner as a management genius who has avoided the trap of big organizations by "just letting the staff do it their way."

For the moment, the weaknesses gathering in destructive force below the surface are masked by a favorable market or long, hard hours of work, or both. When sudden trouble or even unexpected opportunity comes, the entrepreneur will be no different from the corporate executive; survival will depend on strengths, and success will depend on handling weaknesses.

Walton L. Stinson is an entrepreneur who was almost undone by success. When Stinson was 10 years old he "went over to a friend's house after school and he had a shortwave radio which he let me listen to. . . . I put on a pair of headphones and I heard signals coming in from around the world. It caught my childhood imagination and off I went and never stopped running."

A dozen years later, in 1973, Stinson and partner Steve Weiner, having decided to enter audio retailing, toured 14 markets before selecting Denver as the site of their ListenUp store. Everything the partners owned, including personal audio equipment valued at $10,000, went into the business. Weiner moved in with Stinson and his wife, who brought in the only regular cash through a job as an office manager. When the audio manufacturers' representatives came to pay their first visit to the new store, "by and large, they thought it was a joke; they gave us maybe 90 days to survive."

The manufacturers' reps were wrong, and by 1983 the store was prospering, by far the most successful audio store in the Denver market. Then, as Stinson puts it, "we got a tiger by the tail and we hung on." The tiger was the compact disc. Stinson and Weiner had seen the possibilities of this innovation long before other retailers and even many manufacturers. When record stores proved hesitant to stock the new medium, ListenUp expanded into the record business. To dramatize digital audio, ListenUp hosted several charity concerts at which musicians left the stage one at a time gradually revealing to the stunned audiences that they were actually listening to a digital tape recording. "We were nationally prominent. We were written up in *Business Week*. I was a delegate to the Compact Disc Group, which helped formulate the national marketing for the CD."

As the new technology took off, ListenUp boomed, doubling its sales from $6 million in fiscal year 1983 to $12 million in fiscal year 1986. Employment went from 30 to nearly 100. As the business accelerated, Stinson "got a glimpse of what might happen and it scared me half to death. I said, 'I am going to lose this company.' That is what I thought." The reason for this sudden fear was Stinson's realization that he just did not have the skills to handle a $12 million company with 100 employees. "It was going to swamp me."

This is the entrepreneur's nightmare of success when the weaknesses begin to overpower the strengths, in Stinson's case with terrifying speed. Most entrepreneurs fail in the first few years. Others survive because of two or three strengths, normally some high technical capacity, a sense of a market, and a willingness to work brutal hours. As long as the business does not grow too fast and is not is seriously battered by market conditions or competition, these strengths continue to ensure survival. Instinctively knowing this, Stinson had considered trying to hold back his company's growth in the early 1980s, but he had then decided to push ahead. Now he had reason to question that decision.

"I called a professor of mine from college, a man I have always trusted. I said, 'I've got a problem and I'm scared. I don't have the skills to do what I need to do to keep up with the growth of this business. I am either going to have to turn it over to somebody or else I am going to have to sell it or I am going to have to go out of business. What should I do?' " Stinson's former professor recommended none of these options; instead he suggested that his former student enroll in an MBA program.

Stinson followed the advice even though he had been able to solve earlier, smaller crises by his own version of on-the-job training, first learning sales "by trial and error," and later teaching himself all the firm's back office functions such as media buying and purchasing. When they first started, "I said, 'Steve, how do you set up a file cabinet?' And he said, 'Alphabetically.' And I said, 'Oh, okay, that makes sense.' Then I had to figure out how to manage cash because I figured that if I didn't, we would run out of it and go out of business." The first system was simple but effective: "I just thought about it for awhile and I said, 'Well, if I never spend money unless I have the money, then I can't run out of money.' "

As the business got more complicated, Stinson and his partner began to subscribe to different publications that answered their questions. At times they received 100 a month, canceling some subscriptions and adding new ones as their needs changed.

Stinson regularly spends 20 to 30 hours a week reading. His technique is to "scan for an article or book that relates to a problem that I am having right now, and when I find that, I study it in depth and sometimes I even memorize concepts, formulas, things like that." This pattern goes back to his youth, "when the first thing I wanted to learn was electronics. . . . I was 10 years old and none of my teachers cared about it, none of my peers cared about it, and that is where I set the pattern. I learned from periodicals and a few textbooks, and that set the pattern for my life."

The MBA course at the University of Colorado reintroduced Stinson to structured, disciplined learning. The course met one full day a week and required 15 hours a week of homework. "The sacrifice was tremendous, but I don't think it was as great as the sacrifice I would have made if I hadn't done it." The course expanded Stinson's knowledge, improved his skills, and by creating time pressure, required him to better organize his time on the job.

One of his newly developed skills was crucial in that reorganization. Stinson found that although he no longer had as much time to talk to customers and employees, "letters are an extremely powerful way to communicate with others." Earlier, he had struggled several hours on a one-page letter. But in the MBA course "they made me write. Every week they had me write 100-page papers, 50-page papers. If I sat in front of the typewriter and spent an hour on one page, that was it, I wasn't going to make it." Today, Stinson encourages every customer to write him, and they do in the hundreds. With his new skill, he answers every letter personally, a process that makes him one of the best informed retailers not only in his market but in his industry.

ORGANIZE YOURSELF AT A HIGHER LEVEL

Today, Stinson's ListenUp is stable and steadily growing and is one of the best managed specialty retailers in its industry. Three principles support Stinson's success and they apply to any manager at any level in any industry.

First, rapid growth, whether a sudden business expansion or a promotion to a higher rank, always exposes weaknesses that were invisible or didn't matter at earlier levels. Think of yourself as a company, successfully organized at your existing level. If suddenly, like Listen Up, you accelerate, that organization that used to function quite effectively starts to show strain. The faster the acceleration, the greater the strain.

Second, the strain that you feel at such moments is not mysterious or even negative. You are not under pressure because of other people or even outside circumstances. You feel tension because you are increasingly aware of the gap between your present capabilities and the requirements of your new job. This is always the most important source of tension, never more keenly felt than when you make a sudden, unexpected acceleration forward. It was exactly this same recognition that scared Walt Stinson "half to death" and made Alex Kroll exclaim: "Tension? Desperation was more like it!"

Third, as illustrated by Kroll and Stinson but also applicable in every situation, the most important action you can take at this point is to recognize your weaknesses. Fully. Head on. This was also Baum's approach in facing his lack of knowledge of manufacturing. "If there was anything lower than a weakness, this was it." Ignoring or attempting to isolate weaknesses at this point will only increase the tension level, encouraging you to rationalize or evade. This is always a mistake and will result in failure sooner or later.

Once you have recognized that you cannot isolate your weaknesses, you can deal with them by compensating for them, either by working longer and harder yourself or by bringing in someone with the strength you lack. Or you can follow the path chosen by Kroll, Baum, and Stinson and make the great psychological effort to overcome your weaknesses by reorganizing your mental processes at a higher level. The third is never the easiest choice, but it is always the most personally rewarding. As Kroll, Baum, and Stinson all found, by turning weaknesses into strengths is the only sure method to grow.

SCULPTING YOUR JOB, SCULPTING YOURSELF: THE ESSENTIAL STRATEGY FOR SUCCESS

5

In 1985 Apple Computer, Inc., "was in deep yogurt. We needed a big win and it was obvious to me that this could be that win." For John Scull, then the 29-year-old marketing manager for Apple desktop publishing, that win could be scored by using his product as a "Trojan horse" to introduce Apple to American business.

Apple urgently needed something to cheer about to raise its inside morale and outside reputation. Since late 1984, the company had been reeling, first from the bitter firing of founder Steve Jobs by CEO John Sculley, followed by a 20 percent layoff. Rapidly losing its famed élan, Apple also faced real doubts as to whether it could shift from being the innovative leader in the home and school computer market to a heavyweight player in the business market.

Starting from a standstill, in the midst of major corporate upheaval, Scull and his team launched their product within six months, going on to give Apple that big win. As Scull had predicted, desktop publishing helped get Apple in the door of business offices all over the nation.

Timing was critical. John Scull's desktop publishing effort came at just the right moment to support Apple Chairman John Sculley's overall objective redirecting Apple's energies toward the business market. Although desktop publishing was not the only tactic that helped Apple meet this objective, Scull believes it would be fair to say that what VisiCalc was to Apple II and what Lotus 1-2-3 was to the IBM PC, desktop publishing was to the Macintosh computer. It showed off one thing the machine was very good at as a way of demonstrating its overall strength.

By the end of fiscal year 1987, with Mac's beachhead in the business market well established and expanding, Apple's sales and profits were both roaring at a 40 percent annual rate, and no one was questioning the California company's capacity to play in the business market. By then, Scull had moved on to a new assignment as Apple's marketing manager for emerging markets. As the title suggests, the assignment is important, open-ended, and deliberately short on public details. However, that does not prevent Scull from reminiscing about his five years at Apple, particularly the amazing desktop publishing launch.

CAREER ACCELERATION STRATEGIES

Both prior to and during the launch, Scull's career illustrates four critical strategies that can help any executive accelerate career progress:

1. Find and develop your strengths.
2. Keep overcoming weaknesses.
3. Focus on essentials first.
4. Use nonessentials to create a personal style or statement.

Find Your Strength

The first strategy will be familiar: Find your strengths as quickly as possible and don't be afraid to move around in your early career while you are searching. Scull graduated from the University of Oklahoma with a major in economics. Needing to earn money for graduate school, he took a job teaching math and coaching at a small private school, where he discovered a talent and a love for teaching.

After earning his MBA at Harvard, Scull went to work for a large bank in New York, planning on a career in international finance. "It just wasn't me at all. It was a large bureaucratic organization. There was no risk taking, no willingness to change. I was trying to get them to bring in personal computers, and this was 1981. I was there about half a year, and it was obvious that I had made a mistake. You have to understand when you make a mistake, cut your losses, and go."

Like many who work at Apple, Scull feels an almost mystical attraction to the personal computer. He sees the PC leading the way into the emerging information age in the same way the Model T automobile created the automotive age. Seeking a way into the industry, Scull went to work as a marketing representative for a personal computer sales organization. "At that point you either went with a sales organization or one of the emerging manufacturers, none of whom had a dominant leadership position or even much of a sales strategy." The marketing strategy at that point was basically to throw products out on the market and see what happened.

Scull studied the industry and decided "the key to the whole thing was distribution, understanding the sales process from the customers' point of view." To his strength in teaching and a conceptional strength in marketing gathered at Harvard, Scull now added a step missed by many well-educated marketing people— hands-on sales. That experience has always given him what he calls "a reality check" in dealing with computer marketing.

With his Harvard MBA he certainly could have landed a higher level job than marketing rep in the new industry. However, he consciously chose a position that would give him something he lacked, a pattern he repeated at Apple.

From Conscious Goal to Consummate Strategy

Scull's career illustrates a second familiar strategy: Consciously overcome a weakness and a career opportunity seems to follow almost immediately. At Apple, Scull joined the elite team working under Steve Jobs on the introduction of the Mac. Using his teaching, marketing, and sales strengths, Scull helped to establish sales channels as well as to create training and communication programs for dealers.

Successful on that job, he made a surprising shift. He volunteered for a job, which "was like taking cod liver oil. It's going to taste bad, but it's going to be good for you." Scull believes you can learn "by just listening to people and intellectualizing." He prefers, however, to get his hands on a job. "You learn it better and deeper and get a gut instinct." The "cod liver oil" job was as a marketing communications manager. Here he "had to learn not only the administrative, but the logistical and technical aspects of putting together advertisements, public relations plans, sales promotions, trade shows, events, and conferences." It was a job he simultaneously "loved and hated. I know my strengths and weaknesses and I loved the strategy, which is what I am good at, but not the detail work because I am not a good detail person."

Then why did he take a job dominated by details? The answer is direct. Scull's aspiration is to become a company president after first earning credibility as "one of the really top marketing people in this business. And people who don't get their hands dirty in all aspects of the marketing formula don't ever really understand their business well enough. . . . As a marketing manager, I see myself at the center of a wheel with a variety of spokes. My job is to be the best at overall strategy and then be the number two person in all of the individual components. Ideally the individual component people are the experts. If they are not quite an expert, then I have to know their specialty well enough that I can train, coach, develop them."

In line with a concept he calls "value added leadership," Scull was upgrading his skills. "My view of a boss, manager, or leader is that they have to add value to the people they are leading. If they don't add value and are strictly there as a title holder or a person who is the 'manager,' that isn't good enough in a flat organization. There is no reason for someone to be in a leadership position unless they are truly leading."

Powerful Lever for Personal Growth

By consciously aiming at a goal, analyzing himself against that goal, and then directly addressing a weakness that could hinder him, Scull was applying a powerful lever of personal growth, a lever available to any manager wishing to accelerate a career.

Understanding the nature and power of that lever will explain one of the perennial mysteries in every company: why so many executives after a brilliant start are unable to fulfill their early promise. We know instinctively that at the heart of personality, aspiration remains intact, although career defeats and being passed over may cause many to rationalize "I never really wanted to go further anyway." Inner resources are certainly always available to release energy. Look at the incredible burst of energy displayed by supposedly over-the-hill executives whose careers are suddenly threatened by market downturns, competition, or mergers.

If aspiration remains and inner resources are always available, what is missing? One possibility is that the career has reached an equilibrium in which the weight of the weaknesses and the upward momentum of strengths are balanced, making it impossible to fail or progress in a significant fashion. However, since a true equilibrium rarely endures for long, this cannot be the explanation for such a common condition.

For the real cause of careers that have lost momentum, look first at the interaction between executive and job, a place where many stagnated executives never look at all. Every job has its essentials and its nonessentials. Understanding that difference and acting on it keeps executives rising in organizational life.

The essentials are always those few things that are absolutely critical to getting the job done. Sometimes they are simple survival factors. "The first duty of a statesman is to get reelected" is a reminder of one essential in politics. Winston Churchill learned that lesson when his party lost the elections of 1945 despite the fact that Churchill was then the world's premier statesman.

We know the essentials in sports. The baseball manager is hired to win games, the outfielder to get hits and catch fly balls, and the pitcher to prevent runs. We enjoy sports partly because at one level this sense of clarity seems to mirror life and especially work. Of course, sports and work quickly become more complex, adding pleasure to the one and anxiety to the other. Listen to two baseball fans compare two star pitchers and you might think they have completely forgotten the essential task of preventing runs as they debate their idols' abilities to get the most strikeouts, walk the fewest opponents, win the biggest games, pitch the most complete games, and reverse the most losing streaks. Each of these is important, but the ability to prevent runs is the essential.

Sports also mirror work in that what first appears simple grows in complexity. In the lower ranks of line management, the essentials seem quite clear. We hire a salesperson to close sales, an accountant to produce figures, and a foreman to turn out products. Even here, things are not as clear as they seem. We are dissatisfied if the salesperson meets the quota but alienates too many customers, if the accountant presents figures that others cannot understand, or if the foreman makes the production target with too many rejections.

As we move into staff jobs or the higher ranks of line management, confusion grows geometrically. The essentials no longer seem to be constants. How one does the job can seem in many organizations and many situations to be as important as the primary tasks themselves. Nonetheless, for the star pitcher or the star manager, the essential or essentials are always there.

Many well-managed organizations have tried to overcome this confusion with management by objectives, standards, or performance programs. Chrysler CEO Lee Iaccoca says the key to management is to ask everybody who reports to you to set written targets for the next 90 days and then ask each person to come back every 90 days to report and set new targets.[6]

Such objective-setting programs help managers keep focused on the essentials—at least the essentials as the boss sees them. Unfortunately, in some cases, the procedure of jointly setting objectives has degenerated into a bureaucratic and manipulative exercise, a striking case of an act completed perfectly at the physical and mental level that loses most of its power through a failure at the psychological level to consider the needs and feelings of others.

Whether there is a company-sponsored program or not and whether it is honest or rigged, every manager should independently identify the essentials of the job now held and the next job on the ladder. Stagnated executives are not focusing on the real issues and the real essentials. Any executive who makes that slight course correction is likely once again to find the wind behind the sails of her career.

THE DELIVERABLE

Which brings us back to the role of the essentials in the career of John Scull. Having got the job for which he had prepared himself and having seen the opportunity in desktop publishing, Scull now had to mobilize the necessary resources to achieve "the big win" that he was certain was possible.

The first step was to define what he calls the "deliverable." For Scull, every human transaction has a deliverable, the final result. To him, the deliverable for our interview was that all the right questions had been asked and answered. "You think about what it is at the end you want to have. You try to make it tangible.

---

[6]Lee Iacocca with William Novak, *Iacocca: An Autobiography*, New York: Bantam Books, November, 1984.

If you can see it, you can make other people see it. If you can get other people to see it, then you can get there."

Persuading people in a hurry was important "because there was a short time period to do it, a window of opportunity" that had to be seized or lost forever. Scull was sure his vision was deliverable because it was based on "the fundamental view that people buy things because they have a problem that the product can solve."

He ran through the impact that dramatizing the Mac's problem-solving capabilities would have on all Apple constituencies. "It could build up confidence in our sales force that Macintosh was really a serious tool that they could get behind and push; not only our sales force, but our dealers who were critical. Our software developers needed to see that it was a win so they would continue to bring out other products to round it out." It was also important to people inside Apple. "Some people thought we were going down. We had just had a massive reorganization. You had the classic crisis situation where it was the time to take the bold move because, personally, I didn't see much risk in it."

Scull had the glorious experience of feeling that suddenly all his previous experience was paying off, every job "from my teaching and coaching, to sales, sales development and marketing communications." He knew that before his dream was deliverable, he had to identify "the two or three key things we had to do." In the end, there were only two essentials: "educate customers [that] there was a new way of doing things and educate and train our sales channels [that] there was a new solution that they could sell to specific groups of people." To get the big win, both had to be achieved today, tomorrow at the latest.

First, it took physical effort: 80 hours a week for six straight months. Mental effort involved assembling an organization with all the necessary skills and then keeping them focused week after week on the essentials. It took psychological effort to keep the team together, acknowledging "that I made mistakes all the way through," reminding himself to try not to get impatient when someone couldn't see the vision even when he thought he had communicated it two and three times and "they ought to have seen it clearly." Sometimes, when he couldn't get through, he had to go around the system and then remember to make the effort "to go back later and mend the fences." Despite this effort, "the greatest mistakes I made were the places where I didn't discipline myself," when he gave in to the frustration of simply not believing that people couldn't see how important this was.

He had to break down the essentials of educating the customers and the sales channels into specific steps. The deliverable had to be seen in its many faces. "You had to have X number of dealers who were fully trained to be able to demonstrate and sell the product successfully. I had to envision the average. I didn't worry about the bottom 50 percent of our dealers. I worried about the top 50 percent. I could envision a certain type of salesperson who was right in the middle of what we were aiming for. I could envision that caliber of person, what he or she needed to successfully demonstrate and sell the product. I could almost envision that person talking and saying this stuff [the sales presentation] because I had been around long enough. If you can see that, you can say, 'Okay, now what do I need to get that?' "

To get that, he asked himself, "If I were that salesperson, what are the critical things that I would need? I would need good advertising because I want customers to know about the product and be aware of it." He continued through good public relations, creating an aura of success as people began talking about the new product, a brochure, training, or seminar materials. He asked himself, "If I were that Apple salesperson, would I need more?" He went over the question again and again, deciding in the end that although additional selling tools might be helpful, they weren't critical.

Spice and Raisins

Scull divided the essentials from the nonessentials by using an everyday analogy: baking a cake. "I can't cook a cake unless I have flour, eggs, and shortening. If I have extra spice and raisins, great, but if I don't have those core ingredients, I can't bake the cake."

Spice and raisins are very helpful, he adds, because they provide "the personal twist" that makes the individual cooks feel as if they are doing it themselves. Every manager should exploit the opportunity to bring that personal twist to the job through the nonessentials, but only after ensuring that the flour, eggs, and shortening are completely taken care of.

In the desktop publishing launch, the temptation was always to pay too much attention to the spice and raisins. In Scull's weekly review meetings, the essentials, now held tightly to eight things such as training and promotional materials, were reviewed again and again. "The toughest thing" was to hold on to the essentials and resist the temptation to let other things "creep in." It was tough because many of the ideas were "good things, but they weren't better than what was already on the list." Even more important, they would take time, since "every new idea has a multiplier effect."

Throughout the project, Scull remained alert to the danger of letting one more good thing creep in. "Most people think . . . 'Let's do this one more thing. I am the only one who needs to do it and I can do it. I have no problem.' Wrong! Because they are doing it, it causes three or four or five other people to have to do something and that multiplies up."

With the essentials under control, Scull devoted time to the nonessentials, his own spice and raisins. He personally headed one of the teams that went out to train the dealers and salespeople. "I needed to get the feedback and also it added that personal sense that this was really important. Our field force said, 'Wow, this guy must be crazy or this must be really important.' They sensed that both were true. . . . It gave me a chance to work with these guys and not only intellectually interest them but emotionally involve them." Personal enthusiasm was not yet an essential, but it clearly added spice to the cake Scull was baking so artfully.

To contribute to the publicity momentum, he told the Apple public relations people that he would personally talk to any reporter or security analyst with an interest in desktop publishing. "Anyone, anytime because education was critical." Even here, it was a question of identifying the essentials. "The XYZ town flyer might not get top priority, but the *New York Times* would." He divided contacts into As, Bs, and Cs. "Some I might only talk to for 15 minutes, but I would talk to them all."

Sometimes the nonessentials created greater momentary attention than the essentials, such as the time when Scull distributed special T-shirts with the logo from desktop publishing's first brochure. Despite companywide demand, there were only 50 and Scull did it only once. The T-shirt simultaneously became a collector's item, a badge of honor, and an expression of thanks to the people most intimately involved in his project.

Scull's quick identification of and rigorous adherence to the essentials enabled his team to have a full launch—product fully available, distribution channels complete, field force trained, market communications humming and in place—within only six months. These were the eggs, flour, and shortening for the big win the team gave Apple. Scull had been able to handle this part of the challenge because he had earlier identified the essentials in the marketing manager's job and had spent a year systematically learning what he didn't know.

With the essentials in place, he was free to add his own personal twist, bringing into play his specific personal strengths as a teacher, coach, and articulate thinker about the role of computers in society. Mixed with proper skills, the essentials would have produced the cake; the nonessential spice and raisins made it rich and unique.

The problem for most managers with stalled or declining careers is that they have lost track of the essentials, insisting instead on displaying their undeniable strengths on nonessentials. This is why the outplacement firms are so successful in rehabilitating broken careers. They simply identify the strengths and then help the executive find the job that matches those strengths. But this does not help the thousands of executives stranded in companies in midcareer, seemingly unable to move forward. The lack of focus on essentials has yet to become career threatening, but the year-in, year-out anxiety may in the end take a greater toll.

Measuring Yourself

The first step in reviving a stagnated career is to identify the essentials of your job, but not more than three or four. Next, measure your performance on these essentials with the same critical eye you would use in measuring someone else. Knowing what you do, would you hire yourself for your job? Even if the answer is yes, what are the reservations you would have? In which areas would you like to see improvement?

Very quickly into such a self-analysis, you will come to "the parts of the job I like and the parts I dislike." With the slightest effort and honesty, you will be able to identify the correlation between the parts you love and your strengths and the parts you dislike and your weaknesses. Next, you must look coldly at the parts you dislike. Are any of them essentials? In the stalled or declining career, this will always be the case. Also, how essential are the parts you like so much?

How do you identify the essentials? If you have a management by objectives program, the essentials will be identified for you. If you don't, look for the key results your position is supposed to produce: sales volume, net profit, monthly production for line jobs, or the most important services provided for staff jobs.

If you cannot find these three or four things amidst the confusion of your daily job, seek help—from a spouse, a colleague, a boss, or a mentor. A 40-minute conversation with the aim of identifying the essentials of a job almost always produces the necessary answers. Occasionally, one finds jobs where the essentials cannot be identified at all or where there are so many essentials that identification is useless. These jobs are programmed for failure. Faced with such a job, the only course of action is to leave at one's own pace or, if that is not possible, to make one's own best judgment of the essentials and with good humor seek to excel on those. In no case is the right strategy to become inert or defeated.

Happily, truly impossible jobs are rare. More often anxiety on executive jobs is the result of a stubborn refusal to acknowledge or an unwillingness or an inability to perform on one or more of the essentials. This can be especially acute if great energy and enthusiasm is going into the nonessentials.

Why is it so difficult for so many executives to stay focused on the essentials during these mid-career doldrums? It's not as if managers are so happy using their strengths on the nonessentials. Study after study shows career satisfaction steadily declining starting in the late 30s or early 40s and continuing to decline all the way to the early 60s. At that point it starts to rise again, perhaps for no other reason than the sad fact that the end is now in sight.

YOU ARE ON YOUR OWN

Behind this widely observed phenomenon is one of life's most predictable occurrences, a turning point that catches most executives and professionals so completely unaware that their condition could be best described as being asleep on the job. This moment comes, normally in mid career, when every executive's great inherited endowment no longer has the capacity to be the primary career accelerator. Few people are even aware of the loss of this propulsion because so few were aware of its importance in the first place.

Throughout life, we construct an internal drama with ourselves in the center in the starring role. Like the heroes we dream of being, we overcome difficulty after difficulty, slaying dragon after dragon in our steady rise. Then, in midcareer, the dragons are suddenly better organized or technologically improved or simply bigger and smarter.

The reality of our lives is quite different. Although our effort is important, it is overwhelmingly the effort of others that propels our careers in early to mid life. The list of our benefactors is so long and so wide that a few examples will have to suggest its scope.

Everyone recognizes the effort of parents in keeping us alive and healthy and getting us reasonably socialized. Then, there is the effort of our teachers to educate us. The education process did not begin with our teachers. It was created over centuries by the tremendous effort of tens of thousands of people who continually took everything that humanity had learned up to that point, organized it, and then discovered ingenious ways to transmit it in digestible portions. Imagine how far your career would advance if you had to discover for yourself every bit of knowledge you use in just one hour on the job.

Next, there is the whole political and economic organization of our society, a society that not only permits but encourages individual freedom. I traveled to Iran in the days of the Shah's rule. A young manager visited me to enlist the support of the American Management Association in establishing a management association. During the conversation, I naïvely asked him why he didn't bring together a group of managers and form an association. Glancing nervously around, he explained that meetings of three or more persons required the sanction of the government. Until that moment, "the right of free assembly" had simply been a phrase for me, something vaguely remembered from high school civics. We are all carried forward by such easily forgotten legacies. Each of these legacies, from free speech to free libraries, made our progress possible.

The economy in which we work is the most efficiently organized in history, and that organization also carries us forward. In the 1970s, I sat with a group of European managers debating, partly seriously, partly in fun, which nation produced the best managers per capita. Our award finally went to the Italians, not because they produced the most, but because they produced so much in an environment that was then so politically and economically unstable. We reasoned that if those Italian managers worked in an economy like that of the United States, they would have outproduced everyone in the world.

Even beyond these basics, we must look at the organization

of the industries and companies where we work. Someone invented the product or service that created our industry. Thousands of people, from the postal workers to the drivers of delivery trucks, maintain the distribution channels that bring us together with our customers and vendors. In our own companies, a founder provided the original inspiration, other managers created the systems and procedures through which we get things done, and still others trained every fellow worker on whom we depend.

Even fiercely independent entrepreneurs can see how the work of thousands of others made it possible for them to start their companies, from the relative who provided the capital, to the inventors who created the products they make or use, all the way back to the inventor of currency who saved them the bother of selling their wares in exchange for eggs and butter.

If we add up the effort that others have contributed to carry our careers forward, and only the barest outline appears here, what percentage of the total would our own efforts represent? One percent? Five percent? Whatever the percentage at the start, to succeed past mid career our contributions must grow, not diminish, with age and accomplishment. Our invisible endowment from others is a consumable asset and like careless heirs to a fortune built by others, we spend it wantonly in getting established in life and at work. By mid career it is virtually gone in the sense that it can no longer be used to propel us forward, although we will continue to draw upon it to maintain ourselves for the rest of our lives and careers.

From here on, our own efforts will write the tale of our success, as our generation runs out of endowment at more or less the same time. Those with a higher or a more rigorous education can be propelled for somewhat longer. Those raised in stronger families will have deeper emotional resources to draw on. Those who work in better organized industries or for better organized companies will find more opportunities waiting for a longer period. However, by our late thirties or early forties, we are on our own in a way that feels strange and often disconcerting. After all, whether we have ever acknowledged it, until now we have been supported by the efforts of millions.

It Depends on Me

The unfamiliar sense of loneliness, of being on our own, can lead to the painful mid-career crisis so fashionable among successful executives. When that period of personal turmoil ends, with the families overturned and careers abandoned and successfully restarted, the reinvigorated executive proclaims to the world: "I went through Hell but what I really found out was that, in the end, it all depends on me. I have to be my own person." This is the last message signaling childhood's true end, a message that many use, with or without mid-career crisis, to move on to lives of greater success and fulfillment.

Some of the most successful people in American life have started in the most modest or even disadvantaged way. We have seen the examples of Michael Blumenthal, Eugene Lang, and John Jacob. Such individuals learn earlier and better than most that "it depends on me." With that knowledge firmly in place, they seize fully and astutely whatever part of our common rich endowment is available to them. The ironic advantage enjoyed by such individuals is that because they do not expect to be full, automatic heirs to our common endowment, they learn early how to overcome significant barriers.

Take the barrier of racism, one of the highest and most intimidating barriers in our society. John Jacob has confronted and battled that barrier all his life. "I believe that while racism is a problem, it cannot be an excuse, and that the real achievers find ways to achieve in spite of those kinds of barriers, that it is absolutely paramount that you find ways to scale the barriers—whether you go around them, whether you go under them, whether you go over them, or whether you go through them. The key is to find a way to get around that barrier, and it is incumbent upon people who want to achieve to find that way to get around that barrier."

If Jacob can speak with such optimistic passion about a barrier like racism, who can say she confronts a career barrier too great to overcome?

The Greatest Barrier Is Within

For most executives, the greatest of all barriers is the "Establishment Within." Everyone, including those who successfully overturned external establishments in the 1960s and 1970s, finds this opponent stubbornly intractable. Like all establishments, the Establishment Within protects itself by a network of defenses, some crude and some subtle. Its strengths are always on display, ready to be flexed and used—used sometimes, like the military force of a great empire, to achieve ridiculously petty ends. Internal weaknesses, far from being corrected, go on being ignored or covered up behind an external mask of strength. As power and position increase, the once clear essentials lose force in a welter of side issues and novelties. For all this, the Establishment Within, like all establishments, is most formidable and united when it is under attack, especially an attack by a new and external reality.

That new and external reality for many executives and professionals in mid career is the diminishing strength of career strategies that worked so well only yesterday. Careers that once were full of verve and speed lose zest and momentum. Like a bureaucracy suddenly under siege, the Establishment Within fights back with a stream of memos, press releases, communiques from the front, and desperate "to whom it may concerns," in an attempt to cover itself and establish the blame for the deteriorating situation on others. Whipping boys are never far away: the company, the boss, the merger, the industry, the economy, the mortgage, the kids' college bills, the Democrats, the Republicans, the Japanese, the Europeans, and so on. On a bad day, messages assigning blame flood the mind, leaving no room for the most life-affirming message of all: It depends on me.

Locked in this internal witch hunt, the obsessed executive

must still explain why others are moving ahead while facing the same obstacles. When the intracompany memo arrives in the in-basket announcing another promotion for Joe or Jane, the Establishment Within is quick with an explanation—the boss likes him; she's a smooth talker; well, sure, if you want to be a workaholic; or, the all-time favorite (that extends a feeling of generous approval, and an equally warm feeling of absolution for one's own deficiencies) that lucky devil, always the right person at the right place at the right time! If Joe and Jane are astute, and they usually are, they will minimize the resentment of colleagues by declaring themselves to be equally mystified by yet another surprising turn of good fortune.

THE LUCKY MAN

The all-time all-star among those supposedly lucky enough to be the right person at the right place at the right time is the 34th President of the United States, Dwight David Eisenhower. Even as he rose to be the supreme commander of the Allied forces in Europe, went on to be president of Columbia University, and then became one of our most popular and successful presidents, Ike was held up—sometimes in admiration, sometimes in mockery—as an example of how far you could go in American life with a winning smile and a bit of luck.

The legend of the affable, not-too-bright, and somewhat lazy man with the million-dollar smile and the incredible luck started at West Point before the first World War. Eisenhower ranked barely in the upper half of the class "the stars fell on," the class of 1915, which produced 60 of World War II's generals. After West Point, his career was undistinguished. He was never able to get into combat, or even to Europe in World War I. Twenty years later, he was a major, a pleasant man who was especially good at following up on the details.

Then, in September 1941, Ike got lucky. Everyone in the

Army knew the Louisiana maneuvers of that year were critically important. Most Army officers believed the United States was almost certain to enter the two-year-old war in Europe. With the older commanders retired, the young men would show their skills and determine the leadership for the coming war. General George Marshall was there with his ever-present notebook, ready to write down the names of those who impressed him.

Surprising everyone, Colonel Eisenhower performed brilliantly. The strategy he prepared for one of two maneuver teams quickly and decisively destroyed the opposing army. Out came Marshall's notebook and up went Eisenhower. Twenty-seven months later, Ike was named Supreme Commander of the Allied Forces for the D-Day invasion of Europe. What a lucky man!

To the Best of My Ability

Eisenhower himself promoted the useful mystique of his luck. Only in recent years have we learned of the focused effort that created that lucky moment. Several years ago, Merle Miller set out to write a biography of Eisenhower's political years. Miller planned to devote one chapter to Ike's career before entering politics. He was not looking for anything unusual as he began his research, simply the traditional story of Ike, the lucky soldier.

Miller never wrote the political book. Astonished by what he found in Eisenhower's diaries, letters, and in the reminiscences of those who knew him before the war, Miller wrote 800 pages on *Ike the Soldier—As They Knew Him.*[7] What Miller found was not merely a lucky man but a man of fierce determination. From the time he left West Point, Ike set and met his own high standards. He stuck by these standards despite more than two decades of

---

[7]The revised perspective on Eisenhower in this section plus all of the direct quotes are drawn from Miller's excellent biography, *Ike the Soldier: As They Knew Him*, New York: G.P. Putnam's Sons, 1987.

disappointment and frustration. Only after paying that price did he become an overnight success.

Ike had a clear sense of where the right place at the right time was; he just couldn't get there before 1941. So he made the best use he could out of any place he was. Even before the United States had entered World War I, he had seen the clear possibilities in the new technology of aviation, where an ambitious young officer could rise faster than in the traditional Army. His application to flight school was accepted soon after John Doud had given his permission for Ike to marry his popular daughter Mamie. When Ike announced his flight school plans, Doud said he would withdraw his permission for the marriage if Ike pursued such a risky career. After two days of thought, Ike gave up aviation.

Miller quotes Eisenhower as saying that this decision convinced him it was time to develop "a more serious attitude toward life, perhaps I should take a broader look at my future in the military. Possibly I had been too prone to lead a carefree, debt-ridden life. Now I would set my sights on becoming the finest Army officer I could, regardless of the branch in which I might serve." The somewhat immature, affable Ike was beginning to change. His friendliness and pleasant personality would be his greatest strengths all his life, but he began to take note of other essentials.

His determination to excel as an officer "brought me face to face with myself and caused me to make a decision that I have never recanted or regretted. That decision was to perform every duty given me by the Army to the best of my ability and to do the best I could do to make a creditable record, no matter what the nature of the duty." As biographer Miller notes: "While it is easy to make fun of such a simplistic statement, and many of us did make fun of similar statements when he was President, Eisenhower meant what he said, and he did just what he said he would do for the next 33 years in the Army and, for that matter, in the White House. He performed every duty given him to the best of his ability—'no matter what the nature of the duty.'"

Eisenhower carried out his duties in a manner designed to

make every boss sorry to see him leave. General MacArthur was so sorry, in fact, that he unsuccessfully attempted to prevent Ike from being promoted so he could stay longer. Ike's "good clerk" reputation stemmed from his unwavering commitment to handle all the essential details of every job, no matter how small, "to the best of my ability." Over the years, no matter what the external frustration, this discipline to complete the act became not only a habit but second nature.

When he was President, Eisenhower's reputation for laziness grew in part from his refusal to read long and complicated reports and memos. Drawing on his own long years of completed staff work, he insisted that reports and recommendations come to him as very short proposals, ideally on one page. Intellectuals ridiculed him, but his approach required his staff to remain focused on the essentials.

A University for One

If Eisenhower had merely worked on completing the essentials, he would have risen sooner or later because few ever learned this lesson as well as he did. But his spectacular rise was created by combining this determination to carry out the essentials 100 percent with a wide and sweeping knowledge of his chosen field. A wide and sweeping knowledge? Ike? Again, we are indebted to Merle Miller's research in getting behind the myth.

Eisenhower took an advanced course in military history and strategy at a "university for one" established for him by his most influential commander, General Fox Conner. Conner was Ike's commander in 1922–1924 in Panama, a dreary post in the days before air conditioning. As Conner's son told Miller, "Sometimes just lifting food or a drink to your mouth wore you completely out."

For Ike, Panama was a turning point. Conner was convinced there would be another war and that it would come in Eisenhower's lifetime. Eisenhower later said of Conner: "The whole business of the necessity of being prepared for war was a product of something that just seeped into me from the teaching of this man." Drawing on his great knowledge of military history and strategy, Conner taught Ike through the Socratic method, asking questions about famous battles. What was on Lee's mind at this point at Gettysburg? What did he know? What did he think he had to do? Why did he think that? What do you think the outcome would have been if his decision had been the opposite?

Military history, which had bored Ike at West Point where it was a memory course, became important and exciting. Eisenhower said Conner stimulated his interest at a time when many of his fellow officers were becoming "stultified." At Conner's urging, Eisenhower began to read, borrowing book after book from his mentor's extensive library. He read Nietzsche, Tacitus, and Plato, and he read Clausewitz's *On War* three times. "As I read each one, I tried to digest its main themes and important points—I could be sure that sooner or later the General would be asking me about them." Eisenhower began to pin large maps on a drawing board in his workroom to study famous European battles. He took to reading various military technical journals.

Eisenhower's evening conversations with Conner usually lasted until a late hour and continued the next morning, often on horseback. With a strange prescience, Conner specifically coached Eisenhower on the necessity of strong leadership among allies in combatting a common enemy. Eisenhower later won his greatest success with the way in which he kept the French, British, and American military leaders united in a common effort in the critical days of World War II.

Eisenhower left Panama a well-educated officer with a background and a capacity for lifelong study of his craft. The happy-go-lucky, middle-of-the-class student was gone. A few years later when Ike attended the Command and General Staff School, he finished first in his class. No one paid any particular attention at the time, but a few of his classmates must have wondered just what had happened to Ike since West Point. He's such a nice guy, they probably figured. Maybe the professors just like him.

Ike later looked back on his period in Panama as one of "the most interesting and constructive of my life." He added that Fox Conner "has held a place in my affections for many years that no other, not a relative, could obtain."

Other officers at that command no doubt spent their time complaining about their bad luck in drawing such a terrible assignment. "Ah, well, nothing much to be done except make the best of it at the officer's club bar. Cheers and better luck on the next assignment. This one will be over in three years anyway." One wonders what these officers thought 17 years later when Ike got so incredibly lucky in designing the strategy that won the Louisiana maneuvers.

A DYNAMIC STRATEGY

As Ike's example shows, education is a dynamic strategy for moving a career forward. Education simultaneously increases knowledge, broadens the mind, deepens the intellect, and adds a more stable perspective to the personality. By overlooking the debt we owe to our first round of education, we ignore its ever-present power to reinvigorate a career at any stage.

An additional share of humanity's rich endowment of knowledge is available for any executive, who, like Walt Stinson or Dwight Eisenhower, chooses to start studying again. However, rigorous education in mid life will usually take substantially more effort than the education that many of us earlier received almost as a birthright. From here on, we will earn our way. But, as Stinson and thousands of other managers have found, education richly and delightfully expands the capacity for further growth at any age.

Education, says Minneapolis entrepreneur Randy Carlock, "is the single most important thing individuals can do to make themselves more. It is the most important factor in human development." Even beyond the immediate knowledge gained, education expands the whole personality.

On our consulting assignments, my colleagues and I frequently recommend that our executive clients return to school, even for one course. The results are physically apparent six months later. Those executives who have taken up consistent, disciplined studies show no sign of fatigue from this extra effort. On the contrary, they seem to be brighter, happier, more alert and expansive personalities.

Reading and learning in an undisciplined way will have some effect, but nowhere near the impact of a structured, even self-structured effort. Trammell Crow's Don Williams has kept up his reading program for more than 25 years as a way of committing himself "to a lifelong process of growth." The great works of literature have given him a way to "have multiple experiences, which add to the dimensions of your judgments." His continuing education program has also given Williams a deeper perspective on short-term problems, no matter how serious. "Even if we had failed [during recent tough times in the southwest real estate market], I would certainly have regretted that, but it wouldn't have been the end or some catastrophic tragedy because I wasn't my business." To Williams, business losses "are just facts; facts are something to be dealt with, they are not ultimate issues."

FIVE STRATEGIES

The following five key strategies can be used to keep an executive moving or to relaunch a stalled career. Any one strategy will help; together they have an almost unbelievable multiplier effect.

First, recognize that "it depends on me." No matter how insistent the messages from the Establishment Within about how "they" are at fault, try to close down both the transmitter and the receiving station. If the noise won't stop, effect a compromise: "We know that they are at fault, but since we can't do anything about them, let's pretend for awhile that it depends on me and let's see what happens."

Second, identify the essentials and, like Eisenhower, determine to perform every duty to the best of your ability, no matter what the nature of that duty. Aim for 100 percent, not 95 or 99. If your career is stalled, this will inevitably lead you away from nonessentials that show off your strengths to essentials where your weaknesses are on display.

Psychological effort is required as you confront those weaknesses and discover those that must be compensated for or even turned into strengths. Aim to make every part of every essential a complete act. You will feel a rush of enthusiasm and a career response—an unexpected compliment, perhaps, or even, if the effort is great enough and conspicuous enough, a surprising promotion. This is not a signal to relax. Rather, it should be an encouragement to go further to lift your performance that final bit. Going from 98 percent to 100 percent takes more effort than climbing from 80 percent to 98 percent. The results are commensurate with the effort.

Third, turn to the nonessentials of the job and use your strengths to give the job your own special "personal twist." By this point, your career will once again be on full throttle.

Fourth, to move still faster, identify the essentials of the next job on the ladder and train yourself in the skills necessary to handle those essentials.

Fifth, use education to overcome the weaknesses that are holding back your performance on essentials, use it to learn the skills you need to do the essentials at the next level, and use it to widen your grasp of your field. Try to find structured, disciplined ways to study. If not available, design your own structure like Don Williams. Education is the strategy with the unlimited potential to foster and direct your growth. In Randy Carlock's apt phrase, education is the single best way "to make yourself more."

Centering on the essentials while constantly widening your mind and personality through education is the unbeatable combination for endless career expansion.

6
THE PRINCIPLES OF PROGRESS: WHY SUCCESS IS A SYSTEM, NOT A LOTTERY

To discover and make use of the system of success, we must first get past its external reflection, which accents diversity rather than similarities. This book, for example, is about success in American business, and even here, in this fundamentally narrow context, we are at first dazzled by differences—the expansiveness of a Michael Blumenthal, the determination of an Alex Kroll, the decisiveness of a Doug MacMaster, the concentration of a Richard Markham, and the brilliance of a Kendall Lockhart.

The clear and strong impact of these traits can encourage us to search for a pattern by gathering lists of the personality traits commonly found in successful business people. Although such lists appear regularly in management courses and business magazines, they offer little help. This composite ideal and idealized successful manager seems to be little more than the adult model of the perfect Boy Scout. We quickly find ourselves lacking in comparison to this artificial ideal, justifying our retreat to the rationalization that some are just lucky enough to be born with all these traits of success.

In Shakespeare's wonderfully rolling cadences: "Some are born great, some achieve greatness, and some have greatness thrust upon them." Undoubtedly so, but so what? How does that help us? J.W. Marriott, Jr., certainly started life with a big advantage in being born the elder son of a highly successful entrepreneur, but the son's efforts and skills have carried the company to heights the father never envisioned. If ever a man seemed to have greatness thrust upon him, it was Dwight Eisenhower, and we have already seen the years of effort that went into preparing Ike for the moment when destiny would call.

We can't choose the circumstances of our birth, nor can we demand a call from destiny, but we have it well within our grasp to *achieve* greatness, whatever greatness means to us. This is especially true for readers of this book. Through no particular merit of our own, we all live and work in the first society on earth organized expressly to facilitate human aspiration.

Any Sunday golfer can hit one perfect shot for a hole in one, but winning a Masters tournament is a system. Any rock group might just manage to have it all come together in one hit record like "I Want To Hold Your Hand," but becoming the Beatles is a matter of combining aspiration, effort, strengths, and skills in a system that works over time.

Time is the leveler of empires, accomplishments, and legacies. Time reveals whether a success is a shooting star or a new constellation. Laurence Olivier was a London and Hollywood movie star of the brightest magnitude in the 1930s and 1940s. In the 1950s and 1960s he was the ultimate actor's actor, bringing crowds of his adoring fans to the theater and creating sell-out audiences for classic plays. He directed and managed well into the 1970s and 1980s. Even after his remarkable physical energies began to flag, he still delighted television and motion picture audiences with small but dazzling vignette performances. He endured because he grew year after year. Decades after his stunning physical appeal had faded, he held audiences spellbound with his growing skill and mastery.

In his early to mid years, Hollywood publicists regularly announced "a new Olivier." A bright young star, particularly a British star, was invariably hailed as a "young Olivier." All such claims are long since silent. We now know there will never be another Olivier. Although there will be other great, or even perhaps greater, actors, no one will use the same unique blend of strengths and skills to move our minds and hearts with his artistry. Behind all his success was a lifetime of systematic work, the effort of continually risking new and challenging roles and determining what subtle nuance he could use to bring to life a line that had become a cliché.

All sustained success, everywhere, rests on systematic work. Pablo Casals was the greatest cellist and one of the greatest musicians of this century. He learned, grew, and developed to heights that made his concerts an unforgettable experience for anyone who attended. Up until his death in his late 90s, Casals spent an hour every day quietly practicing the scales at his home in San Juan, Puerto Rico. Only death ended the discipline of a lifetime.

Our arena, the chosen field of this book, is business, an environment of tremendous expansiveness for those who decide to grow, for those who want to use their original endowment as a starting place rather than an entitlement. What was true for our pioneers remains true for business people today. In America, one never has to search hard to find opportunities; one must only work hard to exploit them.

THE BEDROCK PRINCIPLE OF PROGRESS

To grow, to develop, and to succeed, we must always begin with aspiration, the bedrock principle of progress. Where is this aspiration? Always within. Each of us owns a hidden self—a deeper, fuller, greater version of ourselves; a once and future self-portrait, never abandoned, never completely realized. This is our aspiration.

The enemies of human progress often understand this better than humanity's friends. One of the first tasks in a vicious attempt at brainwashing will be to try to erase that aspiration from the mind of the victim. Any society that aims to hold down another group will set about systematically dismantling that group's idealized concept of themselves, stealing from them any hint of a heroic past or future. Heroes lift our hearts because they give life to what we secretly hope to be. They are our aspiration incarnate.

Charles Dickens's A *Christmas Carol* is one of our culture's most enduring fables. As we grow more sophisticated, we scoff at its crude plot devices, its wooden characters, and its sticky sentimentality. Yet, watching it or, even better, having it read to us grabs us with a force that catches us completely by surprise, our cynicism suspended in the wonder of the tale. Despite his creaky plot and artificial characters, Dickens grabs and holds us with his universal story of hope, specifically our never-lost hope that one day we too, like Ebeneezer Scrooge, will wake up, recover our true aspiration, and actually become that person within—that person "who knows how to keep Christmas well" throughout the year.

Like Scrooge in his fitful dream, we are held by the ghosts of Christmas Past and Christmas Present and terrified by the specter of Christmas Yet To Come. Yet we never quite abandon the dream of being Scrooge on Christmas morning—"laughing and crying in the same breath"; hurling open the window; trembling like the old miser, fearful that it might be too late; and then joyfully discovering there is still time. Time to become. Time to be.

We can indeed all be Scrooge on Christmas morning by acknowledging our deepest aspiration and by recognizing as Scrooge did that the shape of Christmas Yet To Come depends, not on some phantom, but on ourselves.

DREAMS OF THE FUTURE

Our deepest aspirations are pure vibrations or simply powerful longings, almost dreams of what we hope will be. Robert Goddard is the father of space travel. In 1899, as a young man of 17, he climbed into a cherry tree in the backyard of his Worcester, Massachusetts, home to do some pruning. Compelled by some strong, almost magnetic attraction, the young man climbed high in the tree and stared at the sky. Slowly, in his mind a shape took form, becoming more vivid and real by the second. It was a shining machine that neither Goddard nor anyone on earth had ever seen before—functioning spaceship.

Goddard never experienced that vision again, but he spent the rest of his life trying to build that machine. First, he got a Ph.D. in physics to help convert the vision in his head to reality. The materials and technology he needed simply did not exist, so Goddard used whatever substitutes he could find or invent. In 1926 he launched the world's first liquid fuel rocket. The entire flight time was 2.5 seconds.

Few scientists took any serious interest in Goddard, his peculiar toys, or the papers he published. He was able to continue and expand his work only when Colonel Charles Lindbergh used his tremendous influence to get Goddard a few small grants. Lindbergh, the first man to fly the Atlantic alone, understood the power of aspiration, and he recognized something important was being shaped in Goddard's work.

As Goddard's example dramatically illustrates, although an aspiration begins as little more than a personal vibration, it must be quickly clothed in a vision. Without that clothing, the aspiration cannot move around in the world. Aspirations come in all shapes and sizes. This is a book about and for business people, so the aspirations we encounter are mostly business aspirations: to grow in the job, to become CEO, to make the company number one in its industry, to make the finest product, or to serve our customers better than anyone in the industry. If this were a book about actors, the aspiration would wear different clothes: to be a Broadway star, to win an Oscar, to have a career in which I am considered both the best Hamlet and Lear of my generation, or to leave an audience always feeling they got far more than they paid for. A soldier's aspirations might include: to become chief of staff, to be the finest leader any of my troops have ever served under, to serve my country, or to be a military hero. A journalist might aspire to be a publisher, an editor, or a successful columnist, or to win the Pulitzer prize.

As these examples show, aspirations are without morality; they can be noble or self-serving. Industrialist Armand Hammer, one of the world's richest men, says he never ever had an aspiration to make money; what he wanted was to help people and the money came along. On the other hand, the aspiration of gangster Al Capone was once summed up in one word. All Al ever wanted was *more*.

Getting What We Really Want

Intensity is what matters, not the nobility or baseness of the aspiration. Intensity opens the doors on the inner resources and releases energy. Strong desire floods the being with the tremendous energy to achieve that aspiration; weak desire produces indifferent energy. This principle has nothing to do with what people say they want or how they behave—it has everything to do with what they really want.

Forty years ago, radio audiences roared with laughter week after week over a standard comic figure known only as the reluctant door-to-door salesman. The skit would always open with a vigorous knocking on a door followed by the weak voice of the salesman saying, "There's nobody home . . . I hope . . . I hope . . . I hope." Audiences laughed because they recognized themselves in the humor. On occasion, we all pretend to knock vigorously on doors we secretly hope will never open.

The flow of energy will also be governed by the greatness or smallness of the aspiration. A great aspiration, strongly felt, will release enough energy to sustain a Goddard through a lifetime of neglect. A small aspiration, for example, to become assistant sales manager, if intensely felt will release more than enough energy for its accomplishment, but not anywhere near enough energy to rise to CEO or create a space program.

The purest, strongest, highest aspiration is often youthful longing. This is the truth behind the frequently quoted epigram: "Beware of what you wish for when you are young, for you are sure to get it when you are older." The intensity of youthful aspiration can be so exceptionally high that it produces enough energy to move us toward the goal, sometimes long after we have consciously forgotten it. I frequently meet retired or second career executives who tell me: "It's funny but I am doing now what I wanted to do way back, before I ever got started in the other business."

One of my deepest and most powerful youthful aspirations was to travel. I daydreamed of running away as a seaman on a merchant ship. I plotted imaginary voyages for myself to distant places on a map. In my career so far, I have served in the Navy and have lived for extended periods in San Juan, Puerto Rico; Great Britain; and Belgium. In five years, as head of the international division of the American Management Association, I have traveled almost constantly throughout Europe, Asia, and Latin America. This manuscript is being written in the south of India near the Bay of Bengal. I have a great respect for the power of youthful aspiration. I see its results everywhere. "I wanted to be an executive in the worst way," John Jacob told me in his spacious National Urban League office, "even before I had any idea what an executive did."

Yes, But . . .

Part of the reason that youthful aspiration is so powerful is that it does not have to contend with a fully armed and mobilized Establishment Within. At any age, the whole art of releasing energy to achieve an aspiration consists of working overtime to repel from the conscious mind the Inner Establishment's single greatest weapon, the simple but deadly phrase "Yes, but. . . ." *Yes, but* I'm too old, too young, too bright, not bright enough. *Yes, but* I don't know math, understand computers, speak French, have a college degree. *Yes, but* the boss would never let me do that, will insist I do it her way, thinks someone else can do it better. *Yes, but* that is not my strength, exposes my biggest weakness, will make me look foolish.

The reluctant door-to-door salesman closed his sample kit and left his radio sales territory two generations ago, but his pathetic spirit lives on in our hearts even as we work within and enjoy the opportunities created by a nation whose greatest strength has been the exultant cry, "Yes, we can!" Our own personal "Yes, I can" is so important because at the first sign of a *"Yes, but . . .,"* the inner resources close up shop until further notice, refusing to produce any energy for a venture with such weak support.

The most important principle for releasing energy for an aspiration is simply to let that aspiration breathe awhile before subjecting it to a barrage of *"Yes, but . . ."*s. For just this reason, creative organizations have learned the art of brainstorming. When a team of people want to solve a problem or create an opportunity, they gather for a meeting with an unusual set of rules. During the session, no one criticizes or says *"Yes, but . . ."* to any idea put out by anyone else. You are only permitted to contribute positive additions or constructive suggestions. The start is usually slow, as people criticize their own ideas mentally before putting them forward in the group. After 5 or 10 minutes, momentum picks up; in 20 minutes, the room is alive with energy, laughter, and creativity. Usually such sessions are limited to a relatively short period, probably because we cannot stand the strain of not being able to say *"Yes, but . . ."* for too long. These sessions almost always produce new and original ideas, especially as the group learns to enjoy working in this relaxed and creative manner.

Why can't we hold brainstorming sessions within ourselves, permitting ourselves only to offer positive and constructive suggestions? Try it and you will feel the exhilaration of overcoming the deeply ingrained *"Yes, but . . ."* mentality. See whether you can identify your aspiration, clothe it, see it vividly in all its splendor without once letting a *"Yes, but . . ."* interfere. Try it regularly. We all daydream anyway, sometimes about our highest hopes, sometimes about our darkest fears. Make these sessions constructive rather than a waste of time by focusing on your aspiration and ruling out *"Yes, but . . ."* for the duration of the daydream. You will feel the enthusiasm and energy that signal that your inner resources are awake, alert, and ready to help you achieve your own version of greatness. Do not become discouraged if *"Yes, but . . ."* will give you no peace. You are now face to face with the Establishment Within. It is flexing its strength, trying to intimidate you with the weight of Christmas Past and Christmas Present as well as the fear of Christmas Yet To Come. Wait it out with patience and good humor. Insist quietly but firmly that you and only you own this particular aspiration. There will be time enough to deal with all of the *"Yes, but . . ."* objections later, when this daydreaming session is over, but for the moment let us see again how that aspiration really looks, how it feels.

There will indeed be a time to deal with objections. Daydreaming, positive or otherwise, cannot produce success on its own. Sustained success comes through systematic work, but first we need these sweet dreams to bring us the energy and enthusiasm that can only come when aspiration touches inner resources.

THE SEARCH FOR CHARACTER

We need to understand what will happen to all the energy created when inner resources become inspired by aspiration. It is here that the particular magic of human personality plays one of its most important roles. Our individual human character is what makes us unique, gives our personality the zest and focus that separates us from each other. In considerable measure that character will determine the shape of our aspiration. At a young age, both Michael Blumenthal and Alex Kroll had the highest aspiration to succeed. Blumenthal got two masters and a Ph. D. at Princeton; Kroll became an All-American. Blumenthal rose to the top of two major manufacturing companies; Kroll, to the top of one of America's premier service organizations. Blumenthal determined early to have a career divided between government and business; Kroll devoted his whole career to one company. Both have succeeded in their aspiration far beyond the dreams of most Americans. How they have succeeded in translating a similar individual aspiration into vastly different careers is a function of their different character.

When we search for character, we are seeking to identify that unique amalgam of inherited mental and physical strengths, weaknesses, temperament, and disposition plus the earliest influences of the environment in which we grew up. One group of teachers used to be frequently quoted as saying "If you give us children until they are seven, you can have them the rest of their lives." Accurately quoted or not, the statement reflects something of our belief in the power of inheritance and early training to shape character.

It is through this character that the energy released by aspiration must first flow. This is where the list builders of personality traits for success pick up and eventually lose the trail. In addition to actually giving form to the aspiration, character begins to direct it. If Alex Kroll had not had a persistent disposition that enabled him to lift the bar a little bit more every day, he would be just another of the many who dreamed of being an All-American. If Michael Blumenthal did not have a quick intelligence and an academic temperament, he never would have earned those advanced degrees.

It is here that we most often find deep-seated character weaknesses that must be overturned if our aspiration is to flower fully. The man without patience may envision the perfect spaceship gliding across the night sky, but he will never endure the failure after failure necessary to write the articles that will change our world. An Eisenhower who remains an affable, "carefree, debt-ridden" officer is not likely to get the chance to lead millions in a crusade or to become President.

How intractable is character? Our history books and our legends are crowded with those who overcame temperament to rendezvous with aspiration. Henry V, glorious, shining Prince Hal, the greatest of all Shakespeare's kings, was a wanton playboy, the despair of his father and the court, until he became king. In the early years of our century, Franklin Roosevelt was viewed by many as a spoiled, ambitious lightweight with an admittedly pleasing personality. Yet he became one of our greatest leaders, inspiring our nation during our most serious economic crisis and then leading us successfully through a world war. Roosevelt clearly changed dramatically when, close to his 40th birthday, he was stricken with polio, making him a chair-bound cripple for the rest of his life. His triumphant return to the competitive field of politics signaled that the pleasant young man had been replaced by a man of iron will. Dr. Martin Luther King, Jr., had a quiet temperament, better suited for a thoughtful scholar than the activist leader and organizer he became. His Nobel Peace Prize, awarded when he was only 35, recognized both his aspiration for human freedom and his self-sacrifice in molding himself to serve that aspiration.

Character may be set by age seven, but there is plenty of evidence that it will bend and bend again before an aspiration that is high enough and strong enough to command the full force of our will. When the strongest aspiration is called forth from deep within the very essence of the individual, it can certainly become far more powerful than our character.

That, however, does not teach us how to deal with character when the aspiration is more modest, like merely wanting to become CEO. The energy created by the inner resources when they are touched by a great aspiration passes through the character and becomes a force—character has given it its first real direction. If stubbornness is one major trait of the character, the energy will be directed in a stubborn, unrelenting way. If the temperament is dominated by a low flash point, a wicked temper, a considerable portion of the energy released will go into angry outbursts. A sweet, social temperament will dictate that great energy is spent attempting to win others to the aspiration. A character dominated by unusual inherited stamina will create a channel for the energy by working hard, long hours.

Give a group of young children the same work or play assignment, one that excites them all; do not provide too many detailed instructions; and watch how character determines not only the result, but the method. In one corner, one boy races through the work with such joy that he cannot delay for an instant for fear he will miss the next challenge. At another table, a second boy, a brother to the first, works very slowly and carefully, ensuring that each step in the project is completed perfectly before proceeding to the next. Over there, a girl, the boys' sister, is so engrossed in inventing creative ways to carry out the project that no one ever dreamed of that she is entirely oblivious to paint stains on her smock and the glue in her hair. It is the same assignment, the same family, much the same degree of aspiration and energy, and yet what different results! The energy has become a force, spilling out into different levels and types of accomplishment through channels created by character.

Anyone who has made it to the executive ranks enjoys a character with far more assets than liabilities. Even the lowest level executive has been able to generate productive energy to complete some very impressive acts, something that simply cannot be done through a character overwhelmed by weaknesses or ruined by excesses.

Although smaller aspirations do not have the power to change character, they are frequently strong enough to get us to change our behavior. For many aspirations, that is enough. Anger contained on the job will likely help us progress toward the next promotion, although the repressed force may still pour out at home. A learned behavior of listening carefully may offset a basically stubborn character well enough to lift us to vice president. Hiring and following the advice of an efficient executive secretary has been a sufficient behavior change to speed the career of many a disorganized executive.

If we dream great dreams of aspiration, we must wrestle with character defects. For more modest aspiration, we must attend to behavior, consistently checking the impulsive urge that wastes or misuses energy. As many executives have found, years or even decades of controlling behavior actually end up modifying character in important and productive ways, opening the way for unexpected growth.

Values: The Invisible Organizer

If we have little control over our inherited and early formed nature, we have far greater control over the next important channel where our energy flows—through our values. These values organize our energy and give it even more precise direction. Two young men had the strongest aspiration to change the world as they found it. Their inherited character turned both aspirations into a force that did change history. However, it was their values that determined the difference between the way we remember Adolph Hitler and Thomas Jefferson.

In business, our values shape the fundamental nature of our work—how we approach our customers, our colleagues, our team members, and our suppliers. Is good organization one of our values? If so, despite a disorganized temperament, we will take great pains to organize presentations to customers and to purchase raw materials in a disciplined, orderly way. Through the years, I have met several very effective presidents who contend they owe their success to a "golden rule" set of values. These presidents regularly review each constituency and ask: "If I were that customer, that supplier, that employee, the chairman of the council of the town where our factory is located, how would I want to be treated in this situation?" Their aspiration was to be the president of a successful and admired company. Character determined what kind of company and in what kind of place; values determined the success by organizing energies around a core concept.

For several years, I have been asking senior executives to identify their most important values. One word comes up on almost every list: integrity. This is not because America's business leaders are so much more honest in basic character than other people. Integrity to most of these executives is a far more pragmatic value. Every manager who has scaled the ladder of an organization has learned that although successful executives can be tough or mild, silent or gregarious, likable or ornery, they must all be reasonably consistent. What they say will happen must happen and what they say won't happen must not. When this simple rule is broken with any regularity, trust and confidence erode and it becomes more and more difficult to lead. This is why so many successful executives have consciously adopted the value of integrity, of being reliable in what they say and do. It has become, for the best, more than just a phrase or even a habit; in fact, it has become second nature.

Serving the customer is a value that also appears on most lists. This is another powerful, integrative value because it requires any manager, particularly a president, to focus on the needs of others.

You Are One of Us Now

At age 50, Robert Cavalco left Sunbeam Corp. after 27 years to become the president of Bang & Olufsen of America, Inc. About the only real common point between the two companies was that both have headquarters in Chicago. Sunbeam is a $2 billion manufacturer and mass marketer of small appliances, whereas B&O is the U.S. sales arm of a high-quality Danish audio/video manufacturer. B&O markets through a network of independent audio/video dealers, most of whom are founder entrepreneurs. The year Cavalco arrived, sales at B&O were $18 million and had been flat for three years.

The industry viewed Cavalco with considerable suspicion when he arrived. First, he was replacing a legendary B&O leader who had personally helped many of the dealers in their early, struggling days. Second, all of his experience was with a company known for mass marketing, and this was an industry of fiercely proud specialty retailers. Third, Cavalco is hearing impaired, and he was entering an industry of audiophile enthusiasts, an industry founded on what one dealer calls "the significant audible difference." Fourth, he has a degree in marketing in an industry where few of his customers have college degrees, let alone specialist education. By all definitions, he was an outsider.

Cavalco, an enthusiastic salesman and a sophisticated marketing executive, spent a year learning the industry and trying various standard approaches with no particular success. Then, in 1984, he began meeting with groups of his customers all over the country. He found discontent was "almost unanimous on four or five points." For example, the dealers didn't understand either B&O's product strategy or its distribution policies, and they understood but didn't like its policy on margins.

After the meetings, Cavalco thought about what he had heard, both inside the company and from the dealers. He realized that although the company had a customer service value, it had not been strongly reinforced in the minds of either staff or dealers. He put together a mission statement, driven by the value of customer service and, using his great selling skills, went on the road again to sell his market that things were going to change. The market was skeptical, but interested. B&O's sales began to show signs of life, particularly after the Danes began to ship several new products to the U.S. subsidiary. In the Chicago office, the emphasis began to change to reflect the new service-driven mentality. New trainers were added to B&O's training department, which provides sales courses for dealers' salespeople. Cavalco also expanded B&O's architectural group, which helps dealers create a contemporary look for their showrooms. Today, sales courses have more than tripled and store design work has doubled under the new program. Meanwhile, B&O expects to approach $30 million in sales this year, and the curve continues to move up.

Cavalco has been successful in an industry where so much was against him not so much because of what he knew or even what he did, but because of what he is. The approach that he took may look on the surface simply like the current "close to the customer" doctrine, but it was really built on something deeper than any current management philosophy; it was built on a value that Cavalco adopted 30 years ago. In the late 1950s he was representing Sunbeam to Atlanta's Rich's Department Stores when he found himself sitting across from a young buyer. Both of them were new and "we decided to approach this whole idea of buying and selling from a different view." Under the arrangement, which emphasized a cooperative rather than an adversary relationship, Cavalco took responsibility to be, in effect, the buyer of his own product for the store, with the understanding that "it was also my responsibility to do everything I could to support the buying effort." Sales of the product "exploded, well over a 100 percent increase in the next season."

Cavalco reinvigorated B&O by using a bigger, more sophisticated version of this approach. As he had with the Rich's buyer, he, in effect, got on the other side of the desk by emphasizing that B&O's mission "was to help the dealer sell products rather than simply selling products to the dealers."

Cavalco dramatizes his approach by putting himself personally on the line when the cooperative spirit threatens to break down. Three years ago he learned that one of B&O's top customers had dropped in volume from their normal 2nd or 3rd place to 14th. His sales manager wanted to follow the traditional policy of dropping the faltering dealer and adding someone else. There were plenty of dealers waiting to take on the B&O product in this particular market. Cavalco called the store owner and arranged a meeting with himself, his sales manager, the store owner, and the store's buyer. Cavalco quickly won over the owner to his win-win approach and "then we, in effect, challenged these guys [the buyer and the sales manager] to reverse the negative trend and we promised that we would be involved in it every inch of the way." Within a month, the business turned around. "They went from 14th position to 3rd position in one year. They had a 90 percent increase in business that year and a 50 percent increase the following year and another 50 percent the third year."

Cavalco bases his strategy on what he calls "the power of relationships. There is a tremendous power between yourself and the customer if you don't look at him as a customer but rather as a human being." Cavalco has gone so far as to send his own financial director to work with dealers with accounting problems and to hire management consultants to coach troubled dealers. Not surprisingly, Cavalco reports that all such efforts produce a "constant and continuing enthusiasm," as well as a better than 60 percent increase in sales since he started at B&O.

Cavalco has a great aspiration to succeed. A quintessential marketer, his measure for success for B&O and for himself is sales growth. His character radiates friendliness and a good humor, both traits that help turn the energy generated by his aspiration into a force that is palpable to his dealers, to his staff, and to anyone who meets him. However, strong aspiration merely coupled with good humor and friendliness could simply have produced a friendly but hard-sell salesman, a behavior entirely inappropriate for his industry or for his company in the mid 1980s. Instead, faced with a difficult situation, Cavalco turned to his core values—cooperation and the power of relationships—channeling his great energy into helping his dealers sell rather than simply trying to find a new way to sell to them.

Two years ago, Cavalco took a group of dealers to Denmark to see the B & O factory. On the plane coming back in a group they asked him to put away forever the watch he had received at his Sunbeam retirement party and to wear instead the expensive watch they had all chipped in to buy him. "Bobby," the dealer spokesman said, "we want you to forget Sunbeam and wear our watch, because now, you are one of us."

THE HANDS OF ACHIEVEMENT

The energy still has one more channel to flow through on its journey to human accomplishment, a channel frequently forgotten but of equal importance with everything that has gone before. That channel is skills—the small, detailed expressions of energy through which work is actually accomplished. Think of the large company with great resources in human energy and capital. Think of its stream of products moving down the assembly line. Watch the individual workers: Some individuals here are working with precision, even grace, but over there one group is installing one part in a slapdash, undisciplined way. Move that product in your mind all the way to the ultimate customer. See that small part fail, and watch as the whole product ceases to function. For the lack of one small set of skills, the product fails despite the creativity, ingenuity, capital resources, machines, inventory, skilled salespeople, installers, and advertising copywriters. One small skill makes all the difference.

All our work life is like that. We can have the highest aspiration, can release energy in an abundant flood, and can have a character that reinforces our dream and values that lift our work to the highest level, but without skill, everything is lost. Visit a foreign country. Entranced by the culture, you may want to exchange ideas with the people you meet, but the whole power of your aspiration and the force of your personality are reduced to the 30 words you know in the language. None of your aspiration, your personality, or your values can help you as you inarticulately try to mumble a few primitive phrases. You lack the skill.

No aspiration, no force of energy, no height of values can overcome the lack of the skills appropriate to the situation. We are blind to opportunities without skills—the skill to read a publication with the right attention, the skill to hear the potential in another's idea, the skill to put two contradictory ideas together in a higher synthesis.

Skills operate below the line and above the line. Below the line they are all struggle and we are all thumbs. Remember when you first learned to drive a manual transmission, to swim, or to use a computer? Every small effort had to be conscious. Will I ever learn to engage the clutch, shift the gears, and steer at the same time? How can I breathe through my mouth at just the right second when my arm is over my head so I don't swallow half the pool? Where is the save key? How does it work? If I push the wrong one, will I lose everything I have written on the computer so far? Effort, conscious effort. Depending on our temperament and the nature of the task, it is either a joy or an anxiety.

Then one day, we can just do it. There was a moment somewhere when we crossed the line. We can speed down the road, foot on the clutch pedal, gears shifting, and steering wheel steady while our thoughts are elsewhere. At one particular moment we are floundering in the water and the next we are gliding through it. Perhaps our glide lasts only a few seconds at first, but we know with an unshakable certainty that we can do it! Our fingers on the computer keyboard are hesitant, anxious, and then at one moment we forget about the technology and we concentrate on the work and we are away. In each case, we have crossed the line. What was formerly strain, effort, and even frustration has become easy, second nature. Of course, should we wish to lift our skills to the highest level, we are still below yet another line or lines that ascend to the sky. If we want to be a Grand Prix racing driver, an Olympic gold medal swimmer, or a computer expert, we must refine, hone, and perfect these basic skills.

Nature equips us to acquire skills as long as life and health last. All studies show that although the speed with which we can acquire new skills does decline slightly with age, our basic capacity remains intact and may even in some cases improve. This makes sense. Nature has a big job to do and very little time to do it. We need to accumulate the skills of survival in the shortest possible time. Nature helps us by designing our mental wiring with an initial flexibility and speed that make us practically skill-learning machines. We soak up skills. As children, we go from achievement to achievement, never tiring of the process until we fall exhausted into bed. We have to learn how to talk, walk, and hold things; how to read, write, and handle an abstract idea; how to tell the difference between a flower and a floor, a cat, and a cow. Watch a two- or three-year-old and you will see an intensive seminar on learning new skills. Our early years in school are nothing more than an attempt to socialize us and to teach us the basic skills to ensure our survival in a technological society.

As we grow older, nature seems to lose interest in us, and we are left on our own in the skill-gathering business. The years of lightning speed and a patience in learning skills are behind us, but we still have plenty of capacity for further learning. And nature has left us with one incomparable legacy—a joy in learning new skills, an enthusiasm that will last as long as we do. When you learn a new skill at 7 or 70, you will experience the same enthusiasm, the same sense of renewal and possibility. This accounts for the boundless energy and enthusiasm in those whose careers require constant learning.

Everyone is familiar with the great musicians who, in their 80s and even beyond, continue to amaze us with their prowess, skill, and enthusiasm. This is because their craft requires a never-ending acquisition of new skills, relearning the sonata that one has not played since one's 20s, and taking on a contemporary piece that not only requires new skills with the hands but the skill to understand the sensibility of a new generation. The media interviewers are always in awe of the maestro's incomparable zest for life. "At his age! How does he do it?" He does it by learning new skills every single day and moving his old skills to a new level of perfection. "If I don't practice for a day, I know it," said one musician. "If I don't practice for two days, the critics know it. And if I don't practice for three days, the audience knows it."

Learning new skills is our joy at work. The higher our aspiration, the greater our skills must be; the more demanding our values, the more we must strive to enrich and expand our skills. In the end, our skills are what we use to deliver the goods, to make our contribution, and to bring life to our aspiration. Our growth is a function of the speed, consistency, and persistence with which we pursue the development of the skills we need.

Douglas G. Myers, executive director of the Zoological Society of San Diego, has built a remarkable career at an early age by a willingness, an eagerness even, to seek out new skills. At 37, Myers has been the top executive at one of the world's premier zoos and animal parks for three years. Surprisingly, he has acquired the skills for this position largely on his own. His formal education ended more than a decade ago with a bachelor's degree concentration in business and psychology. Myers is a good manager, and it could be argued that the executive director of a zoo simply has to be long on management skills without too much technical knowledge. Myers doesn't see it that way. By consistent and dedicated application, he has made himself an expert not only on management, but also on many of the technical aspects of his work. His life at work has been one continuing skills seminar.

Myers got his disciplined approach to life and work from his father, who was a deputy sheriff in Los Angeles. "I was raised with the thought that you will put in a full day's work. You will be able to contribute. You will be able to measure your results at the end of the day, what you have accomplished, was it good for the organization you worked for, and was it meaningful to you." Myers started work early. "I remember washing dishes in a restaurant when I was 12 years old to buy what I wanted. I was one of those kids who bought a car at 15 and couldn't drive it until I was 16."

To put himself through college, Myers took a job as a tour guide at Busch Gardens in Los Angeles, one of a chain of European-style beer gardens that Anheuser-Busch opened next to its breweries "to make people feel good about Busch products." As a tour guide, Myers would take customers on a boat trip through a 7-acre lake and describe the 150 species of animals in the park." He also worked as a bartender, host, hamburger chef, and gift shop clerk.

Spotted as a hard worker, he was offered a full-time job at age 22 as an animal trainer. In this job he worked as the assistant to Robert Gardner, a famous animal behaviorist who was a disciple of the "operative conditioning" theories of B.F. Skinner. Later he realized that Gardner was using the theories to motivate him. "He would give me a stimulus, then he would reinforce it to encourage me to continue. He kept me going that way for months for 80 or 90 hours a week, which was a lesson in motivating people that has stuck with me for a long time."

Two years later, at age 24, he was offered the post as director of zoological operations at Busch Gardens (Los Angeles). He didn't even have an undergraduate degree at this point, and he certainly was not a zoologist. "I went into a department where everybody was either a trained zoologist or had 20 years experience of working with animals. They became some of my best teachers." He also changed his major at the college he was attending part-time, picking up a few courses in biology and zoology.

His management skills also expanded because "I learned how to make decisions out in the open by actively collecting good, live data." He knew immediately that he "couldn't walk out into this work force and say, 'This is what we are going to do.' " So he learned to sit and plan and discuss with others, but he made his special contribution, too, by insisting that the group decide in advance "how we were going to measure what we had accomplished at the end of the day."

The Anheuser-Busch organization invests heavily in training, and Myers took advantage of his many opportunities to learn how to improve his management skills. However, he was not content to be the bright young manager with no technical knowledge or skills. "The people I worked with had more patience than anybody I ever met because I worked with questions. I always wanted to know why. At this stage of the game, I still drove my staff crazy: 'Why? How do we know that?' "

This relentless, inquiring mind was a legacy from his youth. His parents' advice had always been "choose your words carefully, learn, ask questions, read."

For the first time, he really began to read. He had never been much of a reader in high school because "I have a photographic memory for a short period and a wonderful memory forever . . . so I could pass all the tests without a problem." He had also become a good listener because he wished to disguise a youthful stutter. The psychological effort to overcome that liability was linked with a strict physical reinforcement. He joined a fraternity in college and, as part of his hazing, he did push-ups every time he stuttered. "Every word was carefully chosen because it cost me a push-up. I learned to slow down and not to stutter." The stutter was gone in six weeks. "Later I talked in front of a microphone to thousands of people every day doing shows at Busch Gardens."

As he moved through the Busch Gardens organization, he perfected his skills, seeing himself always in the dual roles of learner and teacher. In talking about today's operations, he is always the learner; in talking about tomorrow, he is the teacher. To be an effective teacher, he had to first be a dutiful and eager student.

He rose to be director of park operations for Old Country, a Busch Gardens facility in Williamsburg, Virginia. Then, in 1981, he became general manager of the San Diego Wild Animal Park. By the time Myers arrived, the park had an operating cost of $18 million and was entertaining about one million people. At peak season, it employed about 600. Within a year, Myers's aggressive marketing program had lifted attendance by one-half. As his plans took shape for the next year, it became increasingly apparent that "we were stealing market share from the zoo," which is part of the same organization. Perhaps to restore equilibrium, Myers in 1983 was named director of operations for the Zoological Society, which oversees both zoo and park. In 1985 the society promoted him to its chief operating job, executive director.

In every post, in every year, he has expanded both his management and technical skills. His technical reading program now includes every scientific paper published by any member of the staff plus any paper a member of the staff thinks is of particular interest to San Diego Zoo operations.

Every animal keeper in both the wild animal park and the zoo writes a daily report on the condition of the animals in that keeper's care. Myers gets a daily summary of urgent information. Beyond that he reads every individual report, an assignment exceeding 1000 pages a week. If he is particularly pressed for time, he reads the summary carefully and checks the individual reports by his personally developed skill of reading reports "by braille." He takes all the keepers' reports, turns the stack of papers face down and then runs his fingers across the back of each sheet. "A keeper who is really in trouble or who needs something urgently will write bigger and bolder. I know this because I was an animal keeper once. When you want someone's attention, then you write bigger and push the pen or pencil harder and the impression goes through the page." When Myers can feel the urgency, he turns over the paper to see what the problem is.

Even if the keeper reports get unavoidably stacked up from time to time, he always gets to them eventually. "That is where the heartbeat is. That is where it is at. I love to walk through the zoo and see a keeper and say, 'Is your sunbear okay?'" Myers knows the keepers are always pleased because "when you write those reports day after day, you wonder whether anyone really cares."

In addition to his reading program, Myers loves to "put on the khakis" and spend a day working with and learning from his staff. He listens not only to his own experts, but also to people all over the world. Pointing to the phone on his desk, he says, "I have learned in the past seven years that this instrument will go anywhere in the world you want it to." He will think nothing of calling New York or even China to talk to an expert. "I sometimes think we have another facility in East Germany, the people in the zoo there have been so wonderful to us."

Once he has the information, he can "teach the future." Nothing is so illustrative of Myers, the teacher, in action as his preparation for meetings with his board of trustees. There are 12 members on the board, most representing different constituencies—the scientific community, a retired general reflecting San Diego's large military establishment, the medical community, large donors, and civic leaders. Before the meeting, Myers mentally goes over each agenda item 12 times, each time from the perspective of a different board member. He tries to anticipate every possible question and to include an answer in his presentations to the board. Next, he reviews each agenda item from the viewpoint of a mythical "thirteenth member"—the Zoological Society staff. After board meetings or any unusual event, Myers evaluates his performance, seeking to identify missing skills or techniques and trying to find ways to do it better next time.

Doug Myers grew up with high aspiration. The example of

his father's dedication to both his job and his 30-year career as a volunteer Boy Scout leader provided a strong role model. However, his father's financial position meant that although "he morally supported the continuation of education, that was all he could do." Speaking of his younger self in the third person, Myers remembers: "There was a dilemma before Doug Myers: Either he was going to find a scholarship to get him through school or he was going to figure out a way to work and get himself through school. The second one came my way." Without significant academic credentials in a field of technical specialists, Myers has educated himself every day on the job.

From his family, Myers received an aspiration "to actually accomplish something that had an impact on the world." His father shaped his character by instilling several key values, including being honest and straightforward in every transaction. That means always speaking out when he doesn't know something. His strengths are a quick and retentive memory plus an ability to understand the other person's position. However, all these attributes would not have ensured his early and impressive success without the necessary skills: the management skills to plan, organize, create, deliver on budgets, and supervise people; the technical skills to understand and raise money for key projects; the reading skills to get through and the scientific skills to understand dozens of learned articles and a thousand pages of keeper reports every week; the communication skills to digest, prepare, and then present all this information in a way that will be understood by a dozen key people with quite varying perspectives; and above all, the skill "to teach the future."

Skills are the hands of achievement, the unobtrusive, taken-for-granted actions through which aspiration that has become energy takes the final form that will determine our future.

7 THINKING BEYOND YOURSELF: USING THE THREE GUIDING STARS

"It was a declaration. It was like Babe Ruth standing there pointing the bat, announcing he was going to hit a home run. It was telling people, here is what we say we are."

John Betti speaks with enthusiasm when he describes the impact that a written statement of Mission, Values, and Guiding Principles had on the fortunes of Ford Motor Company. Betti, executive vice president of Ford's $12 billion Diversified Products Operations, admits he was skeptical at first. Not that he didn't believe in the importance of values; he just didn't see much point in writing everything down. "I thought you could just show by example."

Ford printed the Mission, Values, and Guiding Principles statements on both sides of a plastic card that could fit easily into a shirt pocket. Copies went to every employee, dealer, and vendor. Betti now believes that by writing down the principles and circulating them, Ford "raised the sight level of everybody in the organization."

Suppliers and dealers were energized by a guiding principles statement promising to "maintain mutually beneficial relationships with dealers, suppliers, and our other business associates." Before Ford distributed the statements, suppliers frequently heard from

145

Ford buyers, "Yes, we understand we are to be partners, but you understand that it is my job to buy this at the right quantity and the lowest price." With the statement went a note inviting questions whenever Ford was not living up to the commitments of its principles.

"When we had these things distributed," Betti recalls, "we had the whole top management, including Henry Ford, talking about [how] these were the rules we would live by. It became easier for suppliers to say to our buyers, 'We hear what you are telling us, but we also hear what your top management is saying and we can read what you stand for on this card.' That, of course, made it a lot easier for our buyers to come back to us and say, 'Here is the way we have been behaving and we have to agree that this isn't treating these suppliers like partners.' "

THINKING BEYOND YOURSELF

The reason the statements worked so powerfully, Betti says, is that "they made people think beyond themselves." Focusing on the good of the whole company had a dramatic impact on Ford. In the early 1980s, the company that invented the car for the masses was rapidly losing sales in its own market to foreign imports. Even intervention by the U.S. government in getting the Japanese to limit imports didn't help much. After losing more than $3 billion in the early 1980s, Ford became, in the words of *Fortune* magazine, "the comeback story of the decade, the world's most profitable car company—and more. It provides a model for how to transform a struggling also-ran into a world-beater."[8]

Although it is impossible to put a dollars and cents figure on the impact of the Mission, Values, and Guiding Principles state-

---

[8]"A Humble Hero Drives Ford to the Top," *Fortune*, Jan. 4, 1988, p. 23.

ment on this turnaround, Betti feels it was "very significant." Such principles keep a company focused on the fundamentals in a long-term context. Focusing instead on short-term bottom line management, Betti says, "is a recipe for disaster. By the time the bottom line gets into trouble, it says that the fundamentals of the business have been in trouble for a long time."

Mission, values, and guiding principles can keep an individual focused as clearly as a company. Each of them lowers our possibility of practicing our own version of the bottom line, "what's in it for me in the short-term" type of decision making.

How we measure a day's, week's, month's, or lifetime's work says everything about how we have organized our own mission, values, and guiding principles. Like many modern organizations, many executives have sought efficiency by compartmentalizing roles—employee, boss, colleague, citizen, child, and parent—hoping, a little desperately, that all the various departments will add up to a total profit. Mission, values, and guiding principles, by making us think beyond ourselves, integrate our work into a meaningful whole.

MANAGING FOR THE MISSION

The world makes way, the old saying goes, for the individual who knows where he is going. A mission in some mysterious way hooks a person into the dynamics of the time. Thomas Jefferson, one of our greatest leaders, wanted only three of his many accomplishments put on his gravestone: "Author of the Declaration of Independence, Of the Statute of Virginia for Religious Freedom, And Father of the University of Virginia." Missing were Jefferson's achievements as President and Vice President of the United States, Ambassador to France, Governor of Virginia, and Secretary of State. Why did Jefferson choose these three? Because each was a key accomplishment in his life's mission: "I have sworn upon the altar of God, eternal hostility against every form of tyranny over the mind of man." He wanted to be remembered for his lifelong effort to carry out that mission rather than for his political fame and glory.

Frances Hesselbein, the visionary national executive director of the Girl Scouts of the USA, calls her life's work "managing for the mission." Like so many leaders, she almost missed her calling. When the Girl Scout troop in Johnstown, Pennsylvania, first asked her to become a volunteer, she refused. She had never been a Girl Scout herself, and she was the mother of a young boy. "I didn't want to do it at all." After a lot of pressure, she agreed to take a troop of 30 ten-year-old girls for several weeks until they found a "real" leader.

Hesselbein led the troop for eight years, until those girls had all graduated from high school. She also served as president of the local Girl Scout Council. Next, the national organization asked her to become a trainer of board members and eventually to become a member of the national board. Later, to fill an emergency vacancy, she joined the staff as executive director in Johnstown. She became national executive director in 1976.

At every stage, she says, "I found values I could believe in. I found intellectual stimulation, excitement, and diversity, and I believed in the principles. It was a natural fit."

"Managing for the mission" means to Hesselbein that "you have to have a broader focus than just your work. You have to see the environment in which the work takes place and the possibilities of the future." She pursues that broader focus through an average of three hours' reading a day. Her briefcase is always bulging with papers, magazines, and books. Everything she reads passes through one strict filtering question: "What is the implication of this for the Girl Scouts?"

Her mission integrates her continual learning with her work. She spotted early three key trends in American life and redirected the energies of her organization toward new needs. The first trend was the growing number of very young children left alone while parents, sometimes single mothers, were away working. Hesselbein wanted to begin a program for these young girls who, at age 5, or in kindergarten, were well below the traditional starting age

for scouting. Many of her volunteer leaders opposed or were luke-
warm to the idea. They contended that scouting is "not a baby-
sitting service," and that these girls were too young to benefit from
a scouting program.

Hesselbein persisted, sensing a great national need within the
mission of the scouts. She eventually found some leaders willing
to undertake the program, which quickly became established as
the Daisy Scouts, now one of the fastest growing youth programs
in the United States.

By studying demographics, Hesselbein also saw American society rapidly shifting toward a multiracial, multiethnic, multiecon-
omic class configuration. The Girl Scouts traditionally were a
predominantly white, middle-class, suburban organization. Although she has changed the emphasis dramatically, she contends
that much remains to be accomplished. The planning system she
installed created action plans for outreach toward every American
minority. No exceptions. The Girl Scouts have recruiting brochures
and posters for American Indians.

Hesselbein also foresaw that the entry of so many women into
the for-pay work force would reduce the number of leaders available
from traditional sources. She began programs to recruit leaders
from new groups. Today, of the 700,000 adult volunteers in the
Girl Scouting movement, 70,000 are men. She also encouraged
programs to recruit career women without children. She found
ways for the Scouts to offer new advantages to their leaders. Today,
the Girl Scouts runs one of the largest adult-education training
programs in the country. Operating their own training center, the
Girl Scouts train about 3000 leaders a year. For example, a course
featuring the principles of corporate management for local council
leaders has been given by the faculty of the Harvard Business
School for 10 years.

Clarity of mission drives Hesselbein's work and her life. She
judges every decision—whether to read a new management best-
seller, hire a new staff member, add a new service, make a speech
in California, or take on another board of directors assignment—
by a single, demanding criterion: How will this help the Girl Scouts?

She even asks that question about articles she reads in the three newspapers she goes through every day. When Peter F. Drucker, the father of modern American management, was asked to name the best managed organization in the United States, he responded without a second's hesitation: "The Girl Scouts. Tough, hard-working women can do anything."

Not everyone discovers a job that is "a perfect fit," a job that simultaneously permits them to create and execute a mission for their life's work. Those who do are seldom weary and never dull. They glow with a special brightness that is the sure signal that aspiration and energy have united with purpose to find in the world a new and continuing adventure.

COMMITTING TO VALUES

Although not everyone gets to manage for the mission, everyone can manage for values. Everything that the Ford statement did for that company, managing for values can do for you. When you commit to a value, even the most mundane value like that of punctuality, it requires you to think beyond yourself; it requires you to organize your work with a broader focus than just the short-term, bottom line approach of "What do I do next?" It requires you to integrate your work with the efforts of others so that your combined projects can get out on time. It pushes you toward essentials, toward completed acts, toward overcoming weaknesses.

That's just one of the simpler values. Take a value like honesty. Sounds worthwhile, you say, the sort of thing everyone should agree with: "Why, basically, I'm a fundamentally honest person already." Try to lift your standard of honesty in the next week and watch what happens. You can't give a social compliment you don't mean, express a concern you don't feel, say you're sorry about something when you're not, or promise to think further about something when you have already made up your mind. The effort to be honest will cause you to pause before you speak, to think about what you are going to say, and to consider the response of others before you speak. The effort is monumental.

As Ford's example illustrates, if we commit to a high value, we need to have it in front of us in some way until it becomes second nature. As a young reporter, I worked in a newsroom with Pulitzer Prize winning editor William Dorvillier. To the top of his typewriter Bill had taped a single question: "Do you really believe it?" For years, Bill looked at that question every time he put a piece of paper in his typewriter. Bill won the highest prize in journalism for a series of calm, well thought out editorials for weeks while he and his paper withstood the fiercest pressure and outright attacks from one of the most influential groups in his community. The single question taped to his typewriter reminded him of his highest value while it sustained him.

Every success story in this book is a story of value implementation, of commitment to something higher. At the physical level, a commitment to values organizes our work through our consistent effort toward cleanliness, safety, orderliness, and punctuality. At the mental level, we pursue such ideals as discipline, communication, and freedom. At the highest psychological level, we touch our concern for others through such values as trust and respect for customers and employees.

Our reaction to success is an unfailing clue to the height of our values. An aspiration triggered by greed will certainly produce success if we follow the process described in Chapter 6. Without values that process is neutral. However, greed-driven success will bring a sour taste. An aspiration built on competitiveness alone will indeed beat the competition, but the victory will feel somehow incomplete. An aspiration resting on an ambition to rise will also succeed, but the results will produce greater fatigue after each success. Only an aspiration based on a value such as self-development through service will produce a sweet, complete, and endless stream of energy.

Making Values Operational

We should identify the values that matter to us in tranquility because there just isn't much time in the heat of action. Hale Champion, the former director of Harvard's Kennedy School of Government who has seen many leaders under fire, says that "when you have to ask yourself before every decision, 'What are my values?' [you] tend not to get a hell of a lot done." The politician who gets things done "doesn't have to ask himself or go through a long exercise about what he thinks is appropriate, what he thinks is reasonable in terms of standards or values. He's got a tough set, he applies them, he doesn't have to ask himself what they are, he knows. That's a great attribute." Champion adds that it is "a great advantage" in dealing with rapidly changing situations to have a set of values that are "operational as well as theoretical."

Operational values are also the key with Harvey Golub, president and CEO of IDS, the Minneapolis-St. Paul–based financial services company. When Golub arrived at IDS, he set out to work on what he views as the four essentials of any CEO's job: mission, business strategy, organizational strategy, and values. He addressed defining values for the organization in a surprising way. Values are very important to Golub because they are what "creates the environment I am comfortable in." Despite having strong views, he played almost no part in the value-setting process until the end. He delegated the work to a committee drawn from different levels in the company. The team worked for nine months, and then recommended five values. After one was eliminated because it was "illogical," the other four were accepted for the whole company.

Golub makes a startling statement: "I wasn't concerned with what they came up with. It was irrelevant." Why? "Because any group of people approaching the issue will come up with a set of values that they are comfortable with." If you select a group with broad enough representation, you will get the values that represent the company.

And, says Golub, *"The issue is never the value. The issue is execution against the value.* You can go to any organization and ask what are their values and they will tell you things like customer service and excellence. That is immaterial. What is material is the impact the values have on the company's performance every day."

Golub is correct. The values individually hanging on banners and wall signs throughout IDS represent the kinds of thing that most companies would subscribe to: superior service to clients, excellence in all actions, concern with treating individuals with fairness and dignity, and teamwork. The difference is the effort behind execution.

The same principle applies to individual executives and their values. If the selection of values is not quite "irrelevant," it is close to being so. The most important step is that the values have been defined by each individual determined to rise in life. Even mundane, physical values like cleanliness and orderliness have an exceptional power simply because they require effort that must be renewed every single day. The effort to keep the office space clean and orderly raises our consciousness of everything around us, makes us more alert and more aware.

Mental values at work center around good organization of ourselves, our department, and, for the CEO, our company. The person who commits to good organization as a value cannot tolerate sloppiness around the edges. Psychological values like the IDS value of treating everyone with fairness and dignity energize the manager and everyone she comes into contact with.

Values that touch all three levels are the most energizing of all. Every good factory manager knows that an outstanding safety program pays for itself many times over. To strive for perfection in safety is a physical effort; loose tools and equipment must be speedily returned to the correct bin. Safety is a mental value that requires everyone to think and organize work in better ways. Safety is also a psychological value in that it demonstrates concern for every worker. When Bob Widham's "rough, tough," and verbally inarticulate workers put on their hard hats, cleaned them, and wore them home, they were saluting themselves with a new pride and speaking volumes about their feelings for their manager.

Identifying Your Values

How do you find the values that are important to you and your career? As always, look inward and outward. An inward search involves the wellsprings of your personality. Beware of choosing a value because it sounds noble or socially acceptable. Ambition is a very positive trait if not carried to excess, particularly when tied to a value like self-development. Don't feel compelled to back away from ambition while substituting the more socially acceptable value of serving others as your principal value.

Golub hit a deep truth when he said that which value you choose is "irrelevant." It is execution that counts. A value of ambition that requires you to carry out your work as a series of more and more complete acts is far more valuable to you, your department, and your company than a value of being of service to others that permits you to disguise weakness as empathy or kindness. That helps no one, not even the person you are allegedly helping.

Your outward search should focus on the values of your company. They always exist, whether or not the company has gone through the discipline of writing them down—something Golub also knew when he asked a representative group to find them and articulate them at IDS. When in doubt, study the personalities of the founder and the most influential CEOs. They have left their mark in the genes of your company.

If you have trouble identifying your company's values, it is because with our associates or our companies we are far better at seeing liabilities than assets. However, survival is a sure test. Most new companies fail within five years. If your company has survived beyond that point, some strengths and positive values are at work. At any particular moment in a company's history, its weaknesses and what might be called negative values can be overwhelming the strengths and positive values. Nonetheless, the latter are always there. The miracle turnarounds, with the new CEO arriving just in time to save the company, are often at the heart the story of a shrewd manager who revives dormant strengths and values in a sinking organization.

Once you identify the values in your organization, ask yourself how well you are, in Golub's word, "executing" them. Again, Golub's approach at IDS offers a very pragmatic model for any manager to upgrade performance on value implementation. Values,

Golub reminds us, only "become operative when they affect behavior," when they become an active criteria for decision making. They are not "relevant" when they merely affect beliefs. After the IDS values were defined, Golub introduced a three-phase implementation program. Any manager can follow Golub's three steps in her own career: eliminate behavior that clashes with the value; reinforce behavior that supports the value; transform neutral acts into value statements.

Eliminate Negative Behavior

First, Golub and his team began "to look for behaviors that weren't congruent with the company's values and eliminated them." They reviewed all products against the customer service standard, for example. Looking at one 30-year-old investment plan product, one of the company's staples, it became clear "in the first 30 seconds" that the product was not as good for the customer as it should have been. "The decision was reached; we eliminated the product. . . . We didn't have to do an analysis or figure out how much money we were making or figure out who in our field sales force would get less money. It didn't fit with the values, so we cut it out."

Behavior that is not congruent with your personal values is an excellent place for you to begin. It is always tempting to halt this important step with two common rationalizations. The first is that, although the value is worthwhile, it just is not prudent or pragmatic to change that behavior this week or this month. Maybe it will be possible in several months. This weakens resolve. Golub demonstrated he was willing to make the tough decision, even if it meant sacrificing short-term gain to upgrade performance on an important value. The individual who adopts a value must make the same commitment.

One reason that deep and true implementation of personal values is so rare—and thereby so successful for those who do it—is that we no sooner decide to implement a value than life immediately tests us. Adopt a value of customer service and within the week, your most unreasonable customer will be on the phone with her most ridiculous request. Determine to be punctual and before you can meet that report deadline for the first time in months, the boss will give you two rush assignments. It is easy to throw up your hands and say, "A nice idea, but what can you do?" What you can do is stick with it. Stay with one of life's deepest truths: If you persevere, what you are not able to do today, you will achieve tomorrow. Measure yourself, not against perfection, but against your effort every day. This process alone will make you stand out from the crowd of managers who shift with every tide without a clear sense of who they are and what they are trying to accomplish.

The second rationalization that gets in the way of implementing personal values is the myth that "they" are somehow preventing you from working toward your values. We can spend days, weeks, or years evaluating other people against high standards and documenting in exquisite detail their many sins against the value. But so what? Eric Webster, the late British management writer, was one of my earliest and most useful mentors. Eric advised me: "You will gain the most use out of any difficulty in life if your first thought in confronting it is 'If there is a problem here, I caused it.' " I have not always been grateful to Eric for his advice, especially on those occasions where initially it was absolutely, positively clear to me that, in this case if in no other, I was the victim of the guile or even maliciousness of others. Frustrating though it was, careful consideration has always disclosed a place where I could have done better. If I couldn't bring myself to admit I caused the problem, I could always see how I contributed mightily to it and how I could do better in the future.

The second message is contained in Eric's introductory phrase, *"If there is a problem here . . . ."* That hidden question has forced me to ask whether there is a problem here at all or an opportunity lurking in disguise. I have not been successful in confronting all of life's problems with the statement, but when I have, I have always benefitted. In value implementation, Eric's phrase can easily be adapted to: "If something or someone is preventing me from implementing a value, I am responsible." Try that approach and you are likely to achieve remarkable and productive results.

Reinforce Positive Behavior

As his second step, Golub began a program to celebrate behaviors that reinforced the IDS values. His program is called VIP, Values In Practice. It consists of short notes to congratulate people on doing something that was congruent with the values. Annual prizes commended outstanding performance on values. "We talk about them [the values] incessantly."

This same type of positive reinforcement can be used to celebrate your own value implementation. Here, we should learn to recognize in ourselves any action where the implementation of the value is the primary motive rather than just the accomplishment of the work. This is essentially what IDS is doing with the VIP program.

Accomplishing the work is important, but the way in which you do it counts also. In the case of the VIP awards, the way you did it may be as important as the work itself. Can we evaluate ourselves in this way? There was one case where I behaved in a certain fashion, got the job done, nothing wrong; but there was another case where I was so conscious of my value that I changed my behavior, perhaps in such small ways that no one noticed except myself. Such recognition, if genuinely deserved, always brings a surge of energy and a sense of achievement. People who evaluate themselves against such a standard and improve regularly are sure to be the VIPs in their organizations before long.

Transforming Routine Actions by Values

Golub moved from eliminating negative behavior and reinforcing positive behavior to the third phase—seeing how neutral acts could be energized by values. "You get people to start looking. You say here is an advertisement that seems to be neutral. How can we make it express the values better? You don't just do the act but you relate how that act is supportive of the values." For example, the company reviewed routine management disciplines with this focus. "If an individual is to be treated with dignity and respect, then he deserves good supervision." Leading from that, IDS developed an upward feedback system so that every supervisor in the company gets an annual performance rating not only from the boss but from his or her subordinates. The rating is an aggregate of how the team rated the boss on such issues as values, strategies, and leadership.

You can energize your work the same way, making any act, no matter how routine, more significant by infusing it with values. For example, take the common act of attending meetings. Most managers consider meetings called by others at best a neutral act and at worst a terrible waste of time. An experienced manager once told me that the art of attending corporate meetings was learning how "to sleep with your eyes open until it is your turn to speak." This is because normally one sits at the meeting table for an hour or more of discussion in which perhaps 10 or 20 minutes are of direct relevance to your job or responsibilities. What to do with the other 40 minutes causes much frustration to many managers. Talking intemperately or too much out of boredom has hurt many executive careers. The person with the capacity to sit, stay alert, and offer comments when and only when they are appropriate is the master of meetings, a highly regarded skill because it is fundamentally rare.

Hewlett-Packard's Sara Westendorf says a trifle indignantly, "My time is too valuable to sleep with my eyes open!" Westendorf has risen fast at HP, ironically not by being overly concerned about promotions, but by making it her top value "to do a top-notch job at whatever my current job is." It just so happens, she adds, "that when I have been successful in achieving top-notch results, the promotions end up coming my way." Westendorf, like the rest of us, has attended her share of meetings where "50 percent of the people get to a topic that doesn't quite apply to their area and you will see in their eyes that they are tuned out." These executives, she adds, "are missing a golden opportunity to learn from the dynamics of what is going on. Always stay involved and when you can't actually be saying or doing something, then use that time to watch."

Why does she make such an effort to watch and listen to discussions that don't affect her area? "We are in a very competitive business environment, and you just can't specialize in your little area and keep yourself and your company successful." She also believes she has a responsibility as a participant to get a meeting back on track if it starts to waste time. Usually the person chairing the meeting appreciates this approach. If in doubt, she asks beforehand. Once in a great while, her advance offer to help refocus a meeting will be refused. What can she do then? "You can still watch. If the meeting didn't get anything accomplished and was really boring, how did it get derailed?" For a woman whose value is to do a top-notch job every minute of every day, there is always something to watch and learn. "Anytime you are just putting in time to collect your check, you aren't going anywhere."

Another executive with another set of values in another situation would use the neutral, routine meeting in another way.

Effective communication is an important value to Rear Admiral David Cooney (Ret.), the president and CEO of Goodwill Industries. Navy protocol would never permit a junior officer to help "get a meeting back on track" the way Westendorf can do at least some of the time at HP. Navy discipline requires junior officers to be quiet until asked or to ask permission before offering a suggestion. For years, Cooney used dead time while sitting at meetings to increase his communication skills by studying the small, individual physical signals that revealed whether the message was getting through.

"If you really watch how another person is behaving when someone is talking to him or her, you can tell whether or not they are hearing, whether or not they are either favorably disposed with the idea or not. If you exercise those tools in your interpersonal communications, you can save a lot of time; you can save a lot of misunderstanding." Cooney recalls observing at several meetings that one very senior admiral "would slide a pencil up and down his fingers. As long as that pencil was moving, that meant he was listening and thinking. When that pencil stopped, that meant he was through" whether the person who was speaking had finished or not.

Two successful managers, two sets of values, two very different environments, one mundane, everyday act used to support and develop those values. The next time you feel like going to sleep at a dull meeting, stop and ask yourself: How can I use this particular moment to support my personal values? What can I learn? What can I contribute? In what way can I walk out of this meeting room in one-half hour having grown to some small degree?

Values truly implemented prevent us from sleeping with our eyes open; there is simply too much going on. When we find ourselves going to sleep, moving through the motions, overcome by boredom, at just such moments we need to ask: What are our values and how could they be used to enrich this moment? Value-driven companies are more alert, more awake, more conscious and that makes them more successful. The same is true for the individual. Sara Westendorf speaks for all of us with her almost indignant statement: "My time is too valuable to sleep with my eyes open!"

Because the task is routine, we do not have to sleepwalk through it. What could be more boring than playing the same musical scales every day of your life? The great musician with the value of aiming for perfection goes through them every day. The value makes her concentration total. The great baseball player with the similar value of playing perfectly does not sit slouched in the dugout dreaming about tonight's date. He is alert, absorbed in watching the opposing pitcher. Why is he lowering his shoulder that fraction of an inch today? And look at the direction of the wind, will that rob the left fielder of a half step? Values dictate our degree of absorption in life. Low values let us sleep much of the time undisturbed. High values demand of us the concentration that can make all of life, even the smallest, most routine acts, at a minimum far more interesting and at the most a high adventure.

GUIDING PRINCIPLES

There comes a time for the most disciplined companies and individuals when values have become so ingrained that they are no longer in any sense abstractions but are firm principles for the organization of work.

Cleveland entrepreneur Larry J.B. Robinson has built or managed a number of highly successful enterprises by turning a set of clear values into guiding principles. The number 12 seems to work for Robinson. He runs his businesses by his 12 Management Precepts, which in turn are carried down to his 12 Basic Steps in Selling Successfully. The authors of such lists are often accused of being simplistic. Robinson's are based on a deep knowledge. He earned an MBA and doctorate from the Harvard Business School, where he also worked as a researcher and wrote publications for the Bureau of Business Research.

Despite his academic credentials, Robinson's precepts and principles are anything but theoretical. He used them to build his family firm J.B. Robinson Jewelers from annual sales of $200,000 to $80 million. He sold the company to W.R. Grace & Co. in 1979, serving as chairman of the jewelry firm while working for Grace until 1987. Both as an entrepreneur and as a corporate executive, he used his guiding principles to expand from 1 store to 96 stores in 25 cities.

Robinson's first value is hard work. "My standards are really too high for comfort. I have always been a perfectionist and it is difficult to get through life that way but it also resolves at a higher level of accomplishments. It is hard for me to settle for anything that isn't an A or 100 percent or a very considerable sales increase over last year." He acquired this work ethic early. "My first mem-

ories are of living above my father's store in the same apartment
with my mother, father and grandparents with no telephone and
no radio." He remembers five uncles in the contracting business
who always wore tennis shoes to work. "They didn't know how to
play tennis and they weren't joggers. They wore tennis shoes because they could run up and down the stairs that way and finish a
job faster." It was a fight for survival. "When you come out of that
depression era, you remain very purposeful."

After Harvard, Robinson started in the corporate world but
returned to Cleveland after his father's death in 1960, because the
liquidators of his father's jewelry store were offering only 20 cents
on the dollar. His first idea was to liquidate the merchandise quickly
at a better price and then return to big business. "I liquidated it
for 28 years after that," he says wryly, "and ended up with 96
stores."

When Robinson started, the typical jeweler sat with a limited
selection and waited for a customer to walk in and spend $10,000
for a 25th wedding anniversary gift. Robinson went after, not the
individual sale, but the volume sale. His money-back guarantees
inspired confidence as did his approach of asking up front what
kind of price range the customer was interested in and then showing
only items within that range.

As he expanded rapidly, starting in the middle 1960s, Robinson began to build his values into a series of guiding principles
or precepts that others could carry out. A Harvard professor later
writing an article about the company said that Robinson "developed
priests" to carry his doctrine to other areas. Robinson preferred to
hire people with no experience in the jewelry business, many times
without any sales experience at all. He then trained them in his
principles. He could make novices effective on the sales floor within
three weeks.

What Does the Customer Want?

The most powerful principle, reinforced again and again in the
training, is The Golden Rule. When in doubt, treat the customer

as you would want to be treated in a similar situation. "My theory, I can't prove it, is that customers will sense if it [the Golden Rule] exists or it doesn't. In companies where there is something like that, customers will sense it and tell others and they will all go back again and again."

Robinson's first Management Precept is: "Ask 'What Does the Customer Want?' " This and his other precepts such as following the Golden Rule have given Robinson a golden touch in business. At radio stations WMJI/WBBG, Cleveland, sales increased from $1 million to $6 million during the two and one-half years he was involved. At KWK/KGLD, St. Louis, the stations' value increased 50 percent during the two years he served as principal partner.

His guiding principles, built on the values of hard work, high achievement, and service, have made him an indefatigable community worker. Approximately 50 percent of the projects funded by his venture capital company are in Cleveland. He teaches Cleveland entrepreneurs at Case Western Reserve University. His biography lists more than 25 present and past civic activities where he has served as director, president, or chairman. A magazine article in the *Cleveland Plain Dealer* once said that Robinson "loves Cleveland the way some men love women."

In explaining his community service, he recalls the words of an early mentor: "In a sense you are a machine. There has been a big capital investment placed in you in terms of a lengthy education. Now you want to make that investment pay off not only in terms of making money but also having the sense of accomplishing something worthwhile in the community and elsewhere." Community work gets the same dedication and hard work as business. Robinson could never be accused of sleeping with his eyes open in any business or community meeting. "If I am running, I want to feel I have gone the distance."

Managers wanting to "go the distance" in their own careers can borrow a powerful technique from Robinson. Being able to convert values to a series of guiding principles is a sure way to keep them operational rather than abstract. For many, principles are a handier guide than just one-word or one-thought values.

Three Key Questions

The individual manager seeking to convert general values into operational principles should ask three questions.

The first question is: *How can my value be converted into a guideline for my work today?* Benjamin Franklin could have said simply "Be thrifty," but he made it operational by his famous maxim: "A penny saved is a penny earned." The latter is an operational guideline for action. Mental orderliness is a strong value, but when Tom Watson hung signs saying "THINK!" in every IBM office, he made it a principle and method of work, not just a value.

Guiding principles need not be fancy or literary or something that you will share with others. Executives wanting to introduce or strengthen the values in this book in their work could adapt its chapters and themes into such guiding principles as: "Always Complete the Act, Physically, Mentally and Psychologically"; "Essentials First"; "The Greatest Growth Comes by Converting Weaknesses into Strengths."

The second question is: *Is the guiding principle as high as we can make it today?* Take the value of customer service. "The customer is always right" is a much higher guiding principle than "We will serve the customer to the best of our ability." Higher still is "The customer will always be pleased by our service." Even higher is the guiding principle that Marvin Bower used to define the client service value of the consulting firm McKinsey & Co.: "Higher than the client expects; greater than the situation warrants."

We should ensure that our personal guiding principles are as high as we can reach. They should make us stretch but not discourage us. There is a point where the height of a principle leaves us with a bit of a so-what feeling; a second, higher point where it begins to inspire us; and a third point where our growing enthusiasm changes to feeling a heavy, onerous duty. We should stop at an elevation just at the point before our maximum enthusiasm is exhausted. At that exact point we should convert our value into a principle that can inspire and direct our energies. Another day, when that principle has been second nature for so long we don't even think about it, we will suddenly find ourselves enthusiastic about a still higher version of that principle. That will be the time to raise our sights once again.

The third question to ask in establishing your guiding principles is: *What span of time is involved in this principle?* At first glance, guiding principles look as if they should be guidelines for action forever. This is seldom the case. Values are the fixed stars on which we should chart our course, but guiding principles are more like the currents we sail in on the way. They shift and change and may be quite different next year.

Could any principle ever commend itself beyond the Golden Rule of treating other people as we would like to be treated? Certainly. Treating others, not as *we* would like to be treated, but as *they* would like to be treated in every situation would open the doors to an even higher truth. However, for the moment, the Golden Rule is so much higher than anyone usually gets or expects, its power alone is sufficient to lift individuals and companies to great success.

Mission, values, and guiding principles touch the principles of progress at every point. Individually or together they can form or clothe an aspiration, releasing energy and giving force to our lives. They are also an invisible organizer. Frances Hesselbein organizes her life around her mission. Harvey Golub reorganized the IDS product line and created an upward appraisal system to meet his commitment to IDS's newly stated values. To live up to his value of being a learner and teacher, Doug Myers organized his work around learning and teaching. Sara Westendorf organized herself around the value of doing "a top-notch job" whatever the assignment. Larry Robinson has trained himself to wake up every day with a list of priorities clear in his head so he can reach for the multifaceted achievements dictated by his values.

By keeping us focused on people and events rather than on ourselves, mission, values, and principles pull us toward acquiring new skills. They demand more of us and enrich us at the same time, while determining in the end not only the height but the depth of our success.

8 REVERSING FORWARD: SUPERHIGHWAY MANAGEMENT

Fred DeLuca, the Subway sandwich shop entrepreneur, got the idea when he and one of his managers were stuck in a traffic jam on the way to a baseball game in New York. "And I said to him, 'This highway is very similar to running our company . . . we know where we want to go and this is the road we want to take and our ability to get there has a lot to do with certain restrictions that are set up, certain restrictions that are built into the system.' "

Looking around, DeLuca suddenly was inspired by many aspects of his analogy. Traffic slowed at a toll booth, "and that toll booth is like my desk where I say to people, 'Listen, before you go any further, stop and check with me.' " He saw that a well-managed company needs to let work flow by priorities. "If you want to be in this lane, drive slowly, and in that lane, step on it." When people want to leave or join the company, "you need some controlled access so they don't disrupt the organization getting on and off." You need rules of the road that "just don't allow anybody to drive in the wrong direction."

With analogy after analogy, DeLuca evolved his concept of Superhighway Management, where you "just set up your company to handle a lot of capacity. Just take whatever you're doing that you can do one at a time and set it up so you can do two at a time

166

or three at a time." Superhighway Management has made Subway the fastest growing food franchise in the United States. The original goal was to open 32 stores in 10 years. Now, Subway is opening more than that total every six weeks.

Superhighway Management demonstrates the power that a dynamic concept can have to change your perspective and allow you to see other possibilities. As DeLuca studied the traffic jam for clues, you need to look around you to understand what the rules are that govern your speed of advancement. You need to look at those rules in a different light, eliminating unnecessary toll booths and making sure you have three lanes where you need them.

The first seven chapters of this book focused on the system for increasing your capacity for growth, or, to draw on DeLuca's analogy, for building a faster, more powerful automobile to take you where you want to go. This chapter looks at the rules of the road that enable you to move more quickly through traffic.

THE RULES OF WORK

Many managers whose careers have stalled or gone off the road never understood enough of the rules of work in the first place. Everyone understands at least a few of the basics. You have to come in on time, do a day's work, and do what the boss instructs you. However, beyond such basics, there are scores of others. In fact, you should assume there is at least one rule governing every single piece of work you carry out. You could even state that the very first rule is: "There is no activity that cannot benefit by a rule."

The first skill in creating Superhighway Management is knowing which rules apply in your work. Start with a few general rules:

1. Planning enhances performance.
2. People all respond to attention.
3. Authority is exceedingly helpful within its own limits.

4. Time is the essence of work, and you can evaluate any work in terms of time.

5. Profit is an index of our effectiveness.

6. Elimination of waste not only increases profits by the savings, but also enhances the level of performance.

You can subdivide any of these rules into other rules that apply in most situations. For example, some related or corollary rules for Rule 1 (Planning enhances performance) might be:

1. a. Using a system to achieve a goal reduces stress.

   b. Developing a habit of stopping and thinking avoids failures and opens opportunities.

   c. Being willing to consult experienced people can solve or avoid many problems.

   d. Bringing two aspects of work together in a better coordination lowers costs and increases productivity.

   e. Applying indices like output, cost, and time to work both measures and enhances efficiency.

These additional five rules, helpful in themselves, reinforce and expose the options of the general rule that planning enhances performance. Ordinary executives operate on a half dozen tested rules. Skilled, experienced managers use a dozen or more. The best executives use even more rules.

Many of the themes in this book rest on rules, stated or unstated:

- If you raise each of your existing capacities, talents, endowments, abilities, and so on by 5 percent, your total performance will increase by at least 100 percent.

- Take one value—orderliness, punctuality, concern for others, cleanliness, safety, and so on—and raise your performance of it to 100 percent; your overall performance will also increase by 100 percent.

- You can achieve anything you want if you put your mind to it.
- No business problem is insolvable to someone who wants to solve it.
- Potential for growth is not even close to being exhausted in anyone working in business today.
- Success is not so much a matter of luck and intelligence as it is a matter of patience and persistence.

RULES GENERATE POWER

One of the most powerful management strengths is the ability to understand the rules thoroughly yourself. This strength multiplies when you exemplify and articulate rules clearly and when you establish a system to ensure that others follow the rules consistently. Military elite organizations like the Marine Corps and the Airborne Parachutists depend on this strength. Japanese companies also show the strength of this coherent approach.

As recently as the 1950s, many U.S. companies had strict rules governing behavior. For example, in that era IBM permitted no executive to come to work without a white shirt. Was it entirely a coincidence that during that period American business led the world in growth and productivity? Rules create discipline, focus, energy, and attention.

Since the 1960s, rules have gone underground in American business. The better managed companies have policies and procedures to give general guidance, but the clear, straightforward "we always do this and we never do that" has disappeared for the most part. There is a lot to be thankful for in that. One secretary who started work on a typing pool of a Fortune 500 company in the late 1940s told me she could not speak while on duty and was once sharply criticized for sneezing too loudly. Few bosses would feel comfortable returning to that kind of environment.

Still, something is clearly missing today. The underlying assumption of the era of liberation that began in the 1960s was that if you gave people enough freedom from external control, they would somehow work out all the important rules for themselves. That has proven to be an illusion. Today many executives are surprised to learn that understanding and adhering to rules can actually accelerate your career—something that would have seemed obvious to their grandparents.

Whether we choose to ignore them or not, rules generate power. The mighty cohesive force of our Asian competitors is proof enough, as is the energy generated by the rare American company that takes the same disciplined, focus-on-the-rules approach.

MANAGING BY INTIMIDATION

"I manage by intimidation," boasts ex-Marine Tom Mitchell, president of Seagate Technology. Since arriving in 1984, Mitchell has increased Seagate's sales eleven fold to $1.3 billion during a period when many competitors have gone out of business in the fiercely competitive world market in personal computer disk drives.

Management by intimidation is not a catch phrase. Mitchell's favorite analogy recalls his days as a Marine officer. "In a platoon, the guy doing the inspection, when he sees a dirty rifle, what does he do? Does he say, 'Son, why don't you step over here for a minute, you really have a dirty rifle. . . ?' He doesn't do that, does he? He screams 'You worm, you filthy, rotten so-and-so. . . .' But the next day, everybody's rifle is clean. . . . That guy doesn't have to explain about cleaning rifles again." Mitchell uses the same approach in his management today. When something is wrong, "you get the guys in here, you single out one manager and you just go on and on and on in front of everybody about it."

"Vivid" is the word Mitchell uses to describe his management style. He adds: "Address this as a business, not as a fraternity."

On one occasion, Mitchell got so upset with two executives that he told them, "I hate you two personally." Despite his vivid personality, Mitchell's management style rests on a lot more than intimidation. He has defined the essentials with a precision rare in even the best managed companies. He has created a pay system commensurate with the pain he passes out. "Beer blasts don't motivate; money motivates." He personally is better organized, more disciplined, and harder working than he asks anyone else to be. Finally, he has staffed his senior ranks with seasoned veterans, all of whom volunteered for this particular duty with their eyes wide open. At the Scotts Valley company, the game may be very rough, but the pots are very big and the rules are straight and absolutely clear.

Up until Seagate reached a size of about $200 million, the company hired 30-year-old's, but the problem was that "everything you wanted them to do, you had to explain to them how to do it." Then Mitchell hit upon a unique personnel strategy. He began to hire "seasoned vice presidents who were at least age 45 and who had worked for a number of companies that had failed, so they knew what failure was all about, and they really needed to be successful in 10 years," good guys who "never made a lot of money."

As Mitchell explains his system: "the guy comes in and he knows that he's going to get the living hell beat out of him to do the job—he knows how to do the job, he does know how to do it, he's seen it, he knows about it conceptually, and all I have to do is say, 'I want this and that and this and that' and the guy goes, 'Yes, I got it. I got it.' "

Although intimidation stands out and grabs everyone's attention, even to Mitchell it is the means, not the end. The results are what count. In the fast-changing, competitive world of personal computer disk drives, long-term results are usually in doubt. But, whatever the long-term outcome, Mitchell has already proven with vivid success that people who have failed and failed again can begin achieving just when many executives are starting to rationalize their lack of success or even their outright failure.

Clarity of Purpose

Mitchell insists that every member of his team concentrate 100 percent on the essentials and the rules. Deviation brings a rough and feared response. Throughout America there are many bosses who illustrate the power of this single focus concentration. At first glance their success completely contradicts popular theories of motivating people. However, their secret is their clarity of purpose, a rare trait still welcomed by many employees. As long as they remain consistent and offer a fair compensation for what they demand of people, their success is often spectacular.

Bosses like Tom Mitchell show what is possible when you follow four rules with total dedication:

> *Rule One:*   I will be successful on the job I have today.
>
> *Rule Two:*   I will identify and concentrate on the essentials of that job until my performance is 100 percent.
>
> *Rule Three:*   The performance on essentials that I considered 100 percent yesterday is not 100 percent today, so Rule Two is never more than momentarily achieved.
>
> *Rule Four:*   I will accept no excuses from myself for my lack of performance on the first three rules. None. Never.

Those four rules alone, if carried out diligently, would ensure spectacular success for any executive, no matter how many times that person had previously failed.

Rules help us because they eliminate confusion, especially confusion at the start of a piece of work. The question "How should I begin?" is often inadequate at the start of a project. It would be better to ask "What is the rule here?" Think of your confusion when you watch a game and you don't know the rules. Americans have trouble even understanding when a cricket match ends. A European no sooner learns that it's three strikes and you're out when a catcher drops a third strike, letting the batter get on base. Our anxiety on taking on a new project often arises from not being sure of the rules.

KNOWING WHEN TO BREAK THE RULES

Rules count and you need to understand or establish them for every key part of your work. You also need to know why and when they don't apply. Failure to understand this rule of rules has aborted more than one fast-rising career. In looking at strengths and weaknesses (Chapter 4) we saw how things are different "above the line" from "below the line." A weakness, for example, took a disproportionate energy until we converted it into a strength. We found the same phenomenon in skills. We expend tremendous amounts of energy in floundering in the water until we learn to swim. After we cross the line, there is a steady, strengthening flow of energy. The essential pattern is repeated in a somewhat different form when we look at rules. A rule or rules that will propel our career at one point will actually retard it at another. Above the line, we must seek a higher rule of organization.

In searching for the line that separates "above" from "below" in following rules, we are looking for one of the most significant divides in management. It is here that we find the difference between a promising group of vice presidents and the one who eventually makes CEO. Up to a certain point, rules help speed progress; beyond that point, unless modified, they promote rigidity and actually slow progress.

One executive whose progress has never slowed seemingly for even an instant is Robert W. Gillespie, who at only age 43 is chairman and chief executive officer of Cleveland's Society Corp. Someone once noted that every 2 years for 20 years Gillespie received a new title until he became chairman. Whether technically correct or not, the comment does convey the rhythm of Gillespie's career at Society, which today is one of Ohio's largest commercial banks with assets of more than $9 billion.

At the start of his career, Gillespie learned the essentials, the rules, and a good bit of finesse from Maurie Struchen, who Gillespie calls "the most thorough and capable salesman I have ever met."

Struchen, who later became one of Gillespie's predecessors as CEO of Society, "wasn't *just* out there shaking hands . . . he was shaking hands, but when it was time to sit at the conference table, he could write a loan agreement by heart."

Struchen imparted the rules of being a good commercial banker to young Gillespie. Even today, Gillespie can rattle off the Gospel according to Maurie:

- Know everything about the company and people you are going to meet before you get to the meeting.
- Identify that company's current needs and solve their problems.
- Never let a month go by without letting a customer or key prospect see your name.

And, the rule of all rules:

- Don't take your customer for granted for a minute.

"One of the things I learned," Gillespie recalls, "is that if an account has been properly taken care of, you can't take it away." The thought of trying to take business away from Maurie Struchen causes Gillespie to declare, "Just forget it!"

Beyond being a thorough salesman and a gifted technician, Struchen taught Gillespie the finesse of the job, the "personal twist." Struchen knew every secretary by name. "He knew if a person had a child who had been ill last time around and he would inquire how that child was doing and very genuinely so. If he knew that someone just had a son or daughter begin college, he would inquire how they had done at the end of their first semester and very genuinely so. . . . Before you knew it, in many cases, I was calling on his old customers and I was trying to out-Struchen Struchen."

When it came to finesse, small details mattered. Struchen never carried a briefcase on a call. "I made the mistake one time of taking out a piece of paper and writing down something, and if looks could kill, Maurie shot me daggers across the room. His theory was that if you care enough about this company to make the call, you have taken the time to learn about it and you will take the time to remember what you've learned and you don't have to be sitting in front of a person taking notes." Of course, nothing ever slipped between the cracks because "the minute we got out of the room Maurie would take out a piece of paper and write it all down, chapter and verse."

Gillespie moved through several commercial banking jobs, always making sure "in our organization, people knew I was earning my spurs." After being with the company nearly 10 years and running the commercial banking department for 2 years, Gillespie went to Harvard's 13-week Advanced Management Program. Before he went, "my bag of tricks was that I was a well-trained, effective commercial lender who had good skills." He came back with "a much better current understanding of the conceptual framework that is required for general management."

An Eye-Opening Experience

The incident that most clearly demonstrates how Robert Gillespie kept widening his perspective is his handling of the bank's programs under the Community Reinvestment Act. In 1977 Congress passed a law requiring commercial banks to take a far more proactive response to community investment. The new law came just after Cleveland had defaulted on its municipal obligations, and local activism was at an all-time high. The new law directed that activism at the commercial banks. "It was a very difficult environment in which to have that kind of external responsibility," Gillespie recalls. "People would frankly come up to me and say, 'Hey Bob, you have to get out of that; that's a ticket to the graveyard.'"

Gillespie had a lot to lose. By this point he was clearly in line for the top job at Society. He thanked his colleagues for their concern and then set to work on the new assignment. "It isn't my

style to say, 'Hey, that one looks dangerous, let's back off there.' "
If you want to lead a company, he adds, you should feel you can
do anything that company asks of you.

Gillespie had his eyes opened by the experience. "Like so
many others, I suppose I came into this thing with a defensiveness
that here were a lot of people who wanted something for nothing,
when, in fact, that wasn't the case. Here were a lot of people who
wanted what they were fully entitled to. They were working people
who wanted a fair shake and nothing else." At Gillespie's recommendation, Society changed its investment policies and eventually
sponsored two community development corporations. The bank
also selected a staff member to work with community groups on a
full-time basis. "I became very closely and personally involved in
these activities and am to this day."

Gillespie had spent his whole working life as a commercial
banker. "I thought that everybody in the world wore a three-piece
suit." In refusing to let past perceptions prevent opening his mind
to new possibilities, he learned a new and extremely valuable rule
that was far more important and appropriate for a future CEO
than the purely financial rules he had learned so well earlier. "In
the banking business, one can't thrive if one's community isn't
thriving."

The turning point came when Gillespie represented Society
at a meeting of a neighborhood community group in a predominantly black neighborhood. After a few minutes, Gillespie realized
that most of the activists in the room were females working to keep
their families together "in the face of real and perceived shortcomings on the part of the institutions that they thought they could
count on. Among them the banks."

At that moment he saw that the existing rules just didn't apply.
*"Whether or not we had been negligent was a question that became
irrelevant.* What seemed clear was that we probably hadn't been
as active or proactive as we could be in that kind of situation."

Robert Gillespie's fast rise was not based on luck. Obviously
referring to his own experience, he says "any person who is going

to emerge as CEO is expending more energy, is working at a level of intensity not common to everyone else." He has applied his strengths with vigor, while learning the essentials of his job early and concentrating on them. These traits would have guaranteed success in time. However, the speed of his success is in part due to the flexibility that has enabled him to master a new job virtually every two years and to understand when the rules that worked in earlier jobs no longer apply.

The soft-spoken, conservatively dressed Gillespie makes it all sound rather matter-of-fact, as if anyone confronted with different jobs and circumstances every few years would have reacted in pretty much the same way. You don't have to look far around you to know how unusual Gillespie's behavior is.

WHEN THE CONTEXT CHANGES

Look at the careers of many executives you know well. For the first 10 or 15 years, progress is swift and dramatic, salaries double every 10 years, sometimes every 5 years. At age 40, the executive is at a higher level and is making more than he had hoped for at retirement. Somewhere in the 40s, the rate slows, the individual hardly notices the loss of acceleration at first. After all, the base is high. Even a 10 percent increase is significant, at least before deductions take their bite.

After several years, however, there is reason to notice the loss of acceleration. The company hires a bright young star in her early 30s, and the grapevine reports she is getting a higher salary than the 20-year executive. What has happened? The executive looks around. Well, yes, Joe and Jane are continuing to move along at their customary mystifying speed, but we have explained that years ago. Looking around elsewhere provides some comfort. Most contemporary colleagues are beginning to level off also—a little more acceleration for Anne, a little less for Andy—but the principle seems clear: Unless you are a workaholic or are lucky enough to be at the right place at the right time, you are going to level off at some point in corporate life and look at how much farther you have come than 90 percent of those you started with.

Before accepting these rationalizations, any executive should take a hard look at the explicit and implicit rules he or she is applying to today's work. *The external and internal contexts in which the rule is applied is as important as the rule itself.* When the context changes, in many cases the rules actually reverse. In mid career it is imperative to understand when to reverse the rules that have carried you forward. Gillespie understood this in dealing with the activist groups, and it succeeded in moving his career forward.

Take our first general rule: planning enhances performance. This rule is about as close to a universal as you can get. However, like all rules, it depends on the context. Since the 1950s, the American Management Association (AMA) has run courses for senior executives aimed at convincing them that planning enhances performance. One long-running course offering this training, called the Management Course for Presidents, is marketed to presidents of small- to mid-sized companies. The impact on most presidents is pronounced. For many, it is akin to a conversion to the idea of planning. If these were lower level managers, they could simply go home with a new and important rule to apply to their work. Since these are not middle managers but presidents, it doesn't work that way.

Almost as soon as the AMA began offering the course, the graduates complained that they could not apply what they had learned. Their vice presidents didn't, couldn't, or wouldn't understand the new rule. In other words, *the context in which a valid rule was being applied worked against its effectiveness. Before the rule could work, the context had to change.* Later, the AMA offered similar courses for vice presidents. The vice presidents usually came back enthusiastic to implement planning. Changing the context changed the result. Many presidents were then able to introduce the rule "Planning enhances performance" with spectacular success.

A Foolish Consistency

"A foolish consistency is the hobgoblin of little minds," wrote the American philosopher Ralph Waldo Emerson. Unfortunately for many rising stars, Emerson's words appear on the walls of very few executive suites. Many mid-career disappointments are the result of continuing to cling to rules that used to ensure success. Somewhere a special committee of a board is meeting to select a new president. One divisional president in that company is sure the job will be his. For more than 15 years, every assignment has been a success. "Look at the results," he told the chairperson of the presidential search committee. "Who has done a better job? Sales, earnings, ROI, quality. Year after year."

However, as the chairperson talked to others, she found that although his team members are fiercely loyal, others in the company deeply resent his success, feeling that he is far too narrowly focused only on the results of his division. He does not deny this. "You bet," he told the chairperson. "I'm paid to get results for this division."

This week the search committee recommended someone else. The committee chairperson was asked why the divisional president was rejected. "An outstanding executive," she replied, "but we just felt he lacked vision." In management, a lack of vision is often a code phrase for an inability to understand when you *must reverse the rules that got you where you are.* Operating in the context of a wider perspective demands both new vision and new rules.

Whether it is the small company president trying to push through planning or the large company divisional president failing to see that sometimes the needs of the whole company must override the rules that made his division successful, the external context always vitally matters. Even the middle-level manager must learn to understand rules in a wider context. The best discipline for this is to practice seeing things from your boss's viewpoint.

By definition, every external context is different. Sizing up which rules apply is one of the first tasks for any new manager brought in from the outside. She quickly discovers that the different context of the new company makes it difficult to apply the rules that made her famous at the former company. If the situation at the new assignment is sufficiently grave, she usually can keep her previous rules and change the context. Otherwise, she is in for a slow process of mutual adaptation.

WHEN THE OLD RULES NO LONGER APPLY

In the 1960s various liberation movements rediscovered the new rule that the old rules no longer apply. There was a great truth in this because both the external and internal contexts had changed. The old rules governing politics, education, and relations between nations, between the citizen and state, between the races, between the sexes, and between leaders and followers had with varying degrees of success guided society for several generations. Then with breathtaking speed technological, educational, and social revolutions simultaneously changed the external context of society and the internal context of the baby boom generation.

Our society crossed some invisible line. Since then, every American institution has been redefining the rules in a changed context. Even those who seem proud to operate by the old rules acknowledge a new context: Ronald Reagan goes to Moscow to talk peace with Mikhail Gorbachev; and before Tom Mitchell is free to manage by intimidation, he must ensure that his system is absolutely fair.

Senior executives often experience violent upheaval when the *external context* changes. The longer the realization is delayed, the greater the upheaval. It took well over a decade for American automobile companies to realize that a significant portion of the American public did want smaller, more fuel efficient cars.

The dramatic recovery of Ford and Chrysler in the 1980s came when they fully acknowledged that the context had changed and then changed the rules to match. Ford's John Betti notes that Ford's rule for quality now starts with the customer's definition. It used to be that the rule for quality was "to meet the standards." As the customer's context changed, this was no longer satisfactory "because those [former] standards are decided by somebody, probably the engineer, maybe with some marketing guy. They may or may not be hooked up with what the customer wants or needs."

The *internal context* in which we apply rules also changes from year to year. "He that hath wife and children," wrote the worldly wise English philosopher Sir Francis Bacon, "hath given hostages to fortune; for they are impediments to great enterprises, either of virtue or mischief." The young, single executive's valid rule "I will never work for one day for someone I don't respect" may well reverse for the parent with three in college to: "I will never work for someone I don't respect for one day more than it takes to discharge my obligation to my children." Both rules are valid, even exemplary, in the internal and external contexts. Conversely, the senior executive who quits, leaving his children without college tuition because "my integrity is far more important than anything else" has ignored the issue of context as clearly as the young, single executive who continues to work for a despised boss because she needs the money to buy a new sports car.

Healthy, happy human beings apply the rules against an inner context that knows when to reverse the rules. This truth is nowhere better illustrated than at the climax of one of America's greatest novels, Mark Twain's *The Adventures of Huckleberry Finn.* Huck, the carefree, untamed youth in all Americans, has traveled the great river with the runaway slave Jim. Through many adventures, he has come to recognize the goodness and human worth of his friend. When Jim is recaptured and is about to be sent back into slavery, Huck wrestles with his conscience. Should he try to release Jim?

On the one side there is everything he has been taught about the rules of property, and in the consciousness of the time, Jim is clearly property. On that side is allied the full force of the law and the rules of organized religion that have taught Huck he will go to jail, and worse, he will surely "go to everlasting fire" if he steals another person's property. Huck wants to be a good citizen and he believes in that Hell with absolute certainty. All of that force is on one side, and on the other side there is only Jim. Then, in one of the most moving moments in all of American literature, the ignorant but pure-hearted Huck decides: "All right then, I'll go to Hell."

Today's readers are confident that Huck will indeed miss the fires of Hell. Our confidence comes not only from observing Huck's dilemma from the changed consciousness of our time, but also from a more universal understanding that substituting a difficult, higher truth for a well-accepted lower rule of behavior is far more likely to put one on the path to Heaven.

Rules are meant to help us progress, not to chain us to yesterday. Thus the final context in which we should evaluate any rule leads to the question: How should this rule be applied in the context of my personal growth? A very common negative example is the executive who is still clinging to the rule "If you want a thing to be done well, do it yourself," even though she is now the leader of a department of 70 people. This is the wrong rule both in the external context and in the context of her own growth. The executive who sits on the not-for-profit board and stubbornly clings to the rule that "Financial surplus is the major index of effectiveness" is missing an opportunity to grow through a widening of perspective. Always obeying the excellent rule to "Stop and think before making decisions" may strangle a growing and potentially useful sense of intuition.

The most important rule in breaking rules is to be sure you know the rule perfectly before you break it. Several years ago, I visited an art gallery presenting a retrospective of the life's work of the famous artist Pablo Picasso. At the start of the exhibition, a large crowd gathered around a group of pictures that looked completely out of place. These were the earliest paintings of this pioneer in modern art. They were well-executed, traditional paintings in which every detail was masterfully taken from life. Like me, most of the audience knew only the later Picasso, the daring revolutionary whose colors and designs changed the way we looked at the world by showing us a world we had never seen. "I didn't know he could paint like that" was the common comment of those standing before the early pictures. Indeed, before he ever began turning the rules upside down, Picasso had mastered every traditional rule of color, design, and perspective.

It is equally dangerous to break the rules because you don't know what they are as it is to apply them and ignore the context. An ability to use rules flexibly and successfully remains one of the most important and one of the most frequently overlooked of the key factors in career success. Rules speed our progress to a certain point. After that, future progress depends on knowing how to reverse forward.

PART TWO

USING THE SYSTEM FOR MAXIMUM PROGRESS

You must walk before you run. This ancient proverb speaks to our transition. The earlier chapters described how you can become a brisk, confident walker on the road to success. These last chapters encourage you to stretch your legs, pick up the pace, and become a runner, who, like Larry Robinson, can always say "When I run, I go the distance."

By now even the most successful of you see daily work in a new light. You know what has propelled your career thus far. You understand which parts of your work are complete acts. You know how to upgrade physical work to mental work and how to ensure that the psychological component is always complete. Your experiments in improving each component of a task you do well are showing you the deep power in this one basic building block of success.

You also see your strengths and weaknesses in a fresh light. By now you have identified which of your strengths are not being exploited to the fullest. Even more important, you are increasingly unwilling to accept the facile answer, "That's just one of my weaknesses. I can't do much about that." If you have started work on overcoming a weakness, you know how exhilarating that hard work can be.

Any of these steps can open the doors to your deepest aspiration, that once and future vision of your greater, more complete self. If you have touched that aspiration while reading this book, you have felt the surge of energy that signals that your inner resources are available to support your future growth.

You are now more clearly focused on the essentials of your job. If your career is stalled or in any danger of going off the road, you first must attend to these essentials 100 percent, however appealing the nonessentials may be. You can permit no rationalization to delay this step. If you have already started on this work, you will feel a renewed sense of achievement and confidence in your future. Stay with this task until it becomes second nature. Then look for places to apply your own "personal twist."

You are also more conscious of the power of values, your own and your company's, to create an environment for success. Remembering Hale Champion's experienced advice, you are sorting out your own values in tranquility so that they can emerge as sturdy guidelines for action in a time of crisis.

Depending on your level and experience, you are looking to discover all the rules that apply to your job or you are trying to identify which previously successful rules actually threaten to hold back your future growth.

You now recognize that more than 90 percent of the work to advance your executive career is psychological effort. It takes psychological effort to complete each act, to build up strengths, to overcome weaknesses, to stick with the essentials, and to find, apply, and then reverse the rules.

You recognize that a life of expansiveness, achievement, and growth rests on your willingness and ability to apply ever greater psychological effort to ever greater responsibilities and opportunities. You will also now understand the role of the Establishment Within, which like all establishments always has one overriding counsel presented in many disguises: Let us preserve what we have. Let us minimize risk. Let us approach change slowly. Let us wait for a better time to try that. From the many examples in this book and your increasingly sharp observation, you now see that those who are going from career success to career success are silencing the voice of that counsel. Like Alex Kroll, they are setting a big goal "that takes your breath away" and then going for it.

Most important of all, it should be marvelously clear to you that whatever you have accomplished so far is merely a prologue. Leveling off is not a fact of life; it is a phantom of the mind. Growth is your birthright and should be your destiny as long as your breath lasts. Even beyond the steps described so far, there are many more opportunities for those who, no matter how far they have already come, now want to "go the distance."

MAXIMUM PROGRESS: BECOMING A SIGNIFICANT INDIVIDUAL

9

Your primary requirement as an executive is to complete the essential tasks before you. *Your job is to make things happen, to achieve results.* Executive work, however, offers you a much wider field for self-development that includes, but also transcends, producing the necessary results. You must first achieve the necessary results or the self-development aspect of your work is valueless. However, if you concentrate only on producing the results, you will miss one of life's most productive opportunities for personal growth.

People grow and develop through interaction with others. Our society provides two major arenas for this dynamic exchange: work and the family. Each has its place in our development and no life can be fully complete without the growth that issues from both. Achievement at work and failure at home brings joyless success; achievement in family life and failure at work gives us a joy that always misses fullness.

To exploit the full potential of your work, you must first separate and later reintegrate the results of your work and your progress through your work. This is a five-level process, going from simple to more complex, from the lowest level of reward to the highest, from the minimum to the maximum in self-fulfillment.

189

However, it is, first and last, a process and you should skip no level, no matter how inviting the next.

LEVEL ONE: PRODUCE THE RESULTS NECESSARY TO ACHIEVE THE ESSENTIALS OF YOUR PRESENT JOB

You must allow no daydreaming about potential for growth, or likes or dislikes, or just or unjust fate. At the end of the year, at the end of the quarter, at the end of the month, at the end of the week, at the end of the day, at the end of the hour, minute by minute, you must achieve the results for which you are responsible.

At this very instant, I am attempting to make this manuscript as complete an act as I possibly can. Gathering, organizing, and finding the right words to share these ideas with you has been one of the great growth experiences of my life. As I work, the date of August 15 is so indelibly imprinted on my brain that I do not need it on my calendar. August 15 is the deadline, the date the manuscript must be in the publisher's hands. This is the result of this work, and every day, indeed now every hour, I must produce the necessary words to achieve that result. Without that result, my personal growth is peripheral.

Your work is the same. Without the results, any talk of growth and progress is an illusion. Whenever we rationalize why the results cannot be achieved, we strengthen the Establishment Within, making it more difficult for us to touch our true aspiration with more than a passing daydream. First and last, results count.

Listen to Harry V. Quadracci, an extraordinary entrepreneur who has built a $385 million printing company in 17 years, starting from ground zero by implementing his highly personal management credo: "Our people shouldn't need me or anybody else to tell them what to do." Achieving that credo means granting exceptional freedom to employees to foster their own growth.

Before employees can enjoy such freedom, however, first come the results. Speaking at a recent Quad/Graphics, Inc., annual Christmas party Quadracci described the results of a fairly typical year: sales up 50 percent; earnings up 100 percent; profit sharing up 100 percent; employment up 50 percent from 2000 to 3200, 4 new jobs every day; 100 new clients, nearly 1 every 3 days; and not a single old client lost. Today, the Pewaukee, Wisconsin, company is one of the largest printers of newsweekly magazines in the world, producing more than 100 million magazines each month.

"We are," says Quadracci, "very ordinary people achieving extraordinary results." Turning ordinary people into extraordinary achievers begins with Quadracci's orientation lecture to new employees, most of whom are high school graduates from rural Wisconsin.

"They are the ones that didn't go on to college," he explains. "They are the ones who did not achieve in high school and now they are going into a technology company, a knowledge company, and they are academic nonachievers. So here they are, looking at their shoes when they come in. They are looking for a job and they are apologizing for not going on to college. So I sit with these kids and I give this little talk." In fact, "this little talk" changes people's lives, gets them to look up from their shoes, and, in his words, "raises their sights." The talk starts with results.

"Remember, overwhelmingly, there is one high purpose in life that draws us together, is the reason why we are in this room together. Higher than company loyalty, higher than your perceptions, higher than anything else. And do you know what that is? *We are all here to make money for the company and to make money individually for ourselves.* That's why we are here at Quad/Graphics. It is not a church; it is not a charity; it is not an orphanage. It is a business, and you are here to make money."

Quadracci then invites those who have come for another reason to raise their hands, because "You've come to the wrong place. Holy Hill [a nearby monastery] is 20 miles to the northeast and they give haircuts at two o'clock."

Business is the world's largest competitive sport, Quadracci goes on to explain. "The name of the game is to win and the people with the best team win." The newcomers have joined a winning team because "we are all partners in this life's work of making money, and together we can make more money than individually, apart."

The unifying concept of people being partners in this "shared expectation," understanding why they are there, has moved Quad/ Graphics at a growth rate of between 40 and 50 percent a year for the past 17 years, with no slowdown in sight.

LEVEL TWO: ACHIEVE MAXIMUM RESULTS ON WHATEVER WORK YOU ARE ASSIGNED

Ordinary results are the standards of the job; they constitute satisfactory performance, which is certainly no worse and probably a bit better than most people at your level achieve. These words should not suggest failure in any way. The way the world is organized, just achieving the required results will get you a better than cost-of-living raise and a promotion in time. And if you work for a hard-driving, competitive company, just achieving the results is not the easiest thing in the world.

Still, achieving the results is not the most difficult thing, either. What it takes, in the apt phrase of Merck's Dick Markham, "is the ability to concentrate over time." We already know the components of that concentration: selecting the essentials of the job, turning each of those essentials into its key tasks, and converting each task into a complete act.

Maximum results are another matter. Maximum results are Quad/Graphics growing at 40 percent year after year; Alex Kroll at 33 creating a worldwide creative system for Young & Rubicam; Kendall Lockhart with no banking experience becoming a Bank of America vice president in five years; Richard Markham rising to vice president of Merck Sharp & Dohme at 37; Larry Robinson going from 1 store to 96; and Robert Gillespie getting a new promotion every two years until he reached chairman of Society at 43. Don't just take these examples. Think of people you know or know of—divisional vice presidents before 35, presidents before 40, entrepreneurs who started companies that just keep growing, and so on. You will see that in every case their rapid rise was due to creating maximum results.

Maximum results come from *anticipating what will be needed and getting it in place before it becomes necessary*. This is more than just focusing on today's essentials; it is making sure that the resources for tomorrow's essentials are being gathered today. Larry Robinson grew his jewelry business so fast because he turned ordinary salespeople into "priests" who could carry his philosophy to other stores.

To learn how to prepare yourself for maximum results, we can turn to Harry Quadracci's "little talk" to the new hires. "Your first task is to learn your job. Your second task is to know your job. Your third task is to improve your job, since only you can tell us how to do your job better. And then, your fourth task is to teach your job to the next person so you can start learning the next task. We are all here together as students and teachers, sometimes more students, sometimes more teachers. . . . learning, knowing, improving, teaching is the way we work together, is what is at the heart of Quad/Graphics." Quadracci's four tasks provide a formula for maximum results that can work for anyone.

First, you must learn your job, whether it is your whole job or just a new assignment to open an office in San Francisco. What do you need to know to do this job? What don't you know? What are the essentials? What skills are required to produce the results? What rules apply to this kind of work? Has someone you know done this work or work that is similar enough to help you find the rules and understand the essentials? It was "up the learning curve once again," says Robert Gillespie, recalling how he felt when switched from commercial banking to retail banking. "But if it took two years, I wanted to do it in a year and a half."

Second, know your job. This means to carry out the complete

act for every critical task. Here one would also find the opportunity to use personal strengths to add a special finesse to the job. Appointed government officials have to be especially adept at quickly learning and knowing how to handle very complex jobs. Knowing the job in a hurry is essential because legislators at confirmation hearings, media, and various constituencies want answers from the new appointee right away. A honeymoon period often doesn't even last a week.

David H. Pingree became Secretary of Florida's $3.5 billion Department of Health and Rehabilitative Services when the department had to cut more than $100 million from existing services within 15 months. The department employed a staff of 33,000, serving Floridians in such politically and humanly sensitive fields as aging and adult services; children's medical services; public health programs; alcohol, drug abuse, and mental health programs; and vocational rehabilitation.

Pingree already had a reputation as a skilled troubleshooter who could make things happen in a hurry. "There seemed to be knowledge by someone [who was influential in the appointments] that if you want something to be done well and quickly in a situation where you need an immediate impact, I am a good person for that job." Getting up to speed in such assignments is a three-step process for Pingree. "Number one, identify what the problems are. Two, recognize quickly the individuals who can help you address those problems and solve them. And three, do not accept less than outstanding performance by those who are there to correct the situation."

Pingree has developed an effective technique for mastering the first two of these points quickly—a technique that can help any manager seeking to know a new job immediately. On taking on a new assignment, Pingree designs a questionnaire to be filled out by each executive reporting to him. The questionnaire asks each person to identify current problems, proposed solutions, the organization's strengths, its weaknesses, its talented managers, plus many related issues. After studying the replies, Pingree goes over each person's response in a two-hour interview.

Five days after taking over as Secretary of HRS—five days that included New Year's Eve and New Year's Day—Pingree had completed reviewing answers with not only his holdover direct reports, but also with four new people he had appointed. "I had people scheduled from eight in the morning until in some cases, midnight, every two hours." Given the pressures on Pingree, he could allow himself no more than five days to know the job.

Once he had a grip on the current situation, Pingree set to work solving problems and establishing priorities for the cuts. He used a team planning approach, involving "advice from as many different sources as possible." After you learn the job and solve immediate problems, says Pingree, who today is vice president of government relations at UNiSYS Corp., you shift to maximizing results by "anticipatory management."

Anticipatory management helps maximize results because it shifts your focus to the third of Quadracci's four steps: Improve your job. To maximize results, you look for ways to get the job done faster, more efficiently, at lower cost, and at greater profit. You search for new opportunities. No one, Quadracci reminds us, knows better how to improve a job you have thoroughly learned than you do.

Improvement is always an imperative. George N. Havens, chairman of Cleveland's Jayme Organization, Inc., is virtually a traveling evangelist for the idea of continuous improvement and growth as a way of life. When Havens joined the five-year-old advertising agency in 1951, he was the eighth employee. "It just might work out," he says with a laugh today. In those days, "we were a small fledgling organization, struggling for survival." In 1972, "the founder decided to retire and Ed [Young, another Jayme executive] and I climbed out a limb and bought control and said we wanted to grow it dramatically and aggressively." Jayme is now among the top 200 agencies in the nation. Billings in 1988 of about $50 million represented both the fifth straight record year and a tripling in the past five years. Havens has set a target of being in the top 100 agencies by 1995.

Havens believes that "growth is essential to life. . . . It is a

very common, almost universal characteristic that everybody wants
to grow, everybody wants to develop, everybody wants to do something different or better." He once attended a management seminar
where the lecturer asked those who wanted to be doing the same
thing in five years to raise their hands. "Of course, nobody raised
their hands." Sounding a bit like Harry Quadracci, Havens adds:
"If we are going to grow individually, then we have to grow as a
company."

The imperatives of growing his business are very clear to
Havens. "Each day in this business you are one day closer to losing
your best account. You need to grow to replace business that you
will inevitably lose. You need to keep up with growing clients who
are getting larger. Every time the merry-go-round goes around
January 1, you must accommodate a set of automatic cost increases
or you simply pull down profits or plateau salaries. Growth is
imperative to maintain an image of a vital, vigorous, successful
organization. Talented people want to be in a place where there
are some additional challenges and the stimulation of growth and
new opportunities."

With slight variations, you can apply all these rationales to
your company, your department, or your job. It used to be, says
Havens, that people sought to find satisfaction and reward in their
leisure time, but today ambitious goals bring a lot of "psychic
rewards to the workplace."

LEVEL THREE: USE YOUR WORK FOR SELF-DEVELOPMENT BY AIMING FOR BOTH MAXIMUM RESULTS AND YOUR OWN PERSONAL PROGRESS

Even at the maximum level, results are still measured entirely by
the material criteria: sales doubled, production costs halved, 90
percent of new hires still on the job six months later, or 25 training
courses held. Even when we use mental and psychological effort,
we still measure a material end product.

In looking at personal progress, the eye is turned inward for the first time. How can I grow in this work? What new skill do I need? Every new assignment opens another possibility. We can either charge into the assignment, confidently using our well-developed strengths and our familiar skills and compensating for our weaknesses, or we can pause and ask, "What can I learn here?"

Ironically, at the start of our careers we do this almost unconsciously because we know there is so much to learn. However, as we get more established, more sure of ourselves, just when we have earned the greatest freedom to search for new opportunities to learn, we go on using the same comfortable, highly effective assets. We cannot doubt there is as much to learn as when we were beginners. However, we have become too accustomed to living on our mental and psychological capital. It is ironic that this happens just when our capacities and opportunities to expand our strengths are at their highest. Not everyone makes this choice.

Part of the great dynamism at Quad/Graphics comes from the way Quadracci has deliberately created "a learning environment." People know they are coming to work to learn. "If you think you just left the classroom, you just joined it," Quadracci tells his recruits. Unlike most print shops, there are no pin-up calendars at Quad/Graphics. Quadracci has filled the walls with murals, limited edition prints "where the skill of the printer is as important to the execution of the work as the artist. . . . And, all of a sudden, again, we start talking about raising the people's sights."

Then there is the enormous personal growth potential in Quadracci's fourth task: Everybody is a teacher. "They were all afraid of teaching, of getting up in front of a group and speaking, but once they get bitten, once they get that self-confidence going, all they want to do is teach."

Ask Quadracci to identify a few outstanding employees who have dramatically progressed, who have spectacularly expanded their personalities in his learning/knowing/improving/teaching system, and he replies matter-of-factly: "Everybody. The whole company." Pressed further for examples, he refers to Quad/Tech, a division that develops new printing technologies. "This is a computer company. We build computers. Invent computers. There are probably 150 self-taught engineers here, hobbyists really." What happens to these inventions? Quad/Graphics uses the inventions to improve its productivity and sells the ideas to other printers.

Why would a company sell new technology to its competitors? The matter-of-fact voice answers with another unorthodox idea: To help lower the cost of printing around the country because "we'd rather be a middle-sized printer in a very healthy print environment than be Number 1 in a lousy printing environment." Another lesson from the little talk: "Other printers are not our competitors. Our competitors are other forms of media. Whatever we can do to bring down the cost of printing against the cost of TV and radio advertising will give us more print." Or, as my old mentor Eric Webster used to say: "To be certain you have two new ideas tomorrow, be sure you give away one good idea today."

If you strive for maximum results while using that effort to promote your growth, like Harry Quadracci, you will be able to say: "I'm more than I ever hoped to be."

One bonus in writing this book was a visit to the office of several of my childhood heros. I was at first disappointed by the small and rather unimpressive waiting room of their New York office. There was barely room across the receptionist's desk for me and the visitor who had preceded me. He had already taken a seat and had buried his head in a New York tabloid newspaper. As I handed my card to the receptionist, the reason for the small reception area suddenly became obvious. Few visitors ever call because the principal revenue earners in the firm are never here. They are always away on urgent business.

The small printed sign on the receptionist's desk announced, "Wonder Woman works here." Turning, I noticed my fellow visitor wasn't moving or even breathing. He was a full-sized, fully clothed papier-mâché version of Clark Kent. His tabloid paper was not the *New York Daily News* but the *Daily Planet*. In the end, the office of DC Comics in no way disappoints. Who would not choose to share in the fun of creativity and imagination rather than sit in fancy chairs, looking at expensive plants.

It is somehow representative of business life in the 1980s that the publisher and president of DC Comics, Inc., is a tall, stylish Radcliffe *cum laude* graduate in art history named Jenette S. Kahn. DC, now a subsidiary of Warner Communications, Inc., owns the rights throughout the cosmos to Superman, Batman, Wonder Woman, Green Lantern, the Flash, Plastic Man—about 1000 characters in all. The core of the business is publishing some 600 comic books a year, although equally important these days are product licensing, television, and movies.

Before coming to DC as publisher 12 years ago, Kahn was a Modern Art Museum Fellow and the creator of three magazines for children: *Kids, Dynamite,* and *Smash.* Although she runs a business built on fantasy, she approaches each task in her work with dedication and seriousness that would make Bruce Wayne proud. In March 1981 when she became president at DC as well as publisher, she was simultaneously the first woman to head a Warner division and, at age 33, the youngest president in the company.

Before receiving that promotion, however, she had to produce some impressive results. When Kahn first arrived in 1976, DC was less than half its present size. It was still a profitable company, but that was mostly because of licensing. The critically important newsstand business was fading, "a diminishing business that was getting worse every year." Deteriorating newsstand sales meant lost profit today. The long-term threat was equally serious since licensing depends on current, viable characters.

By the time Kahn arrived, the traditional distribution system was collapsing throughout the industry. "Over the years, the mom and pop outlets—the candy store, the local drugstore, the soda shop—have disappeared. The friendly neighborhood newsstand where kids could go by themselves is a thing of the past. Comic books were becoming harder to find and yet there was a demand for them."

The emerging distribution pattern was through specialty shops for comic hobbyists. The shops sell current comic books, back issues, and comic book-related material. Unlike the old stores, to get to these shops you had to be old enough to take public transportation or to drive yourself. Today, the largest share of DC's distribution is through 3000 such specialty stores. The average reader (95 percent male) is 23 years old, college educated, and upwardly mobile, and spends about $60 a month on comics. This type of business was "tiny, almost negligible" when Kahn arrived at DC, "but I believed that it would grow, that it would be our future."

Kahn put "tremendous emphasis" on the new approach. Since the specialty shops were not so linked to topical sales, she instituted a nonreturnable, deeper discount policy. She brought in a consultant to work out a different credit plan as well as creating a different type of marketing program and department.

Beyond these marketing changes, Kahn revitalized the creative process at DC. Shortly after her arrival she went to Warner Chairman William Sarnoff with bad news. "I told him, 'We don't have the talent we should have. We seem to have driven them away.'" Kahn advocated rewarding talent fairly because she had left the publisher of her biggest previous success, *Dynamite*, in a dispute over royalty rights. At DC, she found that because of similar disputes "most of the major artists and writers had been blacklisted by a previous administration and were not working for us." With Sarnoff's backing, she began a program of rights and royalties for creators.

Even armed with a fair deal, Kahn still had to overcome artists' and writers' resentment of DC. "This is one place where Radcliffe really did influence me. I had studied art history, and I learned to recognize different artists' styles and tell one from the next and to understand the contribution of each artist. Suddenly, I was in a new industry which actually used some 300 artists and writers to create these comic books." She immediately saw the talent of the artists and the comic books as an art form. This enabled her to give "these artists and writers, who had been treated often badly before, a sense of dignity," a feeling that "they were truly appreciated."

Kahn found that on the first Friday of every month people from throughout the industry would get together to socialize, gossip, and exchange ideas. "And I tried to have a lot of First Fridays at my house. Over time, the staff and I tried to establish a personal contact and maybe even some personal bonds with the talent. We tried to make it clear that DC had a new administration, and an administration run by very different guidelines."

Despite all this, it took over five years for Kahn to win back all of the creative team she wanted. Since she couldn't wait five years, she changed another industry policy. She announced that DC was willing to look at portfolios of new artists. For a decade, the comic industry had introduced few new artists. Even today, "there's a gap between the people in their 50s and the people in their 30s."

Alarmed by the lack of gifted artists and writers available to DC, Kahn hired a consulting firm "to help us figure out how to get more talent into our business." When the consultants said that the problem was that no one had the specific responsibility of recruiting and developing new talent, "we actually created a position of talent coordinator."

Above all, Kahn personally embodied the new attitude. "I made it clear that as a person, I loved comics. It was clear that I read our comics. I collected comic art. I went to conventions and artists' studios. . . . I demonstrated I was someone who had a true respect for the medium and respect for the people, the artists and writers who created the medium."

Her deep regard for talent extended to her own expanding staff. Remembering her resentment over *Dynamite*, she insisted on a bonus pool based on profitability for every DC employee. After a dozen years, Kahn has lost none of her enthusiasm for comics, which she says are on the cutting edge of popular culture. Staying on the cutting edge requires a willingness, even an eagerness to change, to keep up with the times. A few years ago, for example, she felt "it was important to renovate Lois Lane." DC called in a fashion consultant who interviewed a number of women reporters "and all that became a body of work forming the new Lois Lane."

DC also updated Superman "to rousing acclaim and great

sales." With readers getting older, there is greater "interest in human dynamics," so the Man of Steel had some of his powers scaled down. "We made him more of a person."

Even beyond producing such results, Kahn consistently uses her job as a medium for her own development. "I really must say I'm always learning." Her self-dictated studies stay focused on learning the essentials 100 percent. Even after 12 years as publisher of one of the top firms in the field, she feels there are things she needs to know. Every Monday her creative vice president takes her through another stage of comic book editing. How many executives after 12 successful years at the top of their companies would acknowledge such a need for greater training in the fundamentals, let alone do something about it?

Kahn goes further. She and her editor-in-chief periodically read all the comics together "from A to Z." This involves taking home about 30 comics, reading them, and then going through them together cover to cover. "We're looking to see if we are engrossed in the story. We're looking to see if the quality of the artists is both good and consistent. We are looking very much to see if we enjoy this story, and if we didn't, why not."

Kahn "often learns things backwards," doing something first and then learning the technical aspects. Finding herself involved with seven movies based on DC characters, she took a course on screenplay analysis.

Kahn illustrates how one can keep pushing for greater and greater results while using a job for personal growth. She continually renews her enthusiasm for her job, her company, her medium, and her industry. The source of this renewal is the process of "always learning."

LEVEL FOUR: ACHIEVE MAXIMUM RESULTS WHILE ACHIEVING MAXIMUM PROGRESS

Maximum progress is the highest concept we have yet encountered, and it is worth a highest effort. Before aiming for maximum progress, you must first saturate the possibilities for progress at lower levels.

Maximum progress involves seeking out the greatest possibility for personal growth from every new challenge presented by your work, continually disciplining yourself, calling on the energy required to overcome any weakness, and always being willing to learn or upgrade any skill that would enhance your work.

You will find no workaholics at this level, only workaphiles. This is what Robert Gillespie refers to when he speaks of the special "intensity" that it takes if you are going to be a CEO of an important bank at 43. It was this approach that made Gillespie willing to take whatever job came along and then rise to the level he needed.

Dow's Frank Popoff says it's nonsense to worry that one job fits you better than another, because the "first, most important thing in taking on any job is to craft it so you can do it well, after which you craft yourself to do it well." This attitude has not only propelled Popoff's career, it has made him feel from the beginning "as if I were self-employed." So much so that he glories in having "a passion for work" and actually feels "sorry for people who need a hobby to get away from work." This passion comes because "I really feel that we develop ourselves through work, we become serious students of what we do, and then we love what we do."

We make progress when we approach our work in a learning mode, asking what kind of growth is possible in each task, being willing to take the assignments pretty much as they come, and anticipating that each new challenge will give us an opportunity for further growth. Then, like Popoff, in the end "we love what we do."

When we take this attitude, we saturate the possibilities at the level of growth where we are, clearing the way for maximum progress. Take a common example, familiar to everyone. Three science majors are satisfying an undergraduate requirement by taking a course in Spanish in the first year of college. One gets a C, a satisfactory result; one gets an A, maximum result; another gets an A, also maximum result, but during the year develops a deep desire to learn more and progress further, so she takes a summer school program in Mexico.

During the second year, because of shaky fundamentals from the first year, the first student has to struggle to get another C. The result was achieved, but at the cost of more time and effort. The second student again got an A, maximum result. The third student got another A, but with distinction owing to a special paper she prepared in Spanish on Cervantes.

During the third year, the first student, having satisfied the college requirement, does not go on. He forgets Spanish, graduates in science with no particular prospects for graduate school. The second student gets another A, maximum result. With a solid foundation from the first two years, he had little trouble making an A the third year. He used the course to bolster his grade average. He can speak the language but rarely does. Two years after graduation he hardly remembers anything about it. Nonetheless, the three years of A grades lifted his grade average, increasing his chances for admission to a top graduate school. The third student gets another A with distinction. She is now quite fluent, reads Latin American magazines, and is developing a wider interest in Hispanic affairs. She obtains a traveling scholarship in Latin America and takes modern Latin American history as an elective. She later takes a graduate degree in science. Because of her Spanish speaking ability and knowledge of Latin America, she gets a job with a successful multinational company with wide Latin American interests.

The first student met the results and in time got promoted on schedule. The second student met the maximum results and accelerated his forward progress in life. The third student also achieved maximum results. However, she used the experience to widen her overall capacity, not just for Spanish, but her capacity to appreciate and understand foreign cultures.

The first student did not saturate the results level and could not move on. The second student saturated the maximum results level but chose to go no further. Only the third student maximized results and used the experience for personal growth. By focusing on maximum results and using that effort to promote maximum inner progress, she became a wider, more capable personality.

Everyone can relate to the example, but 25 years later when the first student is a successful sales manager, the second is a vice president of marketing, and the third is a CEO and an industry-wide leader, we are baffled by life's vagaries and strange twists.

Life is indeed full of strange twists, but its process is clear. Our actions can always change the scenario at any time. That C student might be another Dwight Eisenhower. A few years from now he may make a total commitment to both maximum results and personal growth and pass both his colleagues before he is 40. The A student who demonstrated such superb maximum progress and inner growth can learn the wrong lesson. She can apply her capacities to nonessentials for three jobs in a row and end up on the street at 40, full of bewildered bitterness about the unfairness of the business world.

Lawrence L. Horsch is a man who has carefully watched a great number of executives run their race. He managed his own venture capital company for 17 years, supporting himself, his wife, and five children on his ability to anticipate which entrepreneurs were going to make it and which were going to fold. "When it's your own dough, you learn to be very careful," he says. Then in 1987 he was asked to come in as chairman and chief executive officer of the very troubled Munsingwear, Inc., a $200 million manufacturer of men's and women's underwear. Through all of his experiences, he has developed some strong views on why some executives succeed and others don't.

"I tell my kids that life is like a long race. Look at your friends in high school. 'Let's grade these people based on their ultimate performance.' Let's keep it simple. We are going to talk about business performance. We're going to talk about net worth and annual income; it's measurable. Line them up for me 25 years from now and you're going to find you are very surprised. Some of those who were the best students and the best this and that went into business, but they got diverted.

"It's like the race [in which] somebody went off to pick blueberries and never got back in the race. Somebody else ran so hard in the beginning they had a heart attack and they couldn't continue the race. You're going to be surprised at the number of people who are going to come up near the top of this rating, who are persistent, who work every day, who are not flashy but keep moving the ball. And they stay on track and they don't get diverted and they have a vision of what they are trying to do."

They are people who strive for maximum results, and those who go the farthest of all are those who also aim for maximum inner development.

LEVEL FIVE: ACHIEVE MAXIMUM PROGRESS THROUGH YOUR WORK

At the highest level, we find those significant individuals who have completely integrated work and inner growth. The person has become the work. It is a cause, a mission; it is "the reason why I am here." That cause or mission can be saving refugees from totalitarianism or serving a better hamburger.

The late Ray Kroc built McDonald's into the world's largest restaurant chain after starting with little money and in ill health at age 52. Kroc expressed his feeling about his mission in life in his usual blunt, too-bad-if-that-shocks-you manner. "I speak of faith in McDonald's as if it were a religion. And, without meaning any offense to the Holy Trinity, the Koran, or the Torah, that's exactly the way I think of it. I've often said that *I believe in God, family, and McDonald's—and in the office, that order is reversed.* If you are running a hundred-yard dash, you aren't thinking about God while you are running. Not if you hope to win. Your mind is on the race. My race is McDonald's."[9]

Seagate Technology is Tom Mitchell's race. His life revolves around his work. In Scotts Valley and in Singapore, Mitchell works in identical offices. "The same furniture, the same carpets, the same lights, the same stuff in the same drawers." Only the view is different. Duplicate offices enable Mitchell to go to work the instant he walks through the door without having to remember where he keeps his pencils. He travels between California and Singapore with only a briefcase because he has identical wardrobes ("I must own 70 suits and a zillion shoes") in each place. Every minute of his life is organized around the challenges and satisfactions of his work.

Frances Hesselbein lives her mission of bringing Girl Scouting to every girl in America. "I start with a reasonable schedule. Then doors open and opportunities turn up and I can't say, 'Call me in six months' because then the opportunity is gone. I often do more than what would seem reasonable. My job is so exciting and the opportunities within and outside the organization are so exciting that I probably do more than a reasonable person would. It feels right for me."

"It feels right for me" could be the slogan of any significant individual as he or she moves through life at a pace that would make others drop. They draw boundless energy from the sheer intoxicating pleasure of the work and the growth arising from the work. Workaholics? Forget it. They are having too much fun. Midlife crisis? As one top executive said to me, "Do you know what they are talking about? I don't. I'm too busy to have a mid-life crisis!"

---

[9]Kroc, Ray, with Robert Anderson, *Grinding It Out—The Making of McDonald's*, Chicago: Henry Regnery Co., p. 136.

An individual who has reached a point where growth is now occurring spontaneously through work seems to move in a different energy dimension. When someone asked Robert Woodruff how he had expanded Delta Airlines from a rural crop duster to one of the top U.S. airlines, he replied, "It was mostly a matter of working all the time."

A person who becomes one with work becomes a significant individual in any field. Think of the leaders in your industry, in your field, or in your region—people who have been successful and great contributors over time. What are the capacities that jump to mind when you think of those people? Commitment, enthusiasm, and, first and last, energy. I can write those words and be absolutely sure that my answers will fit any outstanding leader you can think of in any industry, in any region. Significant individuals share these traits. The key point to remember is that this remarkable energy and enthusiasm are not a great natural endowment that you somehow have missed. What you see is a visible manifestation of matching inner and outer growth so perfectly that the worker and the work are one.

Whenever significant individuals saturate growth and capacities at the existing level of work, life seeks them out for other, expanded work. Ray Kroc became a colorful and controversial baseball team owner, keeping the San Diego Padres in his adopted hometown. Leading public and private organizations ask Frances Hesselbein to serve on their boards. Promotion after promotion seem to seek John Jacob, Robert Gillespie, Alex Kroll, Bob Widham, Doug MacMaster, Frank Popoff, and others mentioned in this book. All of this group seem a little baffled by the thought that others are worrying about the next promotion and the one after that. The consensus attitude of that group could be best expressed as: Do your job and the promotions will come soon enough.

John Jacob, as usual, gets to the heart of the issue: "I have always felt that if you work hard and stay ready and the opportunity comes, you can take advantage of it. The trick is always to be ready."

Often a value, powerfully felt, is the unifying theme that holds together inner and outer growth. That theme in the life of busi-nessman-humanitarian Leo Cherne is human freedom. Now 75, Cherne seems to have lived a dozen lives. The son of refugees from Russia, where his father had been an underground, anti-czarist printer, Cherne "grew up with a hostility to any form of government which pushes people around." In his youth he joined the Metropolitan Opera Children's Chorus ("That career ended when my voice changed"), worked as a merchant seaman in the Caribbean, and wrote muckraking articles for the New York papers while in college. In 1936, shortly after passing his bar exam, he and a partner founded the Research Institute of America. RIA advises corporate clients on economic and regulatory develop-ments. He still serves as the organization's executive director.

Two years later, Assistant Secretary of War Louis Johnson, impressed by the clarity and accuracy of RIA materials, invited Cherne to volunteer ("We cannot even pay your expenses") to help the government complete an industrial mobilization plan for war. Cherne drove to Washington every week "because it was the cheap-est way of getting there and back." Well in advance of the war, the plan was ready.

In 1944 he published a highly successful book entitled *The Rest of Your Life*, which predicted "a managerial revolution altering the character of American business." After the war, President Harry Truman asked him to evaluate the needs of postwar Germany. He served on the staff of General Douglas MacArthur, for whom he prepared the tax reform system that helped create a large Japanese middle class.

In 1946 he joined the board of the nonsectarian International Rescue Committee. Albert Einstein and other intellectuals and academics had founded the IRC soon after Hitler's rise in Germany. Five years later, Cherne became chairman, a position he has held ever since. Thousands of refugees from Europe, Africa, and Asia have benefitted from Cherne's lifesaving efforts. In 1984 he re-ceived America's highest civilian award, the Presidential Medal of Freedom.

The business community continually seeks his advice. When he received the International Platform Association Award, the citation read: "For the accuracy of his social and economic predictions over many years."

When Cherne was advised by his doctor to take up a hobby to relax, he turned to sculpting. Never bothering to learn technique, he began by molding a piece of clay into the head of Dr. Albert Schweitzer. "I didn't know there were tools," he recalls. "I never had any instruction. When it came time to do the hair, I used a comb. How else am I going to make something that looks like hair except with a comb?" Later he took a few classes, learned the tools, and "I've never done hair as satisfactorily since." The head came to the attention of the Smithsonian Institution, which immediately asked for it for their permanent collection. "I don't delude myself," Cherne adds, "I'm not one of the world's great sculptors. I'm competent." Still, every one of his pieces is in a museum or a national collection, and he has presented five to heads of state. Tying in with his lifelong value, almost every piece depicts a champion of human freedom.

Few things in life beat listening to an experienced raconteur with a compelling story. Still, the hour is getting late and Cherne, as always, has more people to see. Despite his rich life, he has proved to be an elusive interview. Ask him "What was going on within Leo Cherne at that point in your life?" and he answers with another riveting story of something the IRC accomplished. Life, his answers imply, is for living, doing, and helping those in need. Leave the reflecting for others. Then, in the final minutes of the interview, Cherne suddenly begins to reflect on the source of his remarkable life of achievement.

"I very clearly have a religious need, but it's not a religious need which is going to be satisfied by ritual or by efforts which other people have organized and which I do not denigrate, but would not satisfy me." Instead, his whole life, especially his work with the IRC, "is my religious need. This is the way I express myself. . . . If I were compelled to call myself something, I suppose

I would say I'm an agnostic. And even that would somehow or other be curiously incomplete, because there is this driving, remorseless impulse. And it's had a consistency, a shape. . . . it's driven me and satisfied me."

Nothing so completely integrates inner and outer growth as a commitment to respond to such a "driving, remorseless impulse," call it what you will.

FINAL BARRIERS: MASTERING YOUR INNER ESTABLISHMENT

10

In less than two decades, Harry Quadracci has built a company of believing achievers. Everyone at Quad/Graphics goes to work every day and sees the living proof of Harry's philosophy: "You are capable of doing anything that you want to do as long as you set your mind to it." This lesson is demonstrated countless times, around the world, through the ages. Why, then, do so many hold back? Quadracci, who has helped change the destiny of thousands, answers that question simply: "Your own lack of self-belief, belief in yourself, is the thing which is your biggest enemy. You are capable of being more than you ever hoped to be. You just have to believe in yourself."

Believing in yourself, in your evolving, ascending future, is a first, indispensable step. A second reason that so many hesitate is that turning that belief into practice always challenges us to abandon our reliance on the past. Every promotion requires you to shed ideas, trappings, and baggage from the past. If the jump was big enough, you had to abandon whole aspects of your personality and acquire new ones.

Early in my career I jumped several levels. I moved from being an individual writer to editor-in-chief, suddenly responsible for the editorial staff and content of an international monthly magazine. I spent months trying to figure out exactly what it was an editor-in-chief did. Even after I had figured it out, it took even longer to convince myself to make the changes I needed to fill the job. Growth always involves parting with the past; the greater the growth, the more of the past we must shed.

LEARNING HOW TO FORGET

Most executives work at developing a good memory, the ability to remember facts and figures, as well as the pattern of past success. Bernard G. Rethore works equally hard at forgetting. Rethore is president and chief executive officer of Microdot Industries, the diversified industrial components division of Microdot, Inc. He brings the confidence of a first-rate mind to his unusual discipline. He was valedictorian of his prep school, carrying 13 major subjects in his senior year, including first-year Russian, third-year Greek, and fourth-year Latin. He received a BA degree (with honors) in economics as a scholarship student at Yale. He earned his MBA from the Wharton School at the University of Pennsylvania, where he was a Joseph P. Wharton Scholar and Fellow. His first business job was in the prestigious Washington office of McKinsey & Co., Inc., where he served as a consultant to senior management in private industry, the U.S. federal government, and the United Nations.

With such a background, why does Rethore say: "I don't bother to remember things"? It is because he is consciously attempting to master "a new thought process." The challenge of world-class manufacturing means that companies like Microdot are reinventing how one manufactures.

In describing his conscious effort to forget, Rethore uses an analogy. Think of your brain as a central computer processing unit. If you try to remember everything you have learned, you are going to use up a lot of your storage space, limiting your remaining capacity to solve unstructured problems. The big payoffs are in solving unstructured problems, the kinds of situations you have never seen before. Rethore clearly understands that "this is just an analogy, with no basis in physiology or anything else." However, it is a creative way to look at a common human problem. If you don't rely on memory, you can expand your capacity to confront problems and opportunities in new shapes and dimensions. Of course, should you need to remember something, you can always bring that data stored off-line into the central processing unit.

Rethore reaches for that stored data as infrequently as possible. "It is the easiest thing in the world to make a decision if you have information. If you go from facts to good information, you can get there." Rethore credits his McKinsey experience with teaching him that facts, not his opinions or biases, must dictate information. In discovering the facts, "you must for the moment get rid of psychologically tainted baggage and try always to go to objective fact or as close to it as you can get." That's why you should avoid stored data.

Rethore's dynamic philosophy arises from the tension between two deeply held assumptions: "the status quo won't work" and "the only way to right answers is good data." Synthesizing them puts the premium on continually reexamining the data in the light of new conditions. One benefit of the approach is that it avoids the psychological burden of ownership of ideas. In the Rethore system you must abandon any idea when confronted by new or better facts. "Memory can be a great substitute for thinking. If you can recall things quickly and put them into some kind of order . . ., then when you are in a one-on-one intellectual combat, you can win the game without ever being challenged to think."

Remembering takes mental effort; forgetting takes psychological effort, especially if, like Bernard Rethore, you have every reason to be proud of your mental endowments and capacities. "The temptation is always just to sit slack at the oars," he says. In what kinds of ways? "Well, the worst thing in the world is going back to a draft of something you wrote previously because you get trapped in your own words, in the logic of that particular expression."

Subverting Your Own Organization

Can you run a $250 million company with this kind of psychological effort? Rethore is trying. His technique is "to subvert my own organization."

He starts by ensuring that members of his top team have views different from his own. "Look for the person who disagrees with you," he advises. Next, challenge everything you've been doing for a few years, especially those things you personally created. Rethore joined Microdot in 1973 and his rise to CEO came in part because of the success of the planning system he installed. Even today, he's proud of his skills as a planner. "In the business environment, I use the weapon of the plan."

In keeping with his commitment to change, in the last year "we junked my planning system . . . it had been around so long that I forgot one of the rules, which is planning systems, like organizations, have to be changed." Contrary to the maxim "if it ain't broke, don't fix it," Rethore believes, "If you haven't changed it in the past five years . . . it's time for a change." In reviewing the planning system, the Microdot team found, somewhat to Rethore's distress, that "a lot of the stuff that I liked isn't necessary. In fact, it got in the way." Rethore admits: "That one really hurt."

To keep expanding the horizons at Microdot, Rethore regularly sends all of the top team a management book to read. He then holds a group meeting to discuss the book. Since he cannot risk the embarrassment of sending out a dud, he reads three or four to find one to circulate.

Abandoning yesterday is not just a task for top management. Two years ago Rethore dreamed up the idea of forming the Microdot in the Year 2000 Board, a group of 22 of the company's brightest younger managers, covering a cross-section of functional disciplines and profit centers. Rethore gave the group an open-ended charter: "Tell us what this business ought to be in the year 2000."

The document, says Rethore, "would knock your socks off." Rethore had the group present its findings at a top management conference. "In essence we were reinvesting their findings in the brains and thought processes of the key players in our planning process." This is what Rethore means by "subverting the organization in a positive way."

Barriers Removed Are Endowments Acquired

Rethore is consciously addressing barriers to change and growth. Every executive in America is faced with similar barriers, and *every barrier removed becomes an endowment acquired.*

To understand this, look around you carefully. In earlier chapters, we began the practice of studying people we knew whose careers are accelerating. Now look at the highest level you can clearly see in your organization. The individuals at the top level have learned to handle the fundamentals discussed in the first eight chapters. You will also notice that these people have one, or possibly two, great endowments or assets. If you look next at people who are not progressing at all, you will see that they are being held back by one, or possibly two, important barriers. Now, imagine the people at the top, one by one, without those one or two assets. Where would they be? Reverse the process with the people being held back by a barrier. Where would they be if that barrier were removed? You can see that removing a barrier has the same or greater force than adding an endowment or capacity.

Following the thought processes in this chapter, removing barriers that are holding you back *can speed your personal growth and progress as much as all the ideas in the first eight chapters combined.* Such is the power of overcoming barriers.

Adversity breeds a talent for overcoming barriers, external and internal. When Larry Horsch had "my own money on the line" picking entrepreneurs, "I would almost never bet on somebody who had inherited most of what he has, simply because he hasn't had to overcome personal adversity." It is no coincidence that so many of the people in this book, and millions of other Americans who are rising rapidly in life, started out in adversity. A generation ago, the high school winners of the prestigious Westinghouse Science Scholarships were in great measure the children of European immigrants; today the awards are similarly dominated by the children of Asian immigrants.

FAMILY TIES

Throughout this book, we have dealt with a number of external barriers; here we are focusing on internal barriers. Where do they begin? How do they start? Almost at birth. With the best of intentions.

When we are born into a family, we inherit a number of features that will shape us. Physically, we may get Uncle Louis's nose and Aunt Phyllis's hair, which may or may not please us, but they will certainly shape us. We will also learn from others at a very early age that we have mother's quick intelligence and father's quick temper. Since this information is coming from figures of great authority, we will accept it, internalize it, and begin to act on it.

This, of course, is only the beginning. Before we know it, we develop habits, attitudes, values, opinions, perspectives, and temperaments, all of which become so embedded in our character that we simply accept them as a valid lens on the world. Although many of these traits represent our strengths of character, all are barriers to our growth, just as the superb memory that made Bernard Rethore such an outstanding student eventually became a self-recognized barrier to his growth.

Take any trait, no matter how positive, and it can become an anchor holding us back. We saw how Bob Smith had to struggle to offset a rich and deep empathy for others, a trait that was a major contributor to his success. Even when we recognize that a deeply held attitude is holding us back, can we change it? Is it really possible? Yes, and affirming examples are all around us.

Consider the barrier of family upbringing. "I came from an environment that had no motivation in it," says entrepreneur Nancy

Vetrone, "where people were satisfied to be where they were. They didn't have big dreams and big hopes, and they didn't have a lot of respect for getting ahead in the world." No one would say that about Vetrone, who in 11 years moved Original Copy Centers to a place on the *Inc.* 500 as one of the fastest growing privately held organizations in the United States. Even at the end of a long day, Vetrone radiates energy and drive. "I couldn't stand it," she says, recalling her early years. "I hated the fact there wasn't any enthusiasm for anything."

Vetrone's second husband Robert E. Bieniek, vice president of Original, who comes from a similar background, adds, "Nancy showed me 13 or 14 years ago that there really is a lot more out there." Vetrone specializes in making others see her vision. Even before she started her firm, "I was always aware I was responsible for opening up the eyes of my children to new and exciting things, to the ballet, to the opera, to anything they can encounter in life that didn't keep them on that mundane level that all my relatives were on." When Bieniek first met Vetrone, a divorced mother struggling to raise her four children, "I was in awe of the way Nancy was open with her children . . . even though they didn't have a lot of money, they dressed right. There was something special in that family that came from Nancy."

Vetrone didn't realize herself what it was that was so special until years later. One of her sons-in-law "brought it to my attention that I was always teaching him new things. . . . I realized that I had done this all my life with my kids. Even when I didn't have any money, I always somehow scraped enough together for us to do something that took them out of that environment, something that said, 'See, there is a lot out there.' "

In 1975, frustrated by her inability to make enough to support her family as an administrative assistant in a public accounting firm, Vetrone "walked in one day and said, 'I am going to make myself president of a small company if you will not give me a promotion.' " Turned down, she opened a secretarial service within two weeks, which she converted shortly into a small printing business. Then one day, she saw a Xerox 9200, and "I came back and told Bob

[Bieniek, who was renting office space from her] I had seen this fantastic machine that I was really in love with." She particularly liked the Xerox because she would no longer be at the mercy of printers. She could learn to run the machine herself. "It was exciting. It was like it was spitting out pennies all the time. When I would hear it click, click, click, it really excited me."

Today, 13 years later, Original operates seven days a week, 24 hours a day out of one of the largest and most modern quick print shops in the nation. Instead of 1 machine clicking out pennies, there are 27 clicking out dollars—5 million of them in 1988. Specializing in Xerox copy services to produce manuals and reports in large volume, Original ships out 15 million copies a month. Just 11 years after striking out on her own, Vetrone made the INC list for the first time, received an Award for Business Excellence from Crain's *Cleveland Business* magazine, and was named the Woman Business Owner of the Year by Cleveland's Women Business Owners Association.

She uses the energy and enthusiasm generated by her own rise in life to spur on others. Remembering her own struggle to overcome an environment of limits, she says: "We don't put a top on people . . . it is unlimited. Open up your brain! Think about what you are doing and come talk to me about it. I have people come to talk to me at 11 or 12 at night." Today, Original employs 96 people, and only 4 employees have ever quit.

The enthusiasm spills over into sales, which have increased (Vetrone can tell you to the final digit) "1224 percent in the last six years!" Four or five years ago, she adds, "we were doing yearly what we are currently doing monthly. We just had a $510,000 month; the average printer will do $180,000 a year."

What has been the most difficult thing about creating and maintaining that kind of growth? "Nothing that I can think of. . . . It is just learning about it and figuring how to do it." Do 14-hour workdays interfere with her personal life? "This *is* our personal life. We are having fun here."

Don't bother to suggest to Vetrone that we are all prisoners of our early environment, that childhood somehow determines our fate. "I wanted to change the entire course of my family," she says, "and I did that."

ESCAPING FROM SCHOOL

After the home has set its mark upon us, we pack up our family inheritance of habits, values, attitudes, opinions, perspectives, and temperaments in our book bags and set off to test them in the classroom and schoolyard. Like homes, schools come in all varieties, from excellent to abysmal, but they all share a common fanaticism to sort us into categories: from A to F, from smart to dumb, from tall to short, from popular to hated, from athlete to klutz, from winner to loser, from honors in math to required summer school English. We carry our homegrown bag of traits through this maze for 12 to 16 years, discarding some in panic or relief, clinging tenaciously to others despite unyielding resistance all around us, and using still others to ease or accelerate our passage.

As Nancy Vetrone refused to accept the attitudes, opinions, and values in her home, many other successful people chose not to accept the verdict of the sorting out and classifying that is part of every education.

Owen Lipstein says his early success is the result of "early failure" at school. At 36 Lipstein would be clearly at or near the top of any list of imaginative, young entrepreneurial publishers. He is founder, partner, and publisher of *American Health* magazine and in recent years he purchased *Mother Earth News* and *Psychology Today*. Lipstein says, "Early failure is not a glib phrase." He was graduated 93rd out of 104 classmates at a top prep school, Hotchkiss. "The only people who graduated worse than I did didn't graduate." Now, the headmaster of Hotchkiss frequently sends his bright graduates to Lipstein with glowing recommendations. "I keep thinking to myself, I never got recommendations like that."

Denied the usual post-Hotchkiss path to Harvard, Yale, or Princeton, Lipstein enrolled at the University of Rochester. He remembers exactly the summer day when he decided to change the direction of his life. "I had a girlfriend in Southhampton. She was a waitress somewhere and I worked as a gardener. Then one day I found out that she was going out with some rich 36-year-old, which I guess is me now. I went back to the tent where I was living and the tent was gone. I just thought to myself, 'You really aren't doing well, Owen. You had better start looking at another way of understanding the world because you aren't doing well in this.' " Shortly after that Lipstein picked up a book by F. Scott Fitzgerald and suddenly realized that "I don't have to learn all these things personally because there are a lot of really smart people, smarter than me, who have things to say about feeling down and out at 18 years old."

Having discovered he could learn from great writers and thinkers, Lipstein went back to the University of Rochester "and they said I should start with Homer and off I went." By his 25th birthday, he had a masters degree in English literature from England's University of Sussex, an MBA from Columbia University, and a job at CBS Publishing as part of the company's acquisition team.

Surviving and overcoming the wounds left by school have left Lipstein with the same up-on-the-toes confidence that propels others who have overcome significant barriers. "If you went to Hotchkiss, it was not hard to get into Harvard, Yale, or Princeton. When I didn't do things conventionally well, for whatever reasons, I learned it wasn't so bad. I was sort of thrown out of the certain elite group that went there. If you didn't go on with them, you were behind for awhile. But it was like one of the Rocky movies; you take a few punches and you say, 'Not so bad.' . . . I realized that social failure, failure among your peers, disapproval of older people, wasn't too bad. . . . it made me ultimately unafraid of failure."

"Not so bad" is an important lesson, one learned by far too few executives. Many spend anxious hours, or even years, handicapped by how they were classified by schools and classmates.

Social acceptance is an overriding value at age 14 or 15. How we were sorted at that age matters terribly to most of us. Ten years later we should recognize that sorting out is an outgrown relic. Because it touched us at a vulnerable passage, the power of the relic to act as a barrier has unbelievable strength. If you were sorted then into one of the easy-to-spot categories such as weak at math, good at sciences, or poor at social skills, you are probably still winning and losing every day based on that assessment—unless, like Owen Lipstein, you are willing to consign that particular relic to the junkyard where it belongs.

Lipstein's life changed the instant he decided to change it. Then all he needed was a method, a technique to recover lost ground, a way to harness his energy. Because he was so open at that moment, the method came quickly in the form of learning from the masters. Through comprehensive reading, the heritage of Western thought became his to apply.

A TOTALLY DIFFERENT THOUGHT PROCESS

School—even its social aspects—is vitally important in our development. Whatever our experience, we come out of school shaped still further. In addition to our personally refined version of the original family inheritance, we now have a useful set of mental and social skills, a great deal more knowledge, and a whole range of new barriers, some of which we believe are our greatest assets.

Bernard Rethore's memory was such an asset. He did well at Yale. He found that his MBA did not involve a great deal of intellectual challenge. Then he went to work for McKinsey, "and I ran right into a wall." For the first time, all of his colleagues "were at least as bright and probably brighter." His education had been based on a method he calls "repetition is the mother of study." And "repetition involved the use of memory, which was wonderful" until he got to McKinsey.

McKinsey bore the stamp of Marvin Bower, a lawyer who had

adopted a lawyer's approach to consulting. As Rethore describes the system, "You examine a lot of data, come up with a hypothesis, test your hypothesis, drive your hypothesis to a conclusion in the interest of doing unstructured problem solving on behalf of helping the client solve previously undefined problems." It was for Rethore "a totally different thought process. . . . I couldn't cop out and take the easy way." The easy way meant using his quick study and memory skills to substitute for real thought.

On his first assignment he joined a consulting team to the vice-chief of staff of the Army, the same lieutenant general to whom Rethore served as aide-de-camp during a tour of duty in the Airborne Infantry between Yale and Wharton. He thought the assignment would be "a piece of cake." After all, "I knew these guys, the subject matter, and the setting." What he quickly found out was "the things that I could either remember or dig up just weren't good enough." For the first time in his life, Bernie Rethore was failing—and on two counts. "For one, my work didn't exhibit enough new thought. Second, I still had an academic style of writing. I was just coming up with the easy answers and I wasn't getting at the questions hidden behind the questions."

Recognizing that he was having "my nose bloodied," he went after it with his characteristic response, determined to "find a way to beat this." He worked harder and talked with every bright consultant he could find. Fortunately there were plenty of those at McKinsey. "This was basically going to school, and it was terribly embarrassing." Looking back, he sees it was not the work itself that was so difficult, it was "changing a thought process . . . that was pretty well ingrained, especially since it had worked so well for the sum total of my experience."

Stepping Through the Looking Glass

He worked and worked. Then one day, he could just do it. How do you change the thought process that's brought you success all your life?

Rethore uses another analogy. When he was training to be an Airborne Infantry officer, he and his classmates confronted a never-forgotten challenge, the 34-foot tower with a simulated airplane door on top. Before you are ready to jump from a plane, you practice jumping off this training tower. When you are strapped into a harness that will hold 10,000 pounds, you know mentally that the harness is not going to snap under your weight. Knowing mentally and psychologically are quite different matters.

"You stand on the edge of the platform and report to an NCO that you are ready to make your exit. Then you exit and drop 10 feet. You take the shock up on your groin, which isn't any fun, but you don't hit the ground. When you stand up there at the beginning . . . the reality is not that you might kill yourself, but you might break a leg, arm, or your back. Thirty-four feet is just enough to make that very real. . . . It is more vivid than when you step out of a plane."

You keep stepping off, day after day. Then "one day you step off and it is just like stepping off your doorstep. There is no way of knowing when you will walk through that looking glass. Some never do and they never proceed with the training and that is the end of it." Changing his thought process was very similar. He worked at it conscientiously day after day, and then one day he just stepped through and "my thought process changed." Once his thought process changed, his academic writing style changed as well because "the writing and thinking went hand in hand."

Rethore can articulate this experience with unusual clarity. Yet everyone who has risen at work has gone through some type of similar change. The faster and higher the rise, the greater the shock of stepping off the tower. The pattern is always fundamentally the same: the scary realization that this time, to survive and grow, you must step into a new dimension. To borrow Rethore's analogy: "Some never do . . . and that is the end of it." Each new job, each promotion, and each effort to grow on the job we have require a new dimension of psychological effort, a renewal of the struggle to define ourselves at a higher level.

The Biggest Step of All

No single-level rise in management requires as much self-redefinition as stepping from vice president to president. For John Jacob, who had overcome so many barriers to reach the presidency of the National Urban League, there were, as usual, a few special complications to be handled.

In February 1979, Jacob moved to New York as NUL executive vice president. He had worked for the organization for 15 years, including service as the top executive at the San Diego and Washington, D.C., offices. He did not expect to be president since the board had never selected an insider for the job. Even more important, the current president, Vernon E. Jordan, Jr., was a year younger than Jacob and previous presidents had stayed on this job until death or retirement. Jacob saw his new job as crowning his career in public service prior to a move into the private sector.

In New York, he turned in his usual more-than-expected job. "As a matter of principle, I never left here before Vernon. I just figured if I am supposed to be his chief operating officer, it doesn't make sense if I'm not here when he's here. We made a terrific team."

On May 29, 1980, Jordan was nearly fatally wounded in an assassination attempt in Fort Wayne, Indiana. Jacob became acting president while still carrying out his administrative duties. Jacob determined to carry out the difficult role with absolute integrity: "Under no circumstances did I want to give the appearance of waiting for Vernon to die, or, now that I have my opportunity, I am going to demonstrate that I am their kind of guy."

Still, he had to take charge and he did. His first priority was Jordan's recovery. He had received the call telling him Jordan had been shot at quarter to five in the morning. By seven that same morning, he was on a Norton Simon jet bound for Fort Wayne, together with Norton Simon Chairman David Mahoney, an NUL board member. In between managing the press, working with the black community, and trying to help the FBI and the police, he arranged for a friend, the chief of surgery at Howard University, to fly out to examine Jordan. At the surgeon's recommendation, Jordan was quickly moved to a New York hospital. "I would go up there every day, weekends included, and stay with Vernon because Vernon said to me, 'I'm shot in my back, not my head.' "

Psychological Restraint

The biggest event in the National Urban League's year is its national conference, attended by more than 12,000 people. This was 1980, an election year, and the presidential candidates were scheduled to appear. At first the organization hoped that Jordan's return would be the highlight of the conference, but in the end he was too ill to appear, so Jacob had to make the keynote address. An experienced and inspiring speaker, Jacob could not help but be momentarily tempted by this overwhelming opportunity to use one of his greatest strengths at such a dramatic moment. Instead, he applied the psychological restraint to move in the opposite but appropriate direction.

"I decided that the keynote address had to be short; it had to speak of Jordan; it had to indicate to our group that I was not trying to give the presidential keynote address, that I was the man who was tending the organization for the man who was in the hospital who was our leader." The speech lasted only 12 minutes and achieved all of Jacob's objectives. It also earned the trust and friendship of Vernon Jordan. "I am sure he liked me before and he respected my ability, but through this whole process he learned to trust me. We became very good and close friends."

Jordan eventually returned, but within the year had accepted a position with a New York law firm. Jacob did not campaign for the president's job but won it after making his impassioned response about preparing for it for 17 years.

As is his habit, John Jacob quickly dealt with the barrier of having to change his mentality after being selected president. Having earlier restrained himself from making a presidential speech, he now had to overcome an executive vice president mentality and make a presidential speech. Three days after his appointment, he made his first speech as president in Greenville, South Carolina. He had accepted the invitation much earlier. "Frankly, I had developed an executive vice president speech." He threw away the old speech and prepared a new one.

His new speech was the beginning of a whole new emphasis for his organization. Jacob came out of social work and views himself as a leader who provides services to enhance his advocacy. Jordan, a lawyer from the civil rights movement, viewed himself principally as an advocate, who incidentally provided social services. Jacob found his message by reviewing the previous 10 years of the NUL's annual State of Black America reports. "Every report had highlighted economic and social issues critical to the survival of the black community, but nobody was bothering to do anything with it."

For example, he told his Greenville audience that "if we don't educate these kids, eliminating the barriers to employment won't mean anything because they still can't get hired." For the first time, a National Urban League leader was saying that the organization had to address issues like teenage pregnancy, black-on-black crime, and households headed by single females.

Jacob went around the country with his presidential speech. "The reaction I got from some trustees and almost invariably from all of our local executives was, 'Who does he think he is to tell us what our programs are supposed to be?'" Jacob stuck with it and "it took about four years to get our locals to buy into the program." As the nation's political and social agenda changed, Jacob began to look more like a prophet. "Now I have to spend less time in explaining to them why we ought to be doing these things."

I AM GOING TO HOLD YOU TO IT

Meanwhile, Jacob also took a hard line on discipline within the organization. There was a long-standing practice that few local affiliates paid their dues. Periodically, the national organization would forgive the back dues and the process would start over. In the days when funding sources were plentiful, both the national headquarters and its affiliates could get away with this practice.

Jacob saw much more clearly than most of his fellow civil rights leaders in 1982 that government funding sources were going to become scarce. He had, after all, run the San Diego office during the administration of Governor Ronald Reagan. He announced that there would be no more forgiveness. Everyone would have to pay what they owed. "They said when you were a local executive, you didn't pay dues. But, I said, 'I am no longer a local executive. Now I'm the national president and you have an obligation to pay your dues and I am going to hold you to it.' "

Jacob believes you must have no confusion about your role in taking any new job. To illustrate this point, he tells a story about a lawyer friend, Sam Jackson. Jackson defended 24 people accused of murder and got 24 acquittals. When asked whether any of them were guilty, Jackson always replied he didn't know because it was his job to defend them based on the facts they presented to him, whereas it was the job of the prosecutor to disprove those facts, the job of the jury to make a decision, and the job of the judge to act as referee. Jackson told Jacob, "I never got my job confused."

When Jacob told the affiliates to pay up, they didn't believe him. The largest affiliate owed $365,000 in back dues. "So we wrote them, set a date when they would come and discuss it. They wouldn't discuss it. We wrote them again and told them they owed us. They ignored it. We put them out."

Being put out of the organization meant the affiliate couldn't use the National Urban League name for its fund-raising. The affiliate eventually brought its case to the floor of the National Convention. Jacob was bombarded and lobbied with appeals to change his position. He sensed, however, "in this setting they are not going to win," since small affiliates struggling to pay their dues were not going to vote with them. "So they brought it to the floor and got wiped out. Then, they were really out. That evening we cut a deal, gave them a payment plan on the back dues, but they had to pay up front on current dues. . . . So we put to bed the dues issue."

Jacob's unprecedented rise to the top of his organization contains many lessons for any executive planning to move higher in executive life. One such lesson is that the behavior completely appropriate at one level is often inappropriate at the next. With Jordan too ill to come to the convention, Jacob's restraint in the 1980 keynote address was an admirable model of appropriate executive vice president behavior. To have carried over that same restraint in the Greenville speech would have delayed action on the new agenda he was setting for the Urban League. Although the lesson seems obvious set against the dramatic scenario of Jacob's career, it should be, but is not equally, obvious in the rise of any sales manager to vice president of marketing, or a vice president of production to president. In a quarter of a century in executive life, I have seen executive after executive stumble initially and perhaps irrevocably over similar hurdles.

"I am no longer a local executive," Jacob answered bluntly to those who accused him of inconsistency in his position on dues. In each new role, a certain degree of inconsistency with past positions is not only acceptable, but is required. In such circumstances, past positions are simply another self-imposed barrier that must be overcome.

WRITING YOUR FUTURE

Part of the strength that barriers hold over us lies in the way they seem to be so concrete a definition of what we are, whereas our aspirations seem remote and therefore impossible. After all, the barriers are all built on "real experiences" that happened to us at home, at school, in society, or at the office, whereas aspiration is all about what we want to happen to us. To make our aspiration more concrete, we must learn to see ourselves as we want to be.

Memphis entrepreneur Susan Bowen has developed a technique to free herself from today's barriers while accelerating toward tomorrow. She first writes her future and then lives it.

Bowen started her company Champion Awards, Inc., in 1970 to produce trophies for saddle clubs. She was swamped by demand immediately and soon had her two sons screwing trophies together after school. By 1971 she had quit her job as a dress designer to devote all her time to assembling trophies. In 1977 Champion added a screen printing division, followed by a specialty advertising division in 1982. Today, screen printing of T-shirts and other apparel accounts for 80 percent of total sales.

Hitting sales of $3 million in 1985 was a turning point. After her sons decided to join the business full time, Bowen held a family conference and decided "to shoot for the moon." It took 15 years to get the first $3 million in sales and just 3 years more to reach $7 million. That performance put Champion on the *Inc.* 500 list of rapidly growing companies for 4 consecutive years. Bowen is now setting up the company with capacity for $10 million. Her motto, which could be a slogan on one of her T-shirts, is "Business is fun, if you do it right."

Shooting for the moon involves first imagining "I am in a certain position. . . . And then I have to go about preparing myself to fit that position." It is very hard, she admits, when you are a housewife to see yourself as a business person or when you are the owner of a small business to see yourself as the owner of a big business. She is currently beginning to focus on what it would require of her to be the owner of a $56 million business, the size of the largest company in her industry.

She actually does visualize what she wants to be, but even more important, she writes it down. "I write hundreds of pages of where I'm going and what I'm going to have to do to get there." She writes because she remembers things better that way. The writing also helps her focus on "how I need to project myself, what my goals are, what I'm going to have to change about me in order to fit into certain positions." The hundreds of pages of dreams, ideas, and projections translate to about five key things she sets out to accomplish every six months.

Recently she has had to improve as a public speaker and prepare herself to appear on a new video advertisement for the company. Organizing the company for $10 million in sales involves developing more people to whom she can delegate. At the time we talked, she had just achieved one of her short-term goals, an article in the local Memphis magazine.

She works around the few barriers that hold her back. Memphis is still conservative enough that "I can't call Joe Smith, a customer, and say, 'Hey, Joe let's meet at the golf course or let's have a drink at the hotel.' I can't do that. And a lot of deals are made that way by men, and most of my customers are men." Bowen works around that barrier by meeting her customers in civic organizations where she is very active. And, in 1988, she was one of the first 15 women invited to join the Memphis Rotary.

REDEFINING OURSELVES

As we get older, we keep building on the definitions given us by home, school, society, and the office. Through experience, we add our own attitudes, convictions, and opinions. By our 30s and 40s, most of us are seeking and have often found some kind of cohesive philosophy or framework to make all our roles add up to a unified concept. Heightened religious feelings or conversion works for many people; vague or specific concepts of the meaning of life work for others. Still others find their deepest affirmation in a network of relationships, and many find in work a cause or an identity that deeply satisfies.

For career success, it does not matter how we unify our self-image. What matters tremendously is whether we take a static or dynamic view of ourselves and our place in the world. If we use our stabilized view of ourselves to justify all our present attitudes, opinions, and inherited endowments as well as to explain why we are no longer growing in our work, then no matter how noble or elevating the philosophy or cause on which our lives rest, we are leveling off. If, on the other hand, we see all our many attitudes, opinions, and experiences for what they are—a vast array of tools, some useful, some not—then we can use our newly found maturity and cohesiveness to keep moving toward the achievement of our deepest aspiration.

Harry Quadracci's truth is absolute: "You are capable of doing anything that you want to do as long as you set your mind to it." But before you set your mind to a task, you must first free it from the barriers that hold you back.

11 THE SYSTEM IN ACTION: FROM JUNIOR MANAGER TO CEO

We have come far. It is time to reintegrate the separate ideas in this book and apply them to your specific job. By now we stand on a knowledge whose parts are:

- Success is not a random lottery, won by chance. It ceases to be a lottery when we understand what it rests upon.

- Success is a system—a system that you can learn and start applying from today on, carrying you to greater and greater success for the rest of your life.

- Your success begins when you want it. Wanting is not a vague wishing; rather, it is a longing that will not be denied. It came to Owen Lipstein at the exact moment he said, "You had better start looking at another way of understanding the world because you aren't doing well in this."

- That longing for success is *the single most important aspect of becoming successful.* "I wanted to be an executive in the worst way, even before I had any idea what an executive did," John Jacob told me. It has that power to shape a life. Released once in pursuit of something you really want, it can inspire you again and again. Alex Kroll learned how to "lift the bar another inch" in high school and has been lifting bigger bars ever since. Dwight Eisenhower, a man of no particular promise, wooed and won the very popular Mamie Doud, and his effort made him rethink what he wanted in life with results that changed history.

- Considerably greater than 90 percent of the effort required for you to succeed is psychological effort—the work you do on yourself. The main task here is to free yourself from what you like and don't like, from what you consider your strengths and weaknesses.

- Freed of biases, likes, and dislikes, approach your work by asking: What are the essentials? Carry out those essentials 100 percent. Make each essential a complete act. Aim for perfection. Then turn to the nonessentials and use the same technique.

- In pursuing success always view the external world as a reflection of the level of your own psychological effort. Whether you can accept this fully as a philosophical concept does not matter. If you can simply train yourself to think this way, you will always find the barrier in you that is holding back the work. Correct *the internal barrier first*, and then tend to the external barrier (and don't be surprised to discover it is no longer there).

- Success is endless. Whatever you have achieved today is a beginning, not a culmination. Are there not barriers to be overcome within you? Clear one barrier and greater success will come. Since each success lifts you and creates another barrier, where can the limit be?

With this foundation in place, let us look at how you can integrate this dynamic approach into your work.

The balance of this chapter is divided into four sections: junior executive, middle-level manager, vice president, and president. Each section builds to some degree on the last, so you should read at least up through the point where you now are in business life. The assumed age breakdown starts with the 20s, moving through the 30s, 40s (vice president), and 50s. You should study the sections on both your age and your level. For example, although entrepreneurs normally carry the title president, their orientation in some areas will be closer to their age.

JUNIOR EXECUTIVE (20s)

In this golden age of youth and possibility, you should immediately establish your own Dwight David Eisenhower Academy for one (wonderful if you can get a few intimate friends to join with you).

The minimum standard for admission is an aspiration, stated in writing, to be CEO of the company where you now work. The Admission Office always welcomes higher aspirations.

Once admitted, all candidates pledge to

- Carry out every task assigned to the best of their ability, no matter what the nature of that task.
- Make every boss sorry to see them leave.
- Widen their mastery of their chosen field and profession.
- Learn from a Fox Connor if one should appear (inevitable once the first three steps are visible).

Having set an aspiration and the terms of work, the next step is to examine the details of your daily assignments. Get a divided notebook with lined pages. In the first section of your notebook, write your aspiration in clear, unmistakable language. Be very specific.

In the second section, write an appraisal of yourself as seen by your boss—as *seen*, not necessarily as spoken to you. Unless you are in an especially well-managed situation, your boss is likely to be a middle-level manager without great experience in giving accurate feedback. Write down what you perceive the boss really thinks, not says. Imagine your boss has been asked to write a confidential memo about you (one that you will never see). The boss must describe your successes, less than successes, failures, strengths, weaknesses, and potential for promotion. You can put anything in this memo you want except you cannot try to explain away any of your deficiencies. If the boss thinks you are never prompt, that's what it should say, not: "Has a difficult commute that gets in the way of promptness." At the same time, list in full all your genuine achievements.

Having written and reviewed the boss's memo, ask yourself, "Would I hire this person for the job I now have?" If the answer is no, your first priority is to take action to rectify that appraisal. If the answer is yes with reservations, those reservations will point you to the first places where the results are not being met 100 percent.

In the third section of your notebook, list the essentials of your job. What does the boss require? The company? Most larger companies try for a quick, initial sorting out of recruits (usually it's mutual) and eliminate those who are clearly not material for the company.

After this first round of sorting out, there is a hiatus, often running three or four years, in which certain allowances are made while the individual and the company try to figure out what this individual does best in this environment. Essentials and results can get a little blurred at this point: "A terrific salesperson with the big items in the line but seems unable to generate much momentum for the smaller product lines. Still, exceeded sales quota by 40 percent on those items composing 90 percent of the budget and missed by only 20 percent on the remaining 10 percent of quota."

Sound pretty good? This is not a passing grade at your version of the Eisenhower Academy. You must sit down and figure out exactly what it would take to get those small items to meet or exceed the quota. Then you must do it. The fact that you like the other products, other buyers, or the feeling you get when you soar past quota in the products you like means absolutely nothing. What counts is that you are not carrying out an essential (as defined by your company) 100 percent. This is where your attention should go. Make a written plan to bring the other products over quota. Set deadlines and start.

When you have your essentials program on track—that is, there are only a very few essential items missing 100 percent and you are making rapid progress on those—you can return to writing in your notebook.

In the fourth section of your notebook, write down three changes in your behavior or attitude that would make your boss sincerely regret to see you leave. Do you always try to have the last word? Do you try to anticipate the boss's deadlines? What steps can you take to help compensate for the boss's greatest weakness? Either make the psychological effort to change or work out a program to improve consistently.

You can begin the fifth section of your notebook concurrently with the fourth, but *never instead of it*—do that and you are simply fooling yourself. Section five will involve heavy notebook writing. Although the steps listed below are related to becoming a CEO, the same principles apply to whatever aspiration you have chosen.

Start by staggering yourself a bit. Write down everything you would need to know and need to be able to do tomorrow if the board of directors made you CEO tonight. Start writing down lists. Here are some items to start you thinking:

- *Communication skills*: Ability to make a speech, draft a forceful memo, preside over a critical meeting where tempers are hot, make a presentation before Congress on a key industry issue (including answering antagonistic questions on TV), and stay in touch with key customers and suppliers and retain their support.

- *Management skills*: Ability to create or reinvigorate a strategic planning system, organize the company to maximize opportunities, establish a control system that lets everybody in the company know the results of their unit and how they are doing individually, and assemble the right data to make the most important decisions necessary for the company's growth.

- *Knowledge*: Understanding of trends in the industry, the nation, and the world with special understanding of how those trends impact the company.

You may feel the urge at this point to comment: "But our current CEO doesn't know some of those things." Who said our objective was for you to equal the performance of your CEO? We want you to start preparing to do far better.

Write everything down in full under the heading "If I were CEO tomorrow" in your notebook. Make it as concrete as you possibly can. Don't just say industry trends; list specific trends and write down how you see those trends developing today. *Cut out every single negative comment.* This is not a critique of company practice or of the CEO. If you became CEO tomorrow, you'd have your plate full of things to do and learn; stay with those. When you have completed what Susan Bowen calls "pages and pages of ideas," move to the next section of your notebook.

You just got a postponement—you won't be CEO for three years. Open a new section of your notebook, divide it into six sections, one for each six-month period. Go back to your lists of things you need to know. Now select the most important skills you will need *in order of priority* to take over in three years. Don't be general; be specific. If you need to be a better planner, what do you need to know? A deep conceptual understanding of the process? How to set objectives? How to create follow-up programs that work? Don't stop until you have a three-year program, six months by six months, listing in detail what you have to learn and do.

Next go back to the first six months. Now, from those most pressing priorities, identify five things you are going to do in the next six months to gain the skills, abilities, or knowledge you need. The steps can be quite small, but they must be specific and they must carry a date for completion.

Perhaps there is a key book on major trends in the industry you have been thinking about reading. Not exactly a page turner, so you have been putting it off. Either read it three times, as Eisenhower read Clauswitz, or study it with detailed notes. Perhaps your most glaring weakness (as CEO) is a lack of financial skills. Virtually every college in the country offers an evening course with a title something like "Fundamentals of Finance for Nonfinancial Managers." Perhaps your company offers a worthwhile course. Do you lack confidence, particularly as a speaker? The very worthwhile Dale Carnegie courses have helped thousands overcome the same problem. No cash for the Carnegie course? Join the excellent Toastmasters Club, which has chapters all over the nation. The charge is minimal and you get a chance to speak regularly. Mix your list with things you will really look forward to doing and some you don't like (your version of John Scull's cod-liver oil job).

Whatever you do, *the minute you complete these first sections of your notebook, start closing the gap between where you are today and your aspiration.*

The next step is to take out your calendar and circle a half day exactly six months from now. This is your review session, your standards of performance with yourself:

- Start with the essentials of the job. Are you at 100 percent? If not, are you on target to close the gap to 100 percent? If the answer is no to both of those questions, you are failing. This Academy does not accept 95 percent. The biggest growth (and the hardest work) lies in the final 5 percent. Give yourself a pass/fail grade.

- Look objectively at those things that you are doing to make the boss sorry to see you leave. At the start of the six months, you laid out three and set a timetable to do something about them. Pass/fail on each item on the timetable.

- Look at the five things you laid out for your own program of professional growth. Pass/fail on each item, but anything less than completion of all items is, you guessed it, failure.

I use a harsh word like failure to dramatize the absolute nature of the effort you have undertaken. You have to adopt a new and difficult way of looking at yourself, holding two seemingly contrary ideas simultaneously in mind: *Never become discouraged* and *never rationalize.*

We normally don't think like this at all. We undertake a task, determined to give it our best. We work hard and achieve some success—a 110 percent success, a 100 percent success, a 90 percent success. When the success is less than 100 percent, as long as it is "good enough," we rationalize. We get lots of help. Faithful spouses or friends, determined to restore our ego and raise our spirits, give plenty of welcome help: "Who but you, after all, could have done as well?" Bosses help out of concern and out of a desire to build morale: "After all, the best batters in the league only hit one out of three." We help. We know how hard we worked and who knows better where to find the best rationalization in this task?

When we outright fail, we go beyond rationalization. We find a *them* to blame. This limits our growth in two ways. First, it helps us avoid the all-important step of searching for the barrier within us. Second, it gets us in the habit of letting *them* be responsible for our destiny—a habit that grows and becomes over time one of the highest of all barriers and the single greatest cause of anxiety in executive suites. So look at your failure grades as what they are—an opportunity to do more, to achieve more, to grow more. Don't hide from them; use them for greater growth.

At the end of your review session:

- Rewrite the essentials of your job (they may have changed).
- Determine where you are performing less than 100 percent and make a new plan (with deadlines) to close the gap.
- Find three more things that would make your boss sorry to see you leave. Make a program to carry out the necessary changes.
- Looking through your three-year priorities for becoming CEO, select five things you are going to accomplish in the next six months.
- Circle a date six months ahead for your next review.

The process is an upwardly spiraling circle, and you can continue carrying it out, with your own personal variations, for your whole career. Be sure to start every review session by writing down the two key ideas that must always dominate, not only the review, but the whole process: *Never become discouraged* and *never rationalize*.

Several things will begin to be apparent once you start the process:

- You will feel better about your work. Rationalizations never entirely cover the anxiety that arises from a less than 100 percent performance. As you no longer seek to rationalize and you start to work on the less than 100 percent portions of your job, anxiety fades.

- People will start to identify you as a rising star. Casual, even backhand, compliments will begin to come your way. By the time you are in your second six-month cycle (probably well before), there will be talk of a promotion, perhaps more than one level. You should do nothing to encourage this; the less you do (your actions are behind the scenes), the faster the promotion will come.

- A mentor or mentors will appear to give you further guidance. Accept it eagerly, but never as a substitute for your own program. Also never accept advice, even from the most well-meaning mentor, that encourages you to settle for less than 100 percent.

- You will become increasingly alert to self-study or other educational possibilities. Take advantage of all of them, whether they fit your program exactly or not. Once you have a work discipline in place, what you need more than anything else is experience. There are two ways to get experience: Get older or absorb the experience of others. The latter is what Owen Lipstein meant by learning from the masters.

- Education, particularly management education, is nothing more than the distilled experience of others, preferably master managers. Take every course and read every book, always with the question: What is the experience here that can help me? Frank Popoff of Dow told me that there is "time enough for the latest popular novel when I have finished my business reading." On the other hand, Frances Hesselbein is one of the widest ranging readers I know, but everything is read with the question: What is the significance of this for the Girl Scouts? Don Williams's fiction reading is concentrated on classics and the best of modern fiction with an eye to giving him a broader perspective on contemporary issues. With reading, as with work, first achieve the essentials 100 percent, then the nonessentials, your own "personal twist."

- Finally, and most importantly, you will find your work more enjoyable as your project proceeds. This is because there is nothing more enjoyable than personal growth, and through your own Eisenhower Academy, you have linked results of your work with your personal growth, perhaps overtly for the first time.

MIDDLE MANAGER (30s)

You are in the great age of choice. You can certainly see how choices made 10 years ago or more are shaping your life today. You are also conscious that many choices or options are still left open for you. Whether you are conscious of that or not, it remains true. Nothing is yet fixed—neither the level of your success nor your point of leveling off. The choice remains entirely in your hands. Your career may have directed you into one of several broad directions, and we will look at each individually. For many people, the present situation may represent a combination.

Fast-Rising Star

By your mid or late 30s, you will have clearly pulled away from the pack with management responsibilities far greater than your age. You will have become used to managing people older than yourself.

Having read the Junior Executive section, you can now appreciate what is propelling you. You have learned to identify and handle the essentials of any job you are given. And, either through mentors or on your own, you are rapidly gaining a much broader knowledge of your company's business than most of your contemporaries.

Your first opportunity is to maximize results. Simple achievement of 100 percent should not be enough for you. Go back and read the section on maximizing results (Chapter 9) and work out a plan to maximize your results. Here you will encounter difficulties that will mean a major growth. You will have to communicate your vision of maximum results to other members of your team who may not wish to follow you for an extraordinary effort. You will have to take pains to understand each person's motivation and how you can release the team's energy toward maximizing results. Do not permit yourself to assign any blame to *them* for any limitation on this effort to maximize results. Your promise is too bright for that.

As you review the essentials to ensure that you are on track and as you establish your plan to maximize results, write out each major task you must accomplish. Next, write down what it will take to carry out that task completely, what physical, mental, and psychological steps you must take to complete this particular task. Create a program and monitoring system on complete acts. You are most likely to find the greatest area of growth in the psychological aspects because you have probably already mastered the physical and mental components.

It is likely that you have already behaved in a manner that will make your boss sorry to see you leave. If there is the slightest doubt, put Section four of the Junior Executive's program into action. Do this whenever you have a problem with a boss.

Next, tackle Section five of the Junior Executive notebook: What would you need to know or be able to do if you became CEO tomorrow? If you had three years, what would be your highest priority for the next six months? Lay out a program and schedule a review. Remember, from you, nothing less than maximum results is expected.

Once you reach maximum results, ask yourself about how you can impact the nonessentials of the job through your special strengths. It is unlikely that you will get to this phase since you are likely to be promoted again just based on the preceding steps.

Technical Specialist

You are the senior accountant, copywriter, computer specialist, researcher, or human resources specialist. Through your 30s you are likely to receive regular raises and title changes, although the scope of your work may change relatively little. You also may end up managing several people. You have established your technical skills and your capacity to gather and assimilate information in a manner that is useful to senior executives. At this point, you must ask very seriously: What is my aspiration?

The fundamental decision is whether this is the work you want to do for the rest of your career. If the answer is yes, you must immediately aspire to be the best, not in your company, but in your field. Recognize immediately that you are operating with an information base that is growing obsolete every day. You may not yet have noticed this creeping obsolescence, but in 10 years many of your contemporaries in the same technical specialty will suddenly become old-fashioned overnight. Unless the company depends in an unusual way on your specialty (research for drug companies), not a great deal of thought goes into expanding your technical skills. You may get good training in management or interpersonal skills, but in most companies you are more or less on your own when it comes to technical growth.

Consider what maximum results would mean in your area, and establish a program for yourself to improve. You have an advantage over the manager described in the preceding section in that you may not have to motivate other team members to achieve your maximum results.

Your third step involves adapting Section five of the Junior Executive's notebook. Get a notebook and write out the highest aspiration you can imagine; for example, if your field had a Nobel Prize, this would be it. Imagine that you must fill that role tomorrow. What do you need to know and be able to do? Write it out in detail, breaking it into six-month sections and work out a plan to achieve five key things in the next six months. Above all, always keep up with changes in your field and return for advanced education regularly, whether you think you need it or not.

Caught-in-a-Rut Middle Manager

You may be working in a specialty where you don't want to spend the rest of your career, but there doesn't seem to be any way out. Every other job you are offered is more of the same with perhaps a few more dollars. You may have reached the point where you have others reporting to you, although that makes you feel even more trapped between the top and the bottom. Your uneasiness grows with every passing year. Is this all there is?

Most definitely not. Depending on how hard you are willing to work to reactivate your career, you can be rapidly on the rise again in six months, a year at the absolute most. The first thing you have to do is to remember what got you where you are now: a natural endowment plus the ability to do a complete act. You must invest further in your endowment and concentrate on making each task a complete act.

Don't waste time daydreaming about future jobs, opening your own business in five years, or retiring to the beach to write a novel. Start with the job you have. Go through the checklist we know so well by now. Essentials, 100 percent? A program to maximize results? Next educate yourself in something *new that is job related*. Dive in and become an expert. A mentor once advised Dow's Frank Popoff to make himself an expert in something of use to the company. He was told to find something nobody else in the company knew anything about. Popoff chose the technology of making glass, and Dow eventually developed products for the industry.

Understand what has been happening to you in two contexts: *My natural endowment is going fast and I am not bothering to replace it* and *I have forgotten how to do a complete act*. Change one of these equations and your career will stir dramatically to life. Change two and it will take off. In undertaking this program, you may become aware that sloppy work habits are causing you to spend long hours at the office with no real career gain. Begin by addressing those work habits. There are dozens of good courses and books on organizing your work more effectively. Completing the act on each major task will take more time at first. However, you will quickly discover that the time you invest more than comes back to you when you don't have to clean up messes later.

Use the energy generated by these initial actions to start the "fast-rising star" program described earlier. If you are not quite yet in this category, you are clearly headed there.

VICE PRESIDENT (40s)

You start with tremendous advantages. First, you know that every point in this book is true because your career illustrates it. You have reached this level by regularly replenishing your natural endowment, learning how to concentrate on the essentials, showing finesse in handling the nonessentials, and achieving maximum results much of the time. Equally important, you have learned consciously or unconsciously to link your inner and outer growth.

You have also applied considerable psychological effort in carrying out your work—in learning to give others credit, controlling your temper or other weaknesses, and training yourself to listen better. You know how to put the needs of others first when the job requires it. You have learned how to overcome barriers within you—from the simplest prejudices you learned in the schoolyard to the more complex barrier of shifting gears from a department level to a company-wide view.

You stand as proof that following all or most of the principles of progress leads to success. Now, one of business life's biggest challenges is in front of you: the ascent to the presidency. You have all the tools you need; the question is how to apply them.

First, some fundamentals. At this level, not 90 percent, but 100 percent of the new work is psychological effort. If for any reason you are still mired in the physical or mental aspects of your work, your first opportunity is to bring your present assignment under control. You need to free yourself for the psychological effort that will fully transform you into a workaphile if any lingering workaholic habits remain. Results, of course, must be under control, with a heavy bias toward achieving maximum results; essentials must be 100 percent.

With these in place, you are ready to turn to the task of becoming president. First, review the chapter on essentials and nonessentials (Chapter 5). Begin to focus on the nonessentials of your job, those extras that contribute greatly when carried out with finesse. When searching for nonessentials, always look first at the customer. What new service would make life easier, more pleasant for that customer? How could we really please as opposed to merely serve? What can you do to become more intimately involved with the customers' real problems? How can you personally use one of your strengths to help solve those problems?

Look next at the employees. I once knew a very successful senior executive who had a natural politician's love of people and was willing to show it. He sent short, hand-written notes congratulating people on all kinds of things, personal and business. Any employee in the hospital was sure to get a note. Because it grew out of a basic strength, this nonessential always seemed genuine to everyone. It also gave him great credibility within the organization.

Drawing on your basic strengths, what nonessentials can you lift to 100 percent, your own "personal twist?" The focus should always be on others rather than yourself, and it should always be on a nonessential part of the work.

Next, you should review values. If the company has a set of values, be sure your units have specific programs to bring those values to life with customers, employees, and communities where you operate. Be the value leader in the parts of the company for which you are responsible. At your level, be second to none at this. Follow Harvey Golub's system (Chapter 7): Eliminate all actions that conflict with the values; reinforce as many actions that support the values as you can; find a way to transform neutral acts to value-laden acts. Start with yourself; when your performance is 100 percent, institute programs throughout your part of the company.

At this stage, you should also broaden your perspective as rapidly as you can. Try to attend one of the long, residential courses offered by many major business schools. If this is not possible, get deeply involved in industry-wide organizations that will expand your ideas as well as give you contacts from whom you can learn.

This is also the time for a careful review of the rules. Can you identify the most important rules you are using in your work? Do any need to be reversed? Evaluate your rules from the highest perspective of your job. Look at the external and internal context in which you are now working. Are your rules always appropriate?

Next, take specific sights on the job you want next. Get a notebook and do a thorough analysis of every task and skill required of the present CEO. Similar in concept to the Junior Executive's notebook, your version should be much more richly detailed. Make sure you write down every task. Then write candidly the present level of your ability to carry out that task. One after the other, list your strengths and deficiencies. Next create a program for yourself to raise your capacity in each required skill to 100 percent. Find ways in your own work to develop the skills you need.

Most important of all, *treat each new challenge first as a growth possibility for yourself and second as a result to be achieved.* The question is: What can I learn here that I need to know? In answering that question, totally ignore your likes and dislikes, as well as what you are good at and what you are not. Reread the chapter on strengths and weaknesses (Chapter 4), and take your example from Alex Kroll and Herb Baum, vice presidents who became presidents partly because they used business challenges to convert weaknesses to strengths. The greatest growth is available to you through this approach.

Work consistently at this level and in one year, two at the most, you will become a president—either in your present company or another.

PRESIDENT/CEO (50s)

Your possibilities for further growth are without limit. You are the master of the most important points in this book. In some cases, the presentation here may have made you more aware of what has been contributing to your success. If so, this will make you a far better teacher of younger managers—one of your most important roles. You can teach by example what you know unconsciously, but you can instruct concretely only what you have learned consciously. In a few cases, you will have no doubt found areas still requiring self-improvement in the performance of your job. These, of course, are your first priority.

Your greatest single advantage over every other manager in your company is that your growth and the company's growth are completely intertwined. Your work and your development are one. Your psychological effort has immediate impact everywhere. To the degree you discipline yourself to make calm, measured decisions, to listen carefully, and to consider the feelings of others, you will be imitated everywhere.

So much so that if there is a recurring negative behavior in the company, the first place you must look for that particular negative is within yourself. Once identified, make the psychological effort to remove that trait. The results externally will be rapid. This will be as difficult for you as for your most junior manager— maybe more so. Psychological effort doesn't get any easier with higher titles. My old mentor's advice "If there is a problem here, I caused it" is, if anything, even more true at the top.

The founder-entrepreneur has special opportunities. The founder lends the company her great personal strengths at the time of founding and in the early years. Once those are installed in the fabric of the company, the question is: What next? Unless the founder makes the psychological effort to grow in scope and competence, the company cannot grow in a healthy manner for long. The founder-entrepreneur has an absolute challenge to make the psychological effort to continue growing; it is literally true that both her and her company's future success depend on it.

Every president's job is different, but every president's job contains two areas rich with potential for combining organizational and personal growth: planning the future and values.

Planning the Future of the Organization

Anthony L. Anderson, president and chief executive officer of the industrial adhesive and specialty chemical manufacturer H.B. Fuller Co., has given considerable thought to the CEO's role in planning. Fuller, a Fortune 500 company based in Twin Cities, Minnesota, began systematic corporate planning a decade ago. With a system well in place, "my impact on this year is zero," Anderson says. "My effect is hopefully going to be seen in two years."

Defining his role toward the future keeps Anderson always on the prowl for new information. Visit his office and you will find chairs and sofas stacked with newspapers, magazines, and other reading materials. "I provide a modest clipping service to a lot of people," says Anderson. The office is very deceptive because Anderson is a highly disciplined and organized executive beneath his "just folks" manner (the janitor calls him Tony).

To the degree that any president focuses seriously on the future of the company, learning is mandatory. Anderson will eventually recycle all his learning back through the formal planning process, leading to important corporate decisions. Part of the impetus keeping Tony Anderson out in front is his company's legacy of doubling sales every 5 years for 45 years. "We've been a growth company for so long we don't know anything but that." Based on his stewardship of the future, Anderson made two controversial decisions—both of which proved to be winners.

In the middle 1970s when the company's sales were about $200 million, Anderson and one of his key managers saw that certain predictable stresses would have to be anticipated and handled before the next doubling in volume could take place. "There were tax matters, safety matters, environmental matters. I could give you a list of 20 important things we were not doing." Anticipating growth, Anderson invested "hundreds of thousands of dollars" to bring aboard the staff experts even before they were needed. The effort continued well into the early 1980s, a time of great profit squeeze within the industry. Growth continued without a break.

In December 1981, Anderson made his second key decision. After one year's planning, he changed Fuller to a national organization focused on specific industries rather than a geographically regionalized, decentralized one. Several years before any competitor dared move out of the industry-wide pattern, Anderson "decided to take this geographically oriented and cultured, 95-year-old company and change it 180 degrees."

The move overnight changed the jobs of 800 of Fuller's then 1500 employees. "They were reporting to a different person. They were in a different organization. They were selling different products to a different industry." At that moment, says Anderson, everything depended on the trust and confidence of the employees. Not without some doubts, that trust was there. Today, "we wouldn't go back to the old ways for anything. We made the right decision and we think we are three to five years ahead of the competition."

Taking a role as a guardian of the future will expand the vision of every CEO and bring extra depth to key organizational decisions. Seeing the shape of the future, Anderson prepared his company by expanding staff in anticipation of growth and reorganizing to meet coming changes. Growth and change are always linked in his mind. "I learned early that if you are going to grow, you just can't keep doing next year what you did last year. You always have to be doing less of what you are doing and more of some other stuff."

Values

Values represent the second area of opportunity for a CEO wishing to grow personally while accelerating corporate development. In every sense, the top executive embodies the values of the company. How that executive makes decisions is a value statement for the rest of the company. Who that executive promotes is a value statement. How that executive spends work time is perhaps the biggest value statement of all. Whatever the words on the plaque in the lobby, employees, close customers and suppliers, and the community will interpret the organization's values by the CEO's actions.

Before a CEO can reinterpret or expand the scope of the company's values, that individual must have defined and acted upon those values. If the values in a company are unstated, the CEO in getting them stated must first make the psychological effort to adopt those values at a personal level, usually at a higher level than the company's present performance. If the values are already strongly in place, the psychological effort must be to embody them at the highest level. No hint of compromise is possible. The CEO must seek out and correct the smallest personal action that conflicts with the values, while searching for personal opportunities to convert neutral actions in value-laden statements. By example and instruction, the CEO becomes the values, a step that will inevitably and dramatically expand the personality of anyone making such a serious effort.

By such action, company CEOs become industry leaders; industry leaders become national leaders; and national leaders become world figures.

When he became president, Tony Anderson inherited a full set of corporate values, or priorities as they call them at Fuller.

Tony's father had set the strict order of ranking, which has never been compromised: first, the customer; second only to the customer, the employees; third, the shareholder; and fourth, the community. Despite being a publicly held company, Fuller has never shied away from telling shareholders they come third. Not that shareholders have had too much to complain about. Fuller ranks in the top 50 of the Fortune 500 in 10-year total return to shareholders.

The growth rate of doubling every five years in an industry where most sales are repeat business dramatizes the success of Fuller's "customer first" policy. As for employee satisfaction, for the past four years, Fuller has been listed in a book describing the best companies to work for in the U.S. Well before that it had a reputation as a company with outstanding employee relations.

However, it is in the fourth priority area—the community— that Tony Anderson has most dramatically shown any CEO how to take a legacy and expand it. Elmer Anderson, who in effect turned the business over to Tony in 1971, is a legend in Minnesota, where he served as state senator, governor, and chairman of the University of Minnesota's Board of Regents. Elmer, as he is always called at Fuller, left the company with a rich tradition of community involvement.

Tony Anderson saw that what his father had "personalized," he had to "professionalize and democratize." Today Fuller gives 5 percent of its pretax income, about $1 million a year, to the U.S. communities in which it operates. Thirty-two local community affairs councils determine the distribution of funds in their community. The logic seems so clear to Tony Anderson: "The people of the company are the ones who created this money; doesn't it make sense to have these people decide where the money ought to go?"

Embodying the value of community involvement means that Tony Anderson, at any one time, is working on four or five community service priorities, things like a social service agency, education, and the arts. "At any point in time, I may be a little more involved here or there, but if you take a 10-year flow of things, I would have been involved in all five activities." It is an obligation to this disciplined man that "I shouldn't spend all my time in any one area."

Tony Anderson's example suggests the scope for any CEO determined to grow both company and self. Planning and values offer infinite possibilities.

BEYOND CEO

For those who have achieved the topmost level in business, other horizons still are open. At this level, we do not focus so much on acquiring more information but on acquiring more knowledge. What at a lower level was skill has become talent; talent, capacity; capacity, a steady ability under pressure. What used to be pleasant behavior has become a strong personality.

Progress from this point on is no longer measured in material gain, or even by success. Work and individual have become totally one; a gain in one is inseparable from a gain in the other. Growth hereafter is measured in contribution to the industry, to the field of the management, to future generations, and to society. With work and individual growth tied by a seamless thread, the focus is no longer on work as such, on ambition, or even on achievement, but on service and the effort to help others achieve their aspirations.

THERE IS MORE IN YOU: TRANSCENDING SUCCESS

12

Many years ago I visited the town of Bruges in Belgium. In the 13th and 14th centuries, Bruges was the most important seaport in northwestern Europe. Then, an accident of history filled the waters of the port with silt and the seafaring ships went to Antwerp, leaving Bruges to this day an almost perfectly preserved medieval town. In the center of that town, from a man who lived 500 years ago, I first received the central message of this book.

Lodewijck van Gruuthuse was one of Bruges's greatest leaders, and he built his house to show it. Even today it draws admiration for its graceful statement of success. Throughout the house, this diplomat-soldier had carved in stone walls his motto: *Plus est en vous* ("There is more in you"). The absolute, uncompromising starkness of the statement struck me the moment I saw it. Whatever you have achieved, whatever you see as limitation, whatever your self-imposed barriers, there is more in you. Wherever you are in life, you have barely begun to grow, expand, live; there is more in you. Like many reading that ancient carving, I felt my spirit soar across the ages.

Lodewijck van Gruuthuse inspired me, but he left not a single clue concerning how to release that more within you. For that I had to travel and learn much more. From the quiet house in Bruges

255

to the bustling offices of Harry Quadracci in Pewaukee, Wisconsin, my journey can be measured in years and hundreds of thousands of miles. Throughout most of those years, I was working with highly successful executives and entrepreneurs in both Europe and the United States. The inspiring lives of these individuals made the message more and more a living reality, reinforced again and again. By the time I heard Harry Quadracci's earnest exhortation, "You are capable of doing anything that you want to do as long as you set your mind to it," I knew I was hearing a simple truth, a truth bonding Quadracci with Lodewijck van Gruuthuse by a tie that transcends nations, eras, and centuries. Also linked in this dynamic but invisible network are many other executives mentioned in this book, people who have learned, in Michael Blumenthal's stirringly simple words that "it depends on me."

Understanding the power locked within this central message—true 500 years ago, true today—still left me without knowing how that *more in you* could be released. Instinctively, I felt there was a system, although it was obvious that many had managed to work their way to success without following any conscious system.

I hired a researcher who spent many days reviewing biographies of business people, going back to business leaders in Colonial times. The researcher also scoured recent business magazines and journals. I even ordered a series of 60 transcripts of interviews with contemporary business leaders. Less than 1 percent of the material in this book comes directly from any of those sources, but they did point me in some useful directions. The material showed me that those who had risen far were not automatically more conscious of what specific actions had moved their careers. Interesting insights were available everywhere, although no one seemed to have complete answers that could be transferred broadly to others.

In selecting my own interviews, my single criterion became that the person had to have risen significantly in organizational life. I traveled across the nation, listening for clues and examples. The well known had risen further and had far more perspective; the less well known, less famous were often more in touch with what actually was happening in their careers today. The interviews provided life and invaluable practical examples to reinforce my growing sense of system.

For the system itself, I had to journey halfway around the world to South India. During a number of trips to India in the last decade, I had become increasingly aware that no other nation has invested such profound thought in understanding the process of human development. What science is to the West, this knowledge is to India; it has commanded the attention of the society's most creative minds for generations. These deep yogic traditions, going back to the dawn of written history, expanded upon generation after generation, untouched by centuries of foreign conquest, are India's great gift to world. Yet because generations of Indian writers, thinkers, and teachers have focused solely on the highest goal of spiritual growth, this gift has seemed of little use to the pragmatic West.

In India, I received the strongest reinforcement of the idea that all growth in life is fundamentally an internal process, and that seemingly coincidental external conditions are shadows of the inner life. During my stays in India, I was above all influenced by the writings and teachings of Sri Aurobindo and The Mother, two of India's greatest visionaries, who lived and worked in Pondicherry in South India for a combined period of about 50 years earlier in this century. From their writings and from scholars of their work, I was exposed to a full, sweeping, and dynamic view of human development that I then was able to adapt into a system of personal growth for executives.

This phase of my journey had come to an end. What had begun as a challenge in Bruges from Lodewijck van Gruuthuse and had then continued through years of pragmatically gathering information and experiences from executives throughout Europe and America had now matured into a system based on the thought of two authentic, multidimensional geniuses who carried out their most important work in South India. I am truly indebted to some magnificent individuals on three continents for this synthesis.

This synthesis is now available to you. Its single most important idea is that your own growth and development are in your hands.

Our one remaining question is: How will you respond to the challenge of Lodewijck van Gruuthuse? The book gives you a complete system to grow at work much further or faster than any distance you have come so far. Success is available to you the second you truly acknowledge that "it depends on me." From then on, the road map is here; it is in your hands to be as successful as you want to be.

As important as success is, I am convinced that the diplomat-soldier of Bruges had far more in mind than even just success when he ordered his stone carver to leave us those words of challenge. The more that is in you transcends success. The crown of professional work is success, but the crown of life is true enjoyment. We can never really mistake this enjoyment for its counterfeit, the transitory pleasure that comes from one of our many entertainments. True enjoyment is, rather, the deep abiding joy we feel when we grow through conscious effort or when we spend an hour with people we deeply love.

For some, work continually provides such enjoyment. When this is true, work may be sometimes tiring, but it can never be, for an instant, tiresome. The program in this book can carry your work to this level. The key is the psychological effort you make to use external work to create opportunities for inner growth.

The more you move in this direction, the more you will transcend lower forms of work and even success and sail toward the realms of pure enjoyment. This is the true executive odyssey, a voyage of personal growth undertaken by those daring enough to seek a career without limits.

It is not necessary to reach such a level to achieve and enjoy success. Except for those who have become one with their work, our highest enjoyment comes from sharing affection with those we love. The Lords of Life are those who have learned how to do both.

For many, however, a greatly accelerating success while enjoying a rich and full life with loved ones will be more than enough. It is important to understand that these two are never in conflict. Whatever conflict exists is, once again, within ourselves. If we are working at a higher and higher level, focused more and more on growth rather than results, there will be more than enough energy, enthusiasm, and, indeed, love for a deeply satisfying personal life. The more we truly enjoy our work, the more richly developed personalities we become as husbands, wives, parents, or friends.

This is the life that is yours for the taking. You are capable of doing anything that you want to do as long as you set your mind to it.

It depends on you.

ACKNOWLEDGMENTS

This book seeks to translate dynamic principles into everyday reality through the medium of interviews with successful executives. I am grateful to the following individuals for sharing their experiences with me:

Anthony L. Anderson, president and CEO, H.B. Fuller Co., Saint Paul, MN.

Diane R. Annala, director, San Diego Foundation for the Performing Arts, San Diego, CA.

Herbert M. Baum, president, Campbell, USA, Campbell Soup Co., Camden, NJ.

John A. Betti, executive vice president, Diversified Products Operations, Ford Motor Co., Dearborn, MI.

Robert Bieniek, vice president, Original Copy Centers, Inc., Cleveland, OH.

W. Michael Blumenthal, chairman of the board and CEO, Unisys Corp., Blue Bell, PA.

Susan W. Bowen, president, Champion Awards, Inc., Memphis, TN.

Peter W. Bruce, J.D., senior vice president, general counsel and secretary, Northwestern Mutual Life Insurance Co., Milwaukee, WI.

Rodney Burwell, president and CEO, Xerxes Corp., Minneapolis, MN.

Robert E. Buuck, chairman, American Medical Systems, Minneapolis, MN.

Randel S. Carlock, president and CEO, Image Retailing Group, Inc., Minneapolis, MN.

Robert Cavalco, president, Bang & Olufsen of America, Inc., Chicago, IL.

C. Hale Champion, former executive dean, John F. Kennedy School of Government, Harvard University, Cambridge, MA.

Leo Cherne, executive director, Research Institute of America, Inc., New York, NY.

Rear Admiral David M. Cooney (Ret.), president and CEO, Goodwill Industries of America, Inc., Bethesda, MD.

Frederick A. DeLuca, president, Subway Sandwiches & Salads, Milford, CT.

Christopher Espinosa, Apple Computer, Inc., Cupertino, CA.

Mark J. Estren, executive vice president, Infotech Technologies, Inc., New York, NY.

Kay L. Fredericks, president and CEO, Trend Enterprises, Inc., New Brighton, MN.

William Gardner, president, Consulting Resources, Inc., Wilmington, DE.

Robert W. Gillespie, chairman, president, and CEO, Society Corp. and Society National Bank, Cleveland, OH.

Harvey Golub, president and CEO, IDS Financial Services, Inc., Minneapolis, MN.

G.A. "Corky" Hall, vice chairman, U.S. Communications, Minneapolis, MN.

George N. Havens, chairman and CEO, The Jayme Organization, Inc., Cleveland, OH.

Frances Hesselbein, national executive director, Girl Scouts of the USA, New York, NY.

Lawrence L. Horsch, chairman and CEO, Munsingwear, Inc., Minneapolis, MN.

John E. Jacob, president and CEO, National Urban League, Inc., New York, NY.

Jenette S. Kahn, president, DC Comics, Inc., New York, NY.

John C. Koss, chairman and president, Koss Corp., Milwaukee, WI.

Alexander Kroll, chairman and CEO, Young & Rubicam, Inc., New York, NY.

Eugene M. Lang, chairman, "I Have a Dream" Foundation, New York, NY.

Lewis W. Lehr, chairman and CEO (retired), 3M Co., Saint Paul, MN.

Owen J. Lipstein, president and publisher, *American Health, Mother Earth News, Sponsorship Marketing*, New York, NY.

Denise Lloyd, publisher, *Bodyshop Business*, Babcox Publications, Akron, OH.

Kendall Lockhart, vice president, Bank of America, San Francisco, CA.

Douglas J. MacMaster, Jr., senior vice president, Merck & Co., Inc., Rahway, NJ.

Richard J. Markham, vice president of marketing, Merck Sharp & Dohme, West Point, PA.

J.W. Marriott, Jr., chairman and president, Marriott Corp., Washington, DC.

Kendrick Melrose, president and CEO, Toro Co., Bloomington, MN.

Bert N. Mitchell, founder and managing partner, Mitchell/Titus & Co., New York, NY.

Tom Mitchell, president, Seagate Technology, Scotts Valley, CA.

Thomas R. Moore, president, Remmele Engineering, Inc., Minneapolis, MN.

Douglas G. Myers, executive director, Zoological Society of San Diego, San Diego, CA.

Sister Carmella O'Donoghue, president, Sisters of Charity of the Incarnate Word Health Care System, Houston, TX.

J. Tracy O'Rourke, president and CEO, Allen-Bradley Co., Milwaukee, WI.

Commissioner James Osborne, territorial commander, Southern Territory, The Salvation Army, Atlanta, GA.

David H. Pingree, vice president of government relations, Unisys Corp., Blue Bell, PA.

Cathy A. Pokorny, president, PROCONSUL, Cleveland, OH.

Frank Popoff, president and CEO, Dow Chemical Co., Midland, MI.

Harry V. Quadracci, president and founder, Quad/Graphics, Inc., Pewaukee, WI.

Bernard G. Rethore, president and CEO, Microdot Industries, Darien, CT.

Larry J.B. Robinson, chairman, The Robinson Group, Cleveland, OH.

Donald J. Schuenke, president and CEO, Northwestern Mutual Life Insurance Co., Milwaukee, WI.

John Scull, marketing manager of emerging markets, Apple Computer, Inc., Cupertino, CA.

Albert Shanker, president, American Federation of Teachers, AFL-CIO, Washington, DC.

Robert F. Smith, president, Strategies & Teams, Inc., San Diego, CA.

Walton L. Stinson, president, ListenUp Corp., Denver, CO.

Nancy Vetrone, president, Original Copy Centers, Inc., Cleveland, OH.

Sara Westendorf, manager, Advanced Manufacturing Systems Operation, Hewlett-Packard, Sunnyvale, CA.

Robert G. Widham, group vice president, Hand Tool/Die Divisions, Stanley Works, New Britain, CT.

John D. Wiedemann, plant manager, Stanley Tools Division, Stanley Works, Shaftsbury, VT.

J. McDonald Williams, managing partner, Trammell Crow Co., Dallas, TX.

I would also like to extend my appreciation to James W. Krause, president of North Central Management Associates, Inc., Excelsior, MN., and to Jan Feldberg of the Napa, California office of the consulting company Synthesis, both of whom arranged important interviews; to my editor John Mahaney, who provided helpful ideas and support at every stage; to John Riddle, my researcher; and to Kathy Miller Yarrusso, whose administrative and secretarial skills kept this project on schedule.

F. G. H.

INDEX